D0569677

COURTROOM
CRUSADERS

ALSO BY MARK LITWAK

Reel Power

COURTROOM
CRUSADERS

Mark Litwak

WILLIAM MORROW AND COMPANY, INC.   NEW YORK

Library of Congress Cataloging-in-Publication Data

Litwak, Mark.
Courtroom crusaders / Mark Litwak.
p.   cm.
Bibliography: p.
Includes index.
ISBN 0-688-07486-3
1. Lawyers—United States—Biography.   2. Trials—United States.
I. Title.
KF372.L57 1989
349.73′092′2—dc 20
[347.300922]   89-34884
                                                                      CIP

Printed in the United States of America

First Edition

1   2   3   4   5   6   7   8   9   10

BOOK DESIGN BY JAYE ZIMET

To my wonderful wife, Tiiu,
and delightful son, David

PREFACE

This book is about lawyers of vision and daring. Catalysts for change, they challenge the status quo, seeking to set new precedents, redress wrongs and build a more just society. They take on unpopular causes and defend the powerless from the powerful. They are priests of a noble profession.

I have written about interesting attorneys involved in provocative cases. They have been selected with occupational diversity in mind. My subjects include three young lawyers prosecuting mobsters, an attorney defending a man accused of kidnapping and rape, a products liability lawyer who earns million-dollar fees, as well as an attorney who works on skid row. They reside in Boston, Los Angeles, and Anchorage, and places in between.

Each is unique, many are mavericks, some are more admirable than others. But they are the real thing, not the one-dimensional stereotypes often portrayed on television and in film. They don't always win their cases and they don't always represent the innocent. All the stories are true, although the names of victims in several chapters have been changed to save them further embarrassment.

I hope this book will give readers insight into the lives of lawyers today. Perhaps it will also encourage law students to consider the many possiblities open to them upon graduation.

Mark Litwak
Santa Monica, California

CONTENTS

Chapter 1

ON SKID ROW

*The law in its majestic equality, for-
bids the rich as well as the poor to
sleep under bridges.*
  —ANATOLE FRANCE

When I telephoned attorney Nancy Mintie, age
thirty-two, director of the Inner City Law Center,she readily consented to an interview, and invited me to accompany her on a tour of a slum hotel in
downtown Los Angeles. After I accepted, she inquired
whether I owned a camera. I did and she requested that I
bring it, along with lots of film. Then she asked, "Are you
big?"

"Big?" I replied.

"Yeah, big," she said, explaining that both she and the
other attorney going on this trip were women.

I informed her that I was five feet nine and weighed 155
pounds—not exactly bodyguard proportions—and asked
her if that was sufficient. She said fine, but I sensed disappointment. Perhaps I'm too sensitive but I think she would
have preferred a bruiser. So would I. This was when I
began to worry.

On the appointed day, I drove to downtown Los Angeles, careful to keep my windows up and doors locked. As I

approached the skid row area, I passed a man muttering incoherently to himself. Men in ill-fitting and tattered clothes congregated on the sidewalks in small groups. A couple slept curled on the ground oblivious to the world. Although many people appeared haggard and dirty, only a few looked drunk or disoriented.

On skid row itself, hundreds of destitute men and women trudged aimlessly about with their meager belongings in hand, like the shell-shocked survivors of some terrible holocaust. I was truly amazed at their number, although I was aware that Los Angeles was the homeless capital of the United States with some thirty-two thousand people living on the street. Many came to L.A. expecting jobs and warm weather, but there were few jobs to be had and the nights were surprisingly cold.

It seemed incredible that minutes from the splendor of Beverly Hills was a neighborhood where shopping carts were the most common four-wheeled vehicle. It was a grim reminder that life is brutal—for some.

I drove into a parking lot and found that the spaces without cars were filled with mattresses and cardboard-box shelters. Even the narrow pathways between cars were filled with sleeping bodies and bundled possessions. Self-conscious about my clean car and neatly pressed clothes, I was concerned that I might be mistaken for a slumlord or some other exploiter of the poor.

I parked in a garage several blocks away and walked to the Center. At the front door a line of destitute men and women patiently waited to enter. In a small reception room, clients spoke in hushed tones, while at two desks, paralegal "advocates" conducted interviews.

I was shown in to see Mintie, a tall, slender Caucasian with soft features and a ready smile. Dressed in a blue-striped button-down shirt, jeans, white socks with pink hearts, and Nike running shoes, she looked like a suburban shopper who had taken a wrong exit off the freeway.

She confessed she was tired, having stayed out late the night before. The police had begun their crackdown on sidewalk squatters, and she had gone along as a legal observer to help anyone who might be arrested. The controversial action was the result of complaints by local merchants who said that homeless men and women camping on the sidewalks were frightening their employees and ruining their businesses. One businessman posted a large sign that read: FEEL SORRY FOR THE HOMELESS?? ADOPT ONE! TAKE ONE HOME WITH YOU TODAY. LET THEM USE YOUR YARD FOR A BATHROOM.

The police asserted that the makeshift living quarters were illegal and a breeding ground for crime. Police Chief Daryl F. Gates claimed that crime in the vicinity had increased 28 percent from the previous year.

Mintie and her allies, however, believed that persecuting the homeless when there was insufficient housing available to them was inhumane and fruitless. Furthermore, they argued, not having a home shouldn't be a crime. The city attorney was sympathetic and declined to prosecute those arrested.

The issue came to a head when Gates issued an ultimatum stating that the squatters had one week to get off the streets or face mass arrest. Responding to public outrage, the mayor agreed that no one would be arrested unless they first refused alternative shelter. The police were supplied with hotel vouchers to dispense.

When forty police officers arrived at Sixth Street and Stanford Avenue to sweep the area clear, they found far more reporters, cameramen, and observers than squatters. Most of the homeless had left two hours earlier when word spread that the police were on their way.

Finally the police encountered a shirtless twenty-five-year-old man from Tennessee, camped on the sidewalk with his wife. Surrounded by a jostling crowd of reporters and photographers with tape recorders and cameras thrust forward, a cop politely informed the bewildered couple that they were in violation of the city's sidewalk ordinance and asked them if they would like a hotel voucher.

"Yes, I would," replied the man, and he was promptly

handed a voucher good for four days lodging at the Ferraro, a single-room hotel about two miles away. "Thank you very much, officer," he said before departing with a shopping cart filled with aluminum cans. "Have a nice day," replied the officer, as the ceremony was duly recorded by the media.

Later the police approached a mentally disabled woman living in a cardboard box with a blind, crippled man whom she cared for. The woman didn't understand the offer the police were extending her. After several attempts, the cops decided to simply pass the couple by. But Mintie intervened, patiently explained the voucher system to the pair, and made sure they received one.

After the police cleared the area of squatters, the Department of Public Works moved in to remove the remaining debris and clean the streets. For Mintie, observing the plight of the homeless was so upsetting that she was close to tears all evening. Although she is a frequent critic of the police, in this instance she praised them for being kind and gentle. Of course, watched by a lawyer and a mob of reporters, they would have been foolish not to have been.

I was introduced to Sharon Hartman, an attorney with the law office of Irell and Manella, who was the second member of our inspection team. Her firm had donated the time of several attorneys to help the Inner City Law Center battle slumlords. I also met Mark Thompson, a staff writer for *The Recorder,* a San Francisco-based legal publication. It seems I wasn't the only journalist recruited for protection. But he was shorter than I.

We squeezed into Mintie's car, a battered Honda Civic left to her by a homeless man who joined the Army to obtain a job, and proceeded to the Ford Hotel about a mile away. Mintie informed us that its 288 units rent for $200 a month, single-occupancy, $250 a month, double-occupancy. The owner realized a net profit of $519,628.08 in 1985. A long-standing owner of skid row properties, he has repeatedly tangled with regulatory agencies.

Mintie sued him and several other landlords on the

grounds that their buildings weren't habitable for human occupancy. Hoping to be dropped from the suit, he had now agreed to let Mintie inspect the building. She is clearly a force to be reckoned with, having sued the previous owner on behalf of six tenants who had been illegally locked out of their rooms and won a settlement of $47,000 for them.

From across the street we surveyed the six-story hotel. After I pointed out that there were no ladder connections between the fire escape landings, Mintie asked us to take pictures. As we removed our cameras, a large black man drinking beer on the top landing objected. Suddenly, out of the corner of my eye, I saw him hurl a quart of beer. "Watch out," I yelled and we scattered, barely avoiding the glass bottle before it shattered on the pavement. If any one of us had been hit, we could have been seriously injured or killed. Hartman seemed shaken; Mintie was nonchalant.

Inside the seedy building, we approached the wire-reinforced registration window. Mintie gave her name to the manager and introduced us as "the inspectors," undoubtedly aware that he would perceive us as some sort of official delegation. If only city hall cared so much. The manager was cooperative, having been informed of Mintie's visit.

Mintie asked to examine the basement first, and the janitor took us downstairs. We had to sidestep dirty laundry strewn down the stairway before entering a dark hallway that smelled of mildew and rot. Wires and pipes lined the walls and ceiling; the concrete floor was littered with malt liquor cans and cheap wine bottles. With flashlight in hand and the intent look of a Klondiker in search of gold, Mintie proceeded to explore each nook and cranny, insisting that every door be unlocked.

She pointed out rodent droppings, cockroaches, a used condom and a broken smoke detector with the savoir faire of an experienced naturalist describing fauna to a group of wide-eyed tourists. She rattled off building code violations like a veteran building inspector, and had

15

us photograph everything, including a freshly painted door and recent electrical work—repairs apparently made for our benefit.

Behind one padlocked door, we found a soiled mattress, makeshift stove, clothes, and a pile of garbage. Someone was living in this dark dungeon. The janitor professed surprise, claiming the occupant must have sneaked in through a basement window.

We proceeded upstairs past a group of construction workers making repairs and past several tenants who carried toilet paper as they walked to the bathroom. An elderly man slowly shuffled down the hall, breathing through a metal device attached to a hole in his throat.

Mintie knocked on several doors and asked tenants if she could inspect their rooms. Everyone consented. She made it appear that the rooms were chosen at random, although she later confided to us that she had arranged to visit certain rooms that belonged to her informers.

The rooms were small—a single bed filled a third of the floor space. A disabled man who had been living at the Ford for five years had decorated his walls with *Playboy* centerfolds and an American flag. The man kept a stick next to his bed for protection; he complained that mice chewed into the bottom of his mattress and made nests in it. Mintie listened carefully and asked whether he had trouble with cockroaches. He showed her the roach motel that management had distributed the night before. Mintie deftly opened the trap and had us photograph its contents. It was fully occupied, as were all the others she opened that day.

I was struck by how pleasant and courteous the tenants were. Most were neatly dressed and took pride in their appearance, striving to maintain their dignity despite the daily humiliations they experienced. Some were mentally disturbed or physically disabled but most were healthy and articulate. They were workingmen and workingwomen who had lost their jobs.

The residents sensed Mintie's genuine concern and told her everything she wanted to know. Even the crazed man who had hurled the beer bottle at us became friendly when he learned the purpose of our visit.

Earl Winslow, a tenant in the process of moving out, introduced himself. He complained about the lack of security in the building and said his room had been broken into and his radio and television stolen. The Ford remains a dangerous place although it used to be far worse. Before Mintie brought her first suit, 258 burglaries had been reported and an even greater number had gone unreported. There was virtually no security, and tenants lived in constant fear of drug dealers and criminals.

Mintie mentioned that her husband, a photographer, had his equipment stolen during a visit to a slum hotel. Slumlords sometimes try to discourage Mintie by encouraging thugs to thwart her. I presume this is why she now invites unsuspecting journalists to accompany her.

We left the Ford chastened but unharmed. Mintie was pleased with the repairs that had been made but wanted more improvements. She wouldn't drop the Ford Hotel from her lawsuit although she conceded its condition was above average for the neighborhood. On our way back to her office, she said she always felt like taking a shower after one of these visits.

Mintie grew up in conservative Orange County, the second of seven children in an Irish Catholic family. Her parents were conservative Republicans and she was a Nixon supporter. In 1972, while her peers were protesting the war in Vietnam, she gave a speech in support of it.

She is uncertain whether her upbringing should be considered working-class or middle-class. Her father was a salesman who sold Mobil Oil products to the company's franchise stations. Later he moved into their public relations department. He excelled at both jobs because he was personable and enjoyed working with people. He later went into real estate. Mintie's mother had her hands full caring for seven children. The family lived in Downey and Haw-

thorne, suburban communities where people might struggle to make ends meet but nobody was ever hungry or
homeless.

In junior high school Mintie began to study music and
decided she wanted to be a pianist. She attended a Catholic
girls high school and graduated second in her class. By
eighteen, she was enrolled in Loyola on a music scholarship
and was living away from home for the first time. She
supported herself with a series of minimum-wage jobs:
waitress, night-shift operator for an answering service, and
ticket seller for the stagecoach at Knott's Berry Farm.

After a year of studying music, she realized she didn't
have the intense preparation needed to become a concert
pianist. Not content merely to teach music, she began to
rethink her career plans. At the time, her brother was a
social worker on skid row. Visiting him, she was shocked to
see people living on the streets. She had never been exposed
to such abject poverty before.

Through her brother, she began to meet homeless men
and women. She especially liked Eugene, sixty, a kind and
compassionate man in whose presence Mintie felt very
loved and accepted. Eugene was orphaned as a teenager,
and about the same time he was partially paralyzed in a car
accident. He had spent most of his life homeless, unable to
work and had lived under a bridge in Elysian Park for more
than a decade.

Mintie also became friendly with Isaac, an older black
man whose lively spirit had not been crushed by all his
suffering. A lovely, warm, and generous man with a great
deal of pride, he had set up housekeeping on an empty dirt
lot. His "home" didn't have walls or electricity to power his
television set; but whenever Mintie visited him, he would
graciously offer her a chair or a seat on his couch and
engage her in lively conversation. His best friend was a large
dog.

Mintie never had an idealized view of the homeless. "I
don't think that poor people are any more virtuous or evil
than anybody else," she says. "But sometimes it seems that

the suffering strips away a lot of the pretenses or the mask that the rest of us use to shield our vulnerability or our humanness. They're just who they are in a way that is very moving once you get to know them."

As she spent more time downtown, she became increasingly disturbed as she observed people living in vermin-infested tenements under conditions she thought had gone out of existence a century ago. "It was almost like I was allergic to suffering," she would later say.

Eugene died of stomach cancer. Isaac was murdered in his "home" by some criminals who strode in, stabbed him, and killed his dog. Mintie, distraught, began to realize how vulnerable the homeless were, and wanted to do something to help them. While she loved music, it simply didn't address the suffering she saw around her.

She was struck by how many poor people were unable to assert even their limited rights because red tape and bureaucratic barriers kept them from obtaining government aid. Without help in filling out the complex application forms, or anyone to question the sometimes arbitrary rulings of the welfare bureaucracy, they ended up on the street when they needn't be there.

Moreover, even those who obtained shelter were frequently exploited. If they tried to assert their rights as tenants, they might come home at night and find their doors bolted and all their belongings thrown out on the street. Those lucky enough to have jobs were also abused, working in sweatshops that ignored health and safety standards and paid less than the minimum wage.

It thus became increasingly apparent to Mintie that people on skid row were in desperate need of legal assistance. She decided to apply to law school and was accepted at several, including Harvard. Choosing UCLA because she didn't want to be saddled with a lot of debt upon graduation, she worked part-time and summers as an advocate in a state mental institution.

As soon as she completed her studies, she approached the Los Angeles Catholic Worker community, which ran a soup kitchen and shelter on skid row. They agreed to let her live at the shelter while she tried to establish a legal clinic.

For an office, she used a corner of a converted garage that served as the waiting room for a medical clinic upstairs. It was a tiny space with no privacy. In the summer it was as hot as a furnace; in the winter people shivered from the cold. She had one manual typewriter and a single phone line. Yet from day one she had more clients than she could handle. A soup line made its way past her door, and when people heard about the clinic, they came in with their problems.

As a member of the Catholic Worker community, she received five dollars a week spending money, which she used primarily for pantyhose in order to look presentable in court. She was assigned her share of chores and would regularly go with the other members of the group to the produce market to ask for donations of unsold food. Everyone took turns cooking.

Mintie's limited culinary skills, coupled with the hodge-podge of ingredients available to her, made for some unusual meals. One evening she served three kinds of Jell-O and popcorn. After several dinners like that, the staff took her aside and told her that her talents would be better utilized if confined to the legal clinic.

After she had run the clinic from the garage for three years, a benefactor gave her a trailer, which Mintie parked next to the garage and used as an office. As her work expanded, she recruited volunteers from the soup kitchen to assist her. One was an insurance broker, another a machinist, a third came from banking.

Practicing law on skid row was a frontier experience. One day an older Hispanic man flipped out, grabbed all her mail, and flushed it down the toilet, claiming the devil told him to do it. Another day a mentally disturbed woman came in ranting and raving, grabbed a pot of hot coffee and started to flail it about. Mintie shoved her out the door and wrestled her to the ground as neighborhood children cheered.

Another time as Mintie was leaving the office, she said "Good afternoon" to a large man standing by the door. For no apparent reason he exploded in anger and starting swinging at her. A blow glanced off her head before she scurried away.

As a result of such experiences, she has learned to be cautious. "It's best not to speak to people you don't know," she says, "because some people are so trapped by their own mental demons that anything you say or do can be misinterpreted and set them off."

For handling potentially violent people, Mintie and her staff have developed a technique that doesn't rely upon arms, force, or threats. The staff, who are mostly women, calmly, firmly, and as sympathetically as possible confront the agitated person and tell him or her that they will have to step outside until they calm down. The Center insists that clients hand over their guns and knives before they receive services. Almost everyone on skid row is armed with a weapon.

Her clients are frequently victims of violence. One day a man came in who had been repeatedly stabbed in the head by attackers trying to steal a few coins. Later that day another man bled all over her carpet from a gash in his leg before Mintie and her staff rushed him to the hospital. That evening as she left the office, she observed the assault and robbery of an elderly disabled man that happened so fast that the muggers were gone before anyone could intervene.

Virtually all the homeless women she has met have been raped and a number of her clients have been killed. Homeless people are an especially vulnerable population, she says, because many are disabled or mentally ill and they're often isolated and alone. Sleeping on street corners, they're easy pickings for predators.

Her clients bring her all kinds of previously intractable problems, which she tries to resolve. Working out of her trailer with a litigation budget of $3,000, she sued a notorious slumlord on behalf of thirteen families. The defendant retained three top law firms, one of which arrogantly bragged that its assets were equivalent to the gross national product of Belgium. But Mintie, unintimidated and laboring under a heavy workload, persevered and won $200,000, the largest settlement from a landlord in the history of Los Angeles and an encouragement for other attorneys to go after slumlords.

In another case, Mintie defended Richard Erhard, a former seminarian, who, while a full-time volunteer at the soup kitchen, was accused of assaulting police officers and interfering with an arrest. When Erhard had seen several white men yelling racial epithets and beating a black man they had pinned to the ground, he intervened, believing the men to be gang members. But they were undercover cops, and for being a Good Samaritan, Erhard had had his face smashed into a brick wall and had been handcuffed and arrested.

Mintie believed the police pressed charges in order to cover up their own misconduct. At the trial, it was simply their word against Erhard's. So Mintie called several character witnesses to testify to her client's honesty. The director of Erhard's seminary spoke, followed by the Roman Catholic bishop of Los Angeles and the police chaplain. She also put on the stand a little Irish Catholic nun who, when asked under oath if Erhard always told the truth, replied, "I'd stake my life on it." At that point Mintie noticed a juror brushing a tear from her eye. To save itself further embarrassment, the prosecution dropped the case before it went to the jury.

But such dramatic, high-stakes victories are rare. Most of the time, Mintie and her staff struggle to obtain for their clients a missed welfare payment or shelter for a couple of nights. Continually battling an implacable bureaucracy is tedious and frustrating, and Mintie and her staff often feel overwhelmed and despondent. It's the clients who keep their spirits up.

"When I try and imagine how I would feel if I were in their shoes," Mintie says, "I think that I would lose much of my humanity in a very short time if I was out there on the street subject to the kind of living conditions that they have to endure. Yet many of them are willing to hang onto their humanity in a really beautiful way. They'll come in and wait long hours after having spent the night on the street or not having anything to eat. And they stay polite, even grateful, for the little bit of service that we're able to provide. It's just a pleasure to work with them and serve them, and their need is great."

Fund-raising has always been Mintie's weakest area. For the first five years, she and her staff worked without salary. She lived at the shelter and subsisted on her $5-a-week allowance. Today the Center operates on a budget of $130,000 a year, derived from government and foundation grants, individual contributions, fund-raising events, honorariums, court-awarded attorney fees, and anything else she can beg. The one source she has never looked to for funds is her clients, who, she says, usually "don't have two dimes to rub together."

In March 1985, Jackson Browne, Brian Wilson, the Bangles, and other performers participated in a small benefit concert called Trouble in Paradise that raised $20,000. The money enabled Mintie to move the Center into a small complex of offices furnished with secondhand desks, file cabinets, and what must be the noisiest photocopier in the Western world.

One of Mintie's few indulgences is having a piano in her office, which she enjoys playing when she has a free moment. A small poster on the wall features an all-American boy and girl with the caption: THEY'RE RICH, THEY'RE HAPPY, THEY'RE WHITE, THEY'RE YOUNG REPUBLICANS IN LOVE. In a closet a collection of large rats is immersed in bottles of formaldehyde—evidence she has used against slumlords.

The staff has grown to six full-time and four part-time staff people, most of whom are women. The full-timers receive modest salaries, with Mintie earning $24,000 a year. The Center currently serves about two hundred clients a month.

Mintie has moved out of the shelter and now lives with

her husband, Arden Alger, several blocks from the Center in a warehouse loft that also serves as his photography studio.

As word of Mintie's legal victories spread, more victims flooded into her office, patiently waiting their turn to tell their stories, many of which are unforgettably tragic.

Gene (a pseudonym), a skinny, six-foot-one man in his late forties, needed help obtaining Supplemental Security Income benefits that were denied him. He was the second child of a nineteen-year-old mother and twenty-year-old father who were Arkansas farmers. The father died when Gene was two months old, and the boy was raised by his paternal grandmother in Missouri. He doesn't know what became of his mother.

In school, Gene was passed from grade to grade even though he couldn't handle the schoolwork. An eighth-grade dropout, today he finds it difficult to read a newspaper and cannot perform even the simplest arithmetic.

He volunteered for the Army and was given an honorable discharge after three months because of lack of vision in one eye. He was married; but his wife attacked him one day, breaking several ribs, and was placed in a state mental hospital. They are now divorced.

An epileptic, Gene has frequent seizures. One third of his stomach has been removed because of ulcers. He lost his teeth from gum disease and misplaced his dentures while living on the street. While he was homeless, his toes became frostbitten and had to be amputated, adversely affecting his balance and coordination.

Gene suffers from recurring schizophrenia and depression, and he is borderline mentally retarded. Under stress, his schizophrenia is activated and he hears voices urging him to kill himself. Having attempted suicide several times by slitting his throat, slashing his wrists, or stabbing himself, he has been intermittently committed to psychiatric hospitals, including a confinement of two years. Once, after being picked up while wandering the streets and saying he was Jesus, he was hospitalized and given shock treatments.

In an attempt to block his mental demons, he often drinks to excess and experiences frequent blackouts and delirium tremens. The police have arrested him more than fifty times for public intoxication.

Given his physical and mental disabilities, Gene's inability to support himself is not surprising. His work history is comprised exclusively of menial jobs, none of which lasted long. Often he would hear voices ridiculing him, become paranoid, and leave to be alone. At other times, he would suffer day-long crying spells for no apparent reason.

Mentally disabled people like Gene often find it difficult to receive government assistance. Once he managed to get on a program but lost his benefits the next day when he failed to show up for an appointment. For the past four years he has survived by selling his plasma to local blood banks. The Social Security Administration has twice determined him "not disabled" and has refused to grant him benefits.

Mintie took on the Social Security Administration and was able to get Gene regular monthly disability checks plus six thousand dollars in back benefits dating from the time he first applied for assistance. The money enabled him to buy a small house-trailer on the outskirts of Center, Colorado, where he presently resides. He recently wrote Mintie a letter stating: "Nancy, I want to let you know, that I just can't find room enough in my heart to thank you for what you did for me. . . . Your friend, now, always and forever, Gene."

Another group of clients waiting to see Mintie were tenants of a dilapidated building in downtown Los Angeles. Teresa Montenegro, thirty, and small, plump, and cheerful, is a refugee from El Salvador eligible for amnesty under the new Immigration Reform and Control Act of 1986. She lives with her two sons—Billy, one, and Eric, three—and her husband, Roberto, who supports the family with whatever day labor he can find.

She came to Mintie to ask for help in getting her landlord to make repairs after awaking one morning and being startled by a foot-long rat scurrying past her, scraping its tail against her leg. So numerous were the rats that they ate the family's food, chewed holes in their clothes, and frightened her sons. At night they scampered about the room searching for food as the family lay in bed, making so much noise the children found it difficult to sleep.

Often the rats climbed onto the children's beds, and on more than one night Eric had awakened crying, "Mommy, Mommy, something bit me." Teresa had recently found scratches on his body, blood on his head, and spots of blood tracked across his blanket—a rat had apparently chewed on his ear and leg as he slept.

The rats were everywhere. They left their droppings in piles of freshly laundered clothes and fouled the carpet so badly that Teresa had to clean it every morning. They brought fleas into the apartment, and the family's legs were covered with rashes and scabs.

Although the children were healthy when they first moved in, now they often had fevers. Eric would refuse to eat and was lethargic. Whenever he discovered a cut on his body, he would blame the rats. He believed the rats did everything to him and couldn't get them out of his mind. Teresa noticed that the joy in his play was gone.

The apartment was also infested with cockroaches. No matter how hard or how much she cleaned and scrubbed, she couldn't get rid of them. Whenever she entered the apartment, she would see a horde on her bed; when she opened the oven, they would swarm out; when she cooked, they would fall from the ceiling into the food. Night and day she brushed them off her body. She slept in pants and covered her children from head to toe. Even then she would feel them against her skin. She would shake the children at night to throw them off, and then pick the insects out of their hair. She found two squashed in Billy's diaper. Once she prepared a bottle for Billy and was just about to give it to him when she noticed a roach floating on the surface. The insects even crawled into the freezer through gaps in the door; she would find them frozen in ice cubes. Management never sprayed for roaches, and the large amounts of roach powder that Teresa placed about the apartment did little good.

For two weeks in December the kitchen and bathroom sinks were clogged. One night filthy water backed up in both sinks, flooding the apartment and fouling the carpet. The manager refused to make repairs, telling Teresa that the tenants below her were to blame, while telling them she was responsible. Teresa stayed up for several nights watching for back-ups. Finally, the manager brought in a plumber to make repairs, but the carpet wasn't replaced and continued to stink.

The bathtub had never functioned well; the water always drained slowly. Drano didn't work; nor could the plumber clear it. Whenever Teresa or the boys took showers the water rose up the sides of the tub and seeped through cracks onto the floor. She would scoop water out of the tub with a bucket, flush it down the toilet, and then mop the floor.

The hot water supply was highly erratic, sometimes lost for up to ten days. She would heat water on the stove to wash the kids and take cold showers herself. The manager claimed cold showers were good because the weather was warm. Occasionally there was no water at all, forcing her to keep bottles of it on hand.

The electricity would frequently be cut off and the food in the refrigerator would spoil. When the lights went out on Christmas she picked up her children and visited a friend so they wouldn't have to spend the holiday in the dark. The manager, claiming the fuses were bad, said repairs would be made; but several days later the problem reoccurred. Furthermore, the room never had any heat. There was a heater but it didn't work and again no repairs were ever made.

Men who didn't live in Teresa's building would loiter

there, laughing and shouting late into the night, running through the dark halls and knocking on doors. Teresa, who worked nights, was so afraid to enter the building in the dark that her boss had to escort her home.

Downstairs from Teresa, Socorino Arollo lived with four of her children and three grandchildren. Her daughter and son-in-law lived across the hall. One day Socorino's eight-year-old grandson Alfonso was playing on the second floor when the lights went out. He tried to find his way downstairs but tripped and fell, breaking an arm. Socorino rushed him to the hospital where doctors inserted pins into his arm and set the bones, but he was able to regain only partial use of the arm and often complained of discomfort.

In March of 1985, Socorino's son-in-law fell and injured his back and kidneys while trying to fix their electricity. He could walk a little but couldn't stand up straight or sit. Two months later he went in for corrective surgery but is still unable to lift heavy objects and hasn't been able to find a job since the accident. One day he surprised burglars in his apartment and they stabbed him with a screwdriver and fled.

When ten-year-old Consuelo took out the garbage, she was accosted by a man who accused her of taking something of his and attempted to search her. She ran to her mother when the man touched her.

On behalf of the residents of Teresa's building, Mintie sued the landlord, an attorney who had gone to school at Berkeley in the 1960s and considered himself a radical. Somehow he fancied himself a benefactor of the poor by making low-income housing available to them. The case against him is still pending. In the meantime, he missed several mortgage payments and lost ownership of the building. The new owner, under threat of litigation, has made extensive repairs and brought in exterminators to rid the building of vermin.

But Mintie is not always so successful. Tyrone Taggert,

for instance, was a polite and quiet man who became enmeshed in a bureaucratic nightmare when he didn't receive his General Relief checks. The checks either weren't sent, were stolen, or were mailed to the wrong address. The process of tracing such checks is long and tedious, and the hapless recipient is often forced to live on the street.

While the Center's paralegals were trying to straighten out the mess, Taggert suffered a mental breakdown. He walked about downtown Los Angeles waving a pipe in a menacing manner at passing cars. When the police arrived, he came at them saying, "If you want me to put the pipe down, you'll have to kill me." They did. Mintie says she is surprised that more of her clients don't crack up.

Not only has Mintie helped many individuals but she has also tackled some of the larger issues affecting the poor. With an attorney from the Legal Aid Foundation, she challenged the practice of landlords illegally evicting tenants by locking them out of their rooms, winning her clients more than forty thousand dollars in damages and frightening other slumlords into dropping the practice.

Mintie has leveraged her efforts by working with other attorneys. She was a founding member of the Homeless Litigation Team, a joint effort of lawyers from the Legal Aid Foundation, the American Civil Liberties Union (ACLU), the Center for Law in the Public Interest, and other public interest law firms.

The lawyers were struck by the large number of vacant hotel rooms existing in Los Angeles County's voucher system while thousands of people were homeless. After interviewing men and women living on the streets, they discovered that the county had erected two simple but effective barriers preventing people from obtaining shelter.

First, the county insisted that applicants have a certified copy of a birth certificate or a driver's license to receive aid, an impossible request for many homeless individuals who typically kept identification papers with valuables and lost both to thieves.

Second, some welfare offices established quotas for the number of people they would serve. Those who arrived after the quota was filled wouldn't be helped no matter how desperate their plight. Many applicants simply didn't have the stamina to sit in a welfare office for eight or nine hours without food only to be told to come back the next day.

The lawyers sued L.A. County in *Eisenheim* v. *Board of Supervisors* and in 1983 won a temporary restraining order ending both practices. The court directed the county to provide homeless people with shelter on the day they applied for it regardless of whether they had identification.

After the decision, homeless people flooded the welfare offices. When the county ran out of hotel vouchers, it issued eight-dollar checks to enable applicants to purchase their own lodging. The checks were dispersed at 5:00 or 6:00 P.M., after applicants had waited all day, and after all check-cashing facilities had closed. Consequently, the recipients were forced to cash their checks at convenience stores that charged a fee of a dollar or more. The remaining money wasn't sufficient to rent a room, so they would buy food and spend the night on the street or in a seedy all-night movie theater. In *Ross* v. *Board of Supervisors*, the lawyers challenged the adequacy of the eight-dollar payment and won a court order in 1986 requiring the county to provide actual shelter for every homeless person who requested it.

Consequently, the county had to greatly expand its list of hotels in the voucher system. Many were dirty, rat-infested tenements lacking heat, hot water, and security. A lot of homeless people took one look at the rooms and decided they would rather stay on the street. In *Paris* v. *Board of Supervisors*, Mintie and her associates filed one hundred declarations describing the dreadful conditions. In 1987 the county negotiated a settlement requiring voucher hotels to supply heat from October to May and comply with county health codes. The county also agreed to rate hotels and fill the best first. Moreover, if a voucher recipient was dissatisfied, he or she would be able to switch rooms or move to another hotel.

Their next lawsuit challenged what is known as the sixty-day penalty. In California those who apply for welfare are required to enroll in a workfare program. They must work off their grant at the minimum wage and seek job interviews in their free time. If they're late for a work project, fail to turn in a form on time, make errors in their paperwork, or are unable to document twenty job searches a month, they automatically lose their benefits and can't reapply for sixty days. As a result of *Bannister* v. *County of Los Angeles,* the regulations were changed in 1985 so that the sixty-day penalty would only apply when violations were intentional.

Finally, in *Blair* v. *County of Los Angeles,* the Homeless Litigation Team challenged the adequacy of the $228-a-month general relief payments given to workfare participants. Since the worst housing in the city costs at least $240 a month, the county's forty thousand General Relief recipients couldn't afford to live indoors. Embarrassed by the suit, the county raised the benefit to $247 a month, and ultimately settled the suit by agreeing to raise payments to $280 a month by July 1987, and to $312 a month by July 1988.

Mintie believes it's intolerable for America to turn its back on the homeless. "I don't understand how we as a community can stand by and let this situation develop," she says. "To me, it's just completely unacceptable and so unnecessary. I try to tell people about it but often I feel I'm howling into the wind. I mean there are little old ladies, helpless mentally disabled people, children, young girls, not to mention the men, living on the street, subject to the most extreme danger and illness and fear and suffering, and we as a community seem to be saying, 'Well, *c'est la vie.*'

"We've forgotten that we have alternatives. We've forgotten that eight years ago, this problem didn't exist. . . . If

model who recently became a mother. Her sister Mary works in a convalescent home, Ann is an artist, and the youngest, Donna, is a college student.

Mintie says there are three causes of homelessness: People either have an alcohol or drug problem, they're mentally ill, or they simply can't earn enough to afford shelter. When she began working on skid row, most of the homeless were drunks or drug addicts. Today this group comprises only 15 or 20 percent of the homeless, although others eventually turn to alcohol or drugs to escape their miserable existence.

Most of the mentally ill on the streets have been released as a result of the movement begun in the 1960s to deinstitutionalize patients not deemed a danger to themselves or others. Proponents of the policy reasoned that many of the patients in mental hospitals could be treated in community care centers. Elected officials embraced the idea and were pleased to be able to reduce funding for mental hospitals. Patients were discharged, but funds for alternative care never materialized.

Mental illness strikes indiscriminately and unless one has a network of family and friends to help, it's amazing how quickly a person can land on skid row. One day Mintie met a middle-aged black man who was so delusional that she could barely communicate with him. He claimed he had worked for NASA, and upon investigation, it turned out that he had been a brilliant scientist who had sold several inventions to NASA. One day his mind snapped, his life quickly unraveled, and he soon found himself homeless. "There but for the grace of God go I," says Mintie, who feels that the same thing could happen to just about anybody.

Perhaps the most tragic stories belong to those who are healthy and sane and find themselves homeless only because they're unemployed. Many are humiliated to be on General Relief, says Mintie. Callous welfare bureaucrats can make the application process even more degrading.

Mintie tells the story of one applicant who was forced to sit on a little girl's rocking chair for his interview.

Few people are homeless because they're lazy, she says, explaining that when mentally or physically disabled people apply for aid, they're routinely asked if they're able to work. Out of pride and a desire to be productive many respond, "Yes." "So they're put on these work projects," says Mintie, "where they inevitably fail because of their physical or mental limitations, and then they're cut off the aid program when they should have been given a disability dispensation in the first place.

"People go to great lengths to work, even in the slave pools around here where work is very hard and they're very exploited. For example, those handbills you find on your doorknob are distributed by guys who work for temporary day-labor agencies. They get on line in the wee hours of the morning to get priority for those jobs. Then they're put in trucks and taken out to various neighborhoods where they'll work carrying heavy bags of handbills. They're not allowed to take any breaks. The foreman drives around to keep an eye on them. If he sees them sitting down or trying to get something to eat, they're fired and not paid.

"Then they bring them back downtown too late to get in a mission line to compete for one of the scarce beds, so they end up sleeping out. They get paid ten or twelve bucks for a ten-hour day, on their feet all day delivering these things. I've had guys with severe shoulder and back injuries who, nevertheless, hobble around with these bags, very painfully . . . because they want to work.

"It's heartbreaking really, because it's a trap. With that kind of money and sleeping on the street you're never going to make enough to get yourself any kind of housing. It's a pipe dream. Nevertheless, these places [employment agencies] are full of guys looking for that kind of work."

Even those with better-paying jobs have a tough time. "We've had clients who work full-time at the minimum wage and still live in their cars because they can't find housing they can afford," she says.

One summer two of Mintie's associates set up a jobs program. They assumed that with their middle-class connections they could get work for those with some education and skills. They spent an entire summer hunting for jobs, typing up resumes and ironing applicants' shirts. By the end of the summer they had placed two men—one of whom became unemployed again when his factory closed three weeks later.

"There would be an ad for a job with the phone company in the newspaper that morning," says Mintie "and they would rush a man down to the application site, and there would be eleven hundred applications already received. And nobody was going to hire a homeless guy out of work in such a competitive market."

Mintie is critical of the county's workfare program. "People are given jobs shoveling other less fortunate homeless people into the crematorium or cleaning toilets in county hospitals, doing things with no value as job experience. And the person is also supposed to go out and complete twenty job interviews a month. But they're not given the proper clothing, or a place to type up a resume or a phone number to receive calls back, or transportation to get to outlying neighborhoods for interviews.

"And so we end up with thousands of guys walking around in the skid row area and going into various little businesses around here asking for job interviews. The store owners are sick of it. They see all these guys and say, 'We're not going to hire any of these raggedy guys come walking in off the streets. Get out of here.' So the job interview portion of the program is a farce.

"And if the workfare participant makes a single mistake—misses a bus or is late to work because he didn't have an alarm clock—then they're thrown off the program for sixty days. It's just so ironic to me that we would punish the homeless that way when we at least shelter and feed murderers and other vicious criminals."

*   *   *

In 1988 there were 715,000 lawyers in the United States of America, but only a relative handful served the poor. Considering the sacrifices that lawyers like Nancy Mintie must make, it is not surprising that most attorneys prefer fields where the pay is better and the working conditions more pleasant. Indeed, most lawyers work for wealthy individuals or corporate interests. Corporations spend tens of billions of dollars on legal services. By contrast the federal budget for legal aid services was $305 million to operate 320 field programs.

In *Lawyers on Trial*, Philip M. Stern refutes the conventional wisdom that corporations and rich people have more legal problems, and more need of lawyers than the poor. Stern notes that in just two decades (1954–74) the number of black landowners in the South shrank from 175,000 to 40,000 because rural blacks didn't write wills. As a result, when they died, ownership of their land descended to their relatives according to state law.

> Over the years those relatives scattered to places unknown, and when the survivors living on the land found themselves unable to pay the taxes and the other heirs couldn't be located to exercise their option to pay the taxes and keep the land, it went on the auction block. As of 1978, there were just four million acres still owned by blacks. It was being sold off at a rate of 500,000 acres a year. For want of a will. . . . For want of a lawyer.

The lack of legal assistance for the vast majority of the public makes a mockery of the ideal that there is equal justice for all in America. It is not a matter of there being too few lawyers. In 1870 the ratio of lawyers in the United States to the general population was 1 lawyer for every 970 persons. By 1984 the ratio was 1 lawyer for every 376 persons. Two thirds of the lawyers in the world practice in the United States. There are three times as many lawyers in America, per capita, as in England, and twenty-one times as many as in Japan.

Yet in our increasingly complex world, most poor and middle-income Americans can't afford to see a lawyer.

Among Americans with legal problems serious enough to merit seeing an attorney, nearly three out of four had either not consulted an attorney, or had done so only once in their lives. The American Bar Association has acknowledged that the middle 70 percent of the population is not being reached or served adequately by the legal profession.

The lack of legal assistance is particularly acute for the poor. Only those persons whose incomes are less than 125 percent of the federal poverty line are eligible for legal aid. Nearly eight million poor people are shut out. And those who are eligible often must endure interminable delays before receiving assistance. Poor people in Brooklyn, New York, seeking a divorce must wait twelve to eighteen months just to obtain an interview with a lawyer.

Moreover, our legal system has barriers that restrict the access of poor and middle-class people to the courthouse while giving unwarranted advantages to moneyed interests. When a manufacturer cheats a consumer, for instance, the monetary claim is usually too small to justify filing suit. The manufacturer can repeatedly cheat millions of consumers out of small amounts of money with impunity.

The solution has been the class-action lawsuit where consumers combine their claims into a single lawsuit. Since the mid-1970s, however, the Supreme Court has restricted class-action suits. In *Eisen* v. *Carlisle and Jacqueline (1974)*, the Court held that before it could hear the claim of the plaintiff-stockholder, he would have to notify the six million identifiable members of the class. To do so would have cost the plaintiff $250,000 in postage, printing, and other costs, more money than he could afford. The suit was dropped.

As a result of *Eisen* and similar rulings, there has been a reduction of more than 40 percent in the number of class-action lawsuits brought in federal courts. Other Supreme Court decisions have removed plaintiffs from the courtrooms by denying lower courts the power to award attorney fees in public interest litigation.

The American Bar Foundation projects that the number of lawyers in the United States will reach one million by the year 2000. But without structural reforms and new incentives, few of those lawyers will serve the people who need them most.

Those who have observed Mintie up close speak of her in glowing terms. Jill Halverson, the founder and director of the Downtown Women's Center, says Mintie and her staff are willing to tackle any problem, "whether it is helping the women locate children or get a birth certificate or help them with Social Security. There is no task too small or too great."

Gene Blasi, a Legal Aid attorney, praises Mintie as a phenomenally good attorney. "I think she is underrated by some lawyers because she doesn't have all the bells and whistles and office support they have. I mean I just gave her my old computer, which is their first word processor. Up until now she has had to deal with a typewriter and white-out."

Not only is she bright and creative, says ACLU attorney Mark Rosenbaum, but she is also absolutely tenacious and extremely thorough. He says her most extraordinary skill, however, is her rapport with the homeless, who are very difficult to communicate with. Mintie has earned their trust.

County Supervisor Ed Edelman calls Mintie an eloquent advocate, explaining that in testimony before the Board of Supervisors she brought attention to the roadblocks the county was placing in front of the homeless. While she didn't always sway the board to her view, they listened carefully to her because of her sincerity and because she spoke with the authority of someone who was intimately familiar with the problem. If nothing else, he says, she has done a great job raising the consciousness of the board.

"She is a remarkable person," states LeRoy Cordova, director of the office of Legal Services of the California State Bar, which gives a small grant to the Inner City Law Center. "It's a real David versus Goliath situation in Los Angeles," he says, "and she is really a hero to a lot of us in legal services." In recognition of her work she received the

State Bar President's Pro Bono Service Award. She has also been honored by the Los Angeles County and Beverly Hills bar associations.

The most unusual thing about Mintie is that she has not become angry or bitter, and remains a pleasant and vital person who doesn't appear to be discouraged.

Her friend Margaret Holub, thirty, a rabbi, describes Mintie in more personal terms as "somebody who not only collects rats to sue slumlords but also remembers birthdays of everyone she works with. And she's really a lot of fun. A person who loves to dance, and play. She's organized a writing group and she's an excellent poet."

Mintie is modest in speaking of her achievements. "Overall, what I see as the best accomplishment of the Center," she says, "is that we are the last place downtown that the homeless can come to when the bureaucracy slams the door in their face. . . . We're a place where the homeless can come walk in the door and have somebody go to bat for them in a caring atmosphere. The people I have working with me, I've sort of handpicked for the size of their hearts . . . even if what we get the person ultimately is some kind of measly benefit, or a night of shelter, or a few days of food, whatever that little thing is . . . [what matters is that] they can come in and talk to somebody who cares."

Chapter 2

FAST EDDIE

Salus populi suprema lex est.
"The people's safety is the highest law."

Caveat emptor.
"Let the buyer beware."

On a brisk January morning in 1968, Linda and Paul Buckley* dressed their children in quilted winter jackets and prepared to leave their home in Bellingham, Massachusetts. They were going to Cape Cod for the day, a trip Linda had been especially looking forward to because upon their arrival there would be a family reunion and she would shop for a bridesmaid's dress for her sister's wedding.

While Linda gathered the last of their belongings, her husband placed Paul junior, aged two and a half, and Jessica, one and a half, in the rear of their station wagon, wrapping them in a cozy fiberfill comforter. Then he returned to the house to help his wife with the remaining baggage.

He met her as she was walking out the kitchen door with a bunch of diapers in hand. As she looked down the driveway past him, she saw thick, black smoke filling the car. She

---

* The names of the plaintiffs in the "Buckley" case have been changed to protect their privacy.

screamed, Paul turned, and they rushed to the car, flinging open the rear doors in a desperate attempt to rescue their children.

By the time they removed them, their children's hands and faces were severely burned. A black tarry goo lay on top of melted and burned flesh. Linda, a nurse, resuscitated Jessica on the spot, and then they rushed the children to a hospital in nearby Milford. After emergency treatment, the Milford ambulance sped the young victims twenty-five miles to the respected Boston Children's Hospital.

Dr. Angelo Eraklis had been alerted to expect the children, and his team of doctors, nurses, and technicians quickly went into action upon their arrival. Eraklis had seen hundreds of burn victims over the years but he had never seen anything like the hard, black caramellike substance stuck to these children. Because Jessica was having difficulty breathing and was in imminent danger of expiring, the doctors hastily tore away the black crust over her nostrils, cleaned out her mouth, and administered oxygen.

Burns are classified in degrees, from first-degree—a sunburn—to fourth-degree when the epidermal and dermal layers of skin have been burned away along with the subcutaneous layer of fat, nerve endings, sweat glands, and hair follicles. Jessica and Paul junior had fourth-degree burns—when the charred skin was removed, only cartilage and bone remained.

The body responds to such severe burns with a call to battle. Stress hormones pour into the bloodstream, blood vessels dilate, and the heart and lungs pump harder. Fluid and blood leak from damaged capillaries, swelling tissues and reducing the amount of blood needed to fill the newly expanded veins and arteries. To compensate, blood vessels begin to contract, reducing flow to the brain, kidneys, liver, and other vital organs. If the cycle is unchecked, the patient goes into shock and dies. Even those able to survive these acute dangers often succumb to infection and stress ulcers.

Fortunately, Dr. Eraklis and his team were skilled at treating severe burn victims. Tracheotomies were performed and breathing tubes inserted in each child's throat. Fluid losses were restored intravenously. Antibiotics and antitetanus toxoids were given, and charred skin was peeled away.

A few days later Jessica was wheeled into the operating room and under general anesthesia dead tissue was removed. She was having difficulty eating, so a gastrostomy was performed, placing a feeding tube directly into her stomach through the abdominal wall. Although Paul junior's burns were less severe, he also required the procedure.

When the children's conditions stabilized, they were turned over to plastic surgeons for a series of operations. Grafts were made to replace burned tissue and restore the skin's integrity as a barrier against infection. Because scar tissue is less elastic than undamaged skin, surgeons recut scars along more natural lines to try to improve flexibility. The doctors also sought to ameliorate the children's grotesque appearance, but the damage was so great that only limited improvement was possible.

After the accident, Jessica refused to talk, forgetting the few words she knew. Swathed in bandages, she would lie in her crib and cry whenever anyone, including her parents, tried to speak to her.

Several months after the fire, Linda and Paul Buckley consulted an attorney. He expressed the opinion that it was unlikely they could recover anything for their children's injuries, suffering, or medical expenses. A second attorney concurred. A third attorney thought that while the case would be difficult to win, there was a Boston lawyer known as Fast Eddie who might be able to help them.

Edward M. Swartz doesn't look fast—he is fifty-three and chubby with a noticeable midriff bulge. Stepping from a stretch limousine, handkerchief in his breast pocket, wearing black-and-white patent leather shoes, he looks as debonair as Jackie Gleason out for a night on the town. When you observe him grilling a witness, however, you realize he is as mentally agile as a gazelle—with the drive of a charging rhinoceros.

He speaks passionately about injustice and, loving to be the center of attention, is quick to supply inquiring journalists with a generous selection of articles recounting his exploits and a slick videotape chronicling his many television appearances and speeches.

He describes himself as an attorney of last resort—someone people go to when other lawyers tell them their case is hopeless. He will advance hundreds of thousands of dollars of his own to investigate cases and pay court costs, and then battle phalanxes of high-priced lawyers arrayed against him. His concern is genuine, his courtroom skills exceptional, and time and again he has persuaded juries to award huge sums of money to his clients. He has become wealthy representing ordinary people injured by the products of Big Business.

When a junior high school student was horribly burned during a chemistry experiment, Swartz agreed to represent her even though it was apparent he wouldn't be able to collect much from her teacher, who had few assets, or from the school district, which was largely immune from suit. So he sued the publisher of her textbook on the ground that it failed to caution readers of the dangers inherent in the experiment. In the first case of its kind, he won a $1.1 million judgment for "negligent publishing." His fee: $300,000.

In another case, Swartz represented a fifteen-year-old Pennsylvania boy who dived into three and a half feet of water in an above-ground swimming pool. The boy smashed his head on the bottom and fractured his spinal cord, which permanently paralyzed him from the neck down. A top personal injury attorney referred the case to Swartz after concluding it wasn't winnable—a prior case clearly established that such pools weren't defective because the risk of diving into them was obvious. Swartz didn't like that ruling and agreed to represent the boy although the circumstances surrounding the accident were almost identical. Indeed, he was suing the same pool manufacturer in the same Pennsylvania county.

Although plaintiff attorneys in above-ground pool cases typically argued that the pools were defective because they gave an illusory perception of water depth, Swartz conceded at the outset that his client knew he was diving into shallow water. He took a different tack, asserting that the pool was defective because it wasn't apparent how serious an injury would result from diving into it. He said that most people would assume the worst that could happen would be a bump on the head.

At trial, Swartz pointed out that the manufacturer never warned its customers of previous quadriplegic injuries that had occurred when people dove into their pools, that the company's ads showed people diving into the pools, and that the company sold a deck it called a diving platform. Swartz asked the pool company's executives why they didn't place warnings on the pool. They replied that when the pools were designed they hadn't realized that diving into them could cause serious injury.

So Swartz argued that if the executives didn't recognize the danger, how could they expect a fifteen-year-old boy to know. The jury returned a verdict of $6.5 million, including $500,000 in punitive damages—a record in conservative Erie, Pennsylvania.

From such judgments Swartz earns a handsome living. He and his wife live in a mansion worth several million dollars on three acres of land in the exclusive Chestnut Hill section of Boston. The house has fifteen rooms, nine bathrooms, a sauna, and a hot tub. On the grounds are an Olympic-size swimming pool and a tennis court. He also owns homes in Palm Beach, New York City, Cape Cod, and Vermont, as well as six cars, including a Porsche, a Jaguar, an Excalibur, and a Rolls-Royce—with driver.

His office is in the John and Ebenezer Hancock House, the oldest brick building in the city of Boston and the place where Ebenezer Hancock is reputed to have paid soldiers of the Continental Army. Swartz saved the building from the wrecker's ball, restored its handmade English bricks, ax-hewn beams, and iron door hinges, and had it designated a national historical landmark.

Swartz is close to his family. His youngest daughter, Sharron, is a budding singer and actress in high school; daughter Joan is a law student at Boston University; and son James is a law student at Georgetown University. Swartz would like his children to join his firm; already working with him are his brothers Frederic, forty-six, and Joseph, thirty-one, and his mother, who serves as the firm's bookkeeper.

Swartz's wealth contrasts with his humble background. His father was an insurance salesman and the family grew up in a tenement neighborhood in Chelsea. By age nine Swartz was working in a meat market. He later sold encyclopedias, insurance, pots and pans, and magazines, and earned money for college by renting pillows on the New York to Boston train run. The proudest moment in Ed's life was the day he bought his dad a brand-new Cadillac.

There were no lawyers in the family; dad went no further than the fifth grade, mom dropped out of high school to work. Other kids in the neighborhood wanted to be airline pilots and firemen, but little Eddie is reputed to have told everyone when he was three that he was going to be a lawyer. Today he can't remember back that far; but for as long as he can remember, his goal has been to become a lawyer.

With single-minded determination he honed his skills in college debates and by acting in school plays and summer stock. He attended Boston University Law School on a scholarship, was editor in chief of the law review, president of the student bar association, represented his school in a national moot court competition, and graduated first in his class.

As graduation approached, he met with the dean of the law school, who was pleased that his prize student was receiving offers from top Wall Street law firms. "To be candid with you, Ed," the dean said, "we haven't placed BU boys in some of these firms, and we certainly haven't placed any Jewish boys there, so that makes it a doubleheader. What are you going to do?"

Swartz told the dean that he was going into personal injury work—a pursuit sometimes referred to as "ambulance chasing." The dean reacted as if a knife had been stuck in his heart. He pleaded with Swartz, "But that's what you do if you can't get a job." Swartz, however, wasn't interested in working for a big firm representing silk-stocking people.

After graduation Swartz spent six months in the Army Reserves, and then he began working for an older lawyer who let him try cases right away. In one of his first trials he represented a one-eyed drunk who had fallen down an elevator shaft while working in a warehouse. Swartz argued that the man hadn't assumed the risk of injury from hazards in the workplace because it was poverty, not free will, that forced him to work under these conditions. He spoke passionately for the man, remembering how as a child he risked amputation feeding a meat grinder with his bare hands.

As the jury foreman announced a verdict for Swartz's client, he slammed the wooden railing of the jury box with such force that he broke it. At that moment, Swartz realized he had a special gift for persuasion. As the years went by, he continued to improve, learning from the veteran defense attorneys he opposed.

In 1963 he became a member of the Massachusetts Attorney General's Office where he drafted and secured passage of the Massachusetts Truth-In-Lending Act. He also began to build his own practice. He worked for the attorney general from six in the morning until three in the afternoon, and then on his own cases from four in the afternoon until midnight. By 1965 he was devoting himself full-time to his own practice.

In those early years, he often had to rely on bank loans to keep his office afloat; and if he didn't win a case he might not be able to meet his payroll and feed his family. Now that he is wealthy, his survival is assured, yet he still drives himself hard. "When I'm in trial, I'm like a litigation machine," he says. "It's a twenty-two-hour-a-day proposition and I'm turning over every stone, and I'm only thinking about that case."

A favorite Swartz tactic is to exploit the defense's pious declarations for safety. He encourages defense witnesses to elucidate on the principles they profess to believe in. He'll ask, "We all agree that we want to save lives and that if we could save a life, cost would not stand in our way, right?" The witness usually responds affirmatively. Swartz carefully builds standards of care out of the mouths of the defendants, and then cites their conduct, demonstrating how they violated the principles they claim they to believe in. The jury is left with the conclusion that the witness is either a liar or a hypocrite.

He is a tireless pursuer of facts. What distinguishes great lawyers from average practitioners, he says, isn't their understanding of the law but their ability to marshall facts. When a six-year-old girl was severely burned in a fire caused by a twenty-six-year-old hair dryer she used in bed to warm herself, Swartz alleged the product was defective because it didn't have a thermal fuse that would automatically shut it off upon overheating. The defense claimed the dryer was made in accordance with the state of existing technology at the time. To refute the defense, Swartz set out to find an old-fashioned dryer with a thermal fuse.

He found one described in an old Sears, Roebuck catalog in the archives of the Boston Public Library and summoned the librarian to court. The judge refused to accept the book as evidence, however, ruling that the product itself had to be produced. Swartz and his staff called hundreds of secondhand electrical shops searching for the dryer. When they finally located one, the defense capitulated and settled the case for $900,000.

Swartz says lawyers too often cloister themselves in the law library, when they should be rummaging the real world looking for solutions. When he was representing a man injured when a tire flew off a tire-changing machine, the defense brought in a line of high-priced experts. Swartz, on the other hand, drove to ten gas stations and asked the mechanics who changed tires about their experiences.

"Man, are you kidding me," one mechanic replied, "those goddamn tires go off all the time. See that dent in the roof?" Swartz recruited two mechanics to come to court. He instructed them not to wear jackets and ties but to arrive in their regular working clothes, knowing full well that the jury would find men with dirt under their nails and oil-stained overalls far more credible than the defense's neatly dressed experts. Swartz's client won a settlement of $750,000.

Swartz loves courtroom demonstrations. He represented a young boy whose penis was lacerated when he rode atop a canister-style vacuum cleaner playing "horsey" while in his pajamas. To demonstrate how sharp the fan blades were, he pulled a frankfurter from his breast pocket and inserted it, sending chunks of meat flying across the courtroom and splattering the judge. "I didn't have to say much after that," he says. The jury awarded his client $130,000.

In another case, Swartz represented a one-year-old girl who was horribly disfigured when a bottle of liquid drain cleaner overturned, splashing her. Swartz believed the bottle should have been designed to reduce the flow of contents in the event of a spill. Wanting to present the jury with a prototype of a better cap, he consulted experts but they couldn't produce one. So he went to the supermarket and bought dozens of products in all kinds of bottles and spent an evening experimenting with them.

When Swartz cross-examined the defendant's expert, he presented a bottle top and asked if it would be appropriate for the drain cleaner. The expert replied that they had considered such a cap and had rejected it because the viscosity of the drain cleaner was such that it would not pour freely. Swartz opened his briefcase and showed the witness and jury that the bottle cap had come from a bottle of maple syrup. The jury awarded $1.7 million to Swartz's client.

Swartz is a master at tugging on jurors' heartstrings. In the drain cleaner case he asked the girl's mother to explain the impact of the accident: "[She] was a very cheerful, joyful, bright child before the accident," said the mother. "She was very outgoing. She was not afraid of anybody. . . .

"After the accident, she started to become withdrawn. She was very insecure. She always wanted somebody around she knew. As she got older and grew, it was very hard for her to even face people. She would hide her face. She didn't want to be with other children. She constantly asked if she was pretty. She thought she was ugly. . . .

". . . [her] total mannerism changed. . . . She became clingy, insecure. She started to get shy and withdrawn, and as she got older, she started to ask questions about why kids didn't want to play with her, why people stared at her. Kids would cry when they saw her. . . .

"Whenever we took her places, kids called her ugly and said she looked like a monster. She got to be very remorseful and sad. She would want to know why. She would say things like, 'I'm ugly. They are afraid of me.' And she got more and more withdrawn. . . . She would go sit in the corner. She just didn't want to be with other kids."

In the hair dryer case, Swartz had the tearful mother of the victim describe each of the girl's operations, her scars, and the daily cleaning to remove bacteria, dirt, and pus from the fist-sized cavity below her breast. "Has she ever expressed any thoughts to you about the future?" Swartz asked.

"No, but she worries," the mother said. "No boy has ever called her; she's never been invited to a party. Once, late at night, we were sitting, just the two of us, and she asked, 'Mother, will I ever be able to get married?' " At this point the mother began sobbing. Swartz slowly poured her a glass of water, giving her plenty of time to cry.

Swartz always speaks extemporaneously, preferring to maintain eye contact with the jury even at the risk of occasionally missing a point. Reading from a legal pad is "yellow death," he says. "I mean I wouldn't buy a vacuum cleaner from someone who tried to sell me one like that. So why should I buy a position from a lawyer who doesn't know his case well enough, or have confidence enough, to communicate it ably in a conversational way?"

His passion for justice extends beyond the courtroom. Each year before Christmas he begins a crusade against dangerous toys. He visits toy stores with a pocketful of cash looking for toy guns that shoot dangerous projectiles, mobiles that can strangle babies, and stuffed animals with ears and eyes that can be easily removed and swallowed. With great fanfare, he releases a list of what he considers the ten worst toys and demonstrates their dangers before news cameras.

Swartz is extremely critical of the fifteen-billion-dollar-a-year toy industry and the 150,000 different toys it sells. He says that the toy companies are often run by marketers and that safety engineers have little influence on design. He has written two books about dangerous toys, *Toys That Don't Care*, and *Toys That Kill*. He has spoken about dangerous toys on *60 Minutes, The Mike Douglas Show, Good Morning America, The Today Show*, and *To Tell the Truth*.

He has a low opinion of the Consumer Product Safety Commission, which is charged with the responsibility of protecting the public from dangerous products; he maintains that the agency is a captive of industry and is afraid to recall dangerous toys from store shelves for fear of antagonizing their manufacturers.

For this reason, he doesn't wait for the Safety Commission to act. He once lambasted the manufacturers of toy electric ovens for failing to include adequate warning of shock and burn dangers. As a result, such warnings are now required and toy ovens can only be marketed for children eight years and older. Manufacturers changed the design of their dolls after Swartz criticized the presence of pins in their hair that could be detached, exposing sharp spikes. Similarly, he was successful in getting manufacturers to design play bottles in one piece so that the caps couldn't be swallowed.

Swartz spent thirteen years battling Fisher-Price after a fourteen-month-old boy choked on a "Little People" figurine that was part of its Play Family School Bus. The parents rushed the boy to the hospital where the figurine was removed, but not before it cut off the child's oxygen supply, causing irreparable brain damage.

Swartz discovered that Fisher-Price had marketed the toy since 1959 but changed its design in 1964 by reducing the size of the figures to make them more aesthetically appealing in order to boost sales. The company never conducted any tests to determine if the smaller figures could be swallowed by children. Moreover, Fisher-Price ignored letters from consumers informing the company of near catastrophes that occurred when the toy became lodged in children's throats.

At trial, Robert Hicks, Fisher-Price's manager of product development, surprised Swartz with the revelation that he had consulted with an anesthesiologist and a pediatrician, both of whom reputedly said the toy was safe. Neither of the doctors was available to testify, according to Hicks, because one was deceased and the other had retired and moved away and his whereabouts were unknown.

Swartz was suspicious. When the trial adjourned for the day, he began to search for the doctors. Late that night he located them, related Hicks's testimony, and was pleased to find that both were outraged over Hicks's claims. The next morning Swartz marched into court with the two elderly doctors and had them testify for the plaintiff.

After the jury adjourned to commence deliberations, Fisher-Price offered to settle the case for $900,000. Swartz declined the offer. In his closing argument, he demonstrated why he is such a feared adversary:

"You heard the doctors testify about the irreversible damage. . . . I think I used the word 'vegetable' in my opening—I apologize to you and I apologize to the parents for doing so. This is not an appropriate description for this beautiful child, this marvelous person, this very special child.

"But this very special child is special because he is going to have the body of a man and the mind of a child. He is going to be seven years old for the rest of his life mentally. . . . Think of all the indignities that go with that, all the punishment that goes with that, all the fear that goes into his everyday existence. Think of how he'll feel as he observes his brother playing normally and doing things physically that he cannot do."

Turning to the issue of damages, he asked the jury to consider what it was worth that the plaintiff "will never play ball again, never ride a bike again, never walk to school again, never live unassisted, never dance with a woman, never normally make love to a woman, never get married, never have offspring?

"How do you put value on the fact that he is going to be captive for the rest of his life, dependent the rest of his life on the good graces of others?

"The defendant has put him in a permanent cell from which there is no escape."

The jury returned a verdict of $3.1 million. For most attorneys this would mean the end of the case. But Swartz forwarded his research to Nancy Harvey Steorts, chairwoman of the Consumer Product Safety Commission, and urged her to recall the toy. Steorts responded that the agency was still studying its data but would follow up on the problem. Despite Swartz's numerous requests, nothing was done.

In 1985 Swartz appealed to the new chairman, Terrence Scanlon, who replied that the agency was aware of three deaths and one case of severe brain damage from the toy, but in three of those cases the children were younger than the ages for which the toys were recommended. Essentially, Scanlon blamed the parents for giving the toy to children too young for it.

Sixteen years after Swartz's client was injured, Fisher-Price continues to manufacture the toy and Swartz continues to lambast the company. Fisher-Price's only concession was to change its packaging, removing the words "nontoxic surfaces" and printing the message "Age 2–6. Regardless of age, this product is not intended for children who still put objects in their mouths." Swartz is not satisfied, however, asserting that the toy shouldn't be marketed to any children under five because they're likely to put things in their mouths.

When Linda and Paul Buckley met with Swartz and related the terrible tragedy that had befallen them, the attorney spotted several problems. First, it was unclear how the fire had started, although a burned match and matchbook were found in the rear of the station wagon. Second, because the injuries were so severe and damages so great, it was unlikely that any defendant would be inclined to settle the case amicably. Swartz realized he would have to wage a protracted struggle against powerful adversaries with the financial and legal wherewithal to mount a vigorous defense.

On the other hand, Swartz felt the facts of the case cried out for justice: Two beautiful babies had been horribly disfigured. Because the victims were children, they couldn't be found contributorily negligent, nor could any negligence on the part of the parents be imputed to them. After some legal research, he concluded that uncertainty as to the cause of the fire wouldn't bar a suit if the product created an unreasonable risk of harm. And the severity of the children's injuries increased the potential award and his fee.

Swartz evaluated the case from several perspectives. As a pessimist he tried to anticipate every possible move of the opposition and the worst-case scenario of what could transpire in court. (He even considered briefly the possibility that the parents were guilty of child abuse.) He realistically weighed his chances of winning against the time and financial risk he would have to invest.

Finally, he considered his own feelings. "There is nothing in my experience," says Swartz, "that compares with the feeling you get when you fight hard and win a major judgment for a client who has been devastated by some awful injury and who now, with this award, has some chance to rebuild his life; it's a very, very satisfying—even thrilling—sensation." And so he decided to take the case.

Swartz sought and obtained the police and Massachusetts State Fire Prevention Bureau reports of the incident. According to the latter, a pad on the trunk floor of the station wagon and the car's upholstery wouldn't by themselves support a flame—they were made from self-extinguishing materials. The comforter, on the other hand, ignited and burned rapidly in laboratory tests. The finding was consistent with the Buckleys' impression that the comforter was ablaze.

Swartz asked an expert on fabric flammability to undertake a study of similar comforters. He didn't ask that the clothing the children were wearing be tested because it hadn't burned—indeed, it had protected the children's torsos.

Swartz's technical expert tested ten comforters and found that the covering fabric was a highly flammable, quick-burning acetate, and that when the Kodel polyester fiberfill was exposed to the high temperatures of the burning shell, it was transformed into a kind of molten goo, almost like napalm. Swartz was distressed to discover that the comforter's construction didn't violate any state or federal laws because there were no flammability standards for blanket materials.

Linda Buckley distinctly recalled buying the comforter in Almy's, a store located in Danvers, Massachusetts. It came in a plastic bag with a picture of a beautiful young lady sleeping on it and the notations: "Heavenly Sleep . . . with a comforter of Kodel® polyester fiberfill. Non-allergenic. Resilient. Extra comfortable. Fluffy." On the comforter was a tag that read, "This comforter is certified to contain 100% virgin Kodel® polyester fiberfill," and, "Count on Kodel, member of the Eastman Kodak family," with the Eastman Kodak logo. There were no warnings on the packaging that the comforter was flammable or potentially hazardous. There was, however, a label warning of the suffocation dangers of the plastic wrapping around the comforter.

After some investigation, Swartz discovered that the comforters were made by a New York company, the Purofied Downs Corporation. He didn't know who manufactured the covering fabric but he could learn that later.

Although Swartz had all the information needed to file suit, he restrained himself, choosing to wait until the children's medical prognosis was settled. It would be foolish to resolve the case and then learn that the children's damages were greater than expected.

Delay was also a good tactic because Swartz didn't want the defendants to know about his suit until he had nailed down all the relevant facts, interviewed the witnesses, and consulted with his experts. He wasn't going to allow his opponents time to prepare excuses or engage in evasive maneuvers.

Two complaints were prepared. Eastman Kodak and Purofied Downs were out-of-state corporations and consequently they could be sued in federal court. The parent company of Almy's, Gorin's, was a Massachusetts corporation, and the suit against it had to be filed in state court, although Swartz would have preferred bringing all charges in federal court because its procedures were simpler and the scope of discovery greater.

In the federal complaint, Swartz alleged that the comforter burned at an excessive and unsafe rate of speed, left a dangerous tarlike residue, was negligently designed and manufactured, and that inadequate warnings were given as to its flammability. He asked for $3 million for Jessica, $2 million for Paul junior, and $100,000 to compensate the parents for being robbed of the joy of raising healthy and happy children.

The state complaint charged negligence and breach of warranty. The latter cause of action was based on the warranty of fitness and suitability that is implied for all products as long as they are used in the intended manner. Alleging that the comforter was not fit as bedding, Swartz asked for $5.2 million in damages.

Swartz filed the complaints in December 1969, almost two years after the fire. Purofied was quick to respond with a Motion to Dismiss on the grounds that the court lacked jurisdiction. Since Swartz could unquestionably obtain jurisdiction over Purofied in New York, it was clear that the motion wasn't made so much to avoid the suit as to get the case away from Boston—home turf for Swartz, the plaintiffs, and many of the witnesses.

Swartz deposed a Purofied sales agent in Massachusetts and through interrogatories (written questions submitted to the other side) learned that a significant amount of Purofied products were sold in Massachusetts, thereby bringing the company within the terms of a statute conferring jurisdiction over out-of-state companies. Purofied's motion was denied.

In its answer to the complaint, Purofied asserted that the plaintiffs had been guilty of contributory negligence. Eastman Kodak denied that it had been negligent and asserted the suit was barred because of the statute of limitations. Swartz wasn't worried because he knew that neither defense could be raised against minors.

A day after filing its answer, Purofied made a Motion for a More Definite Statement. The motion asks the court to require the plaintiff to be more specific in his complaint so that the defendant can better draft an answer—although Purofied had already answered.

It thus became apparent that Purofied was determined to mount a fierce defense. Swartz perceived that many of Purofied's motions were made only to divert his energies, overwhelm him with paperwork, run up his expenses, and wear him down—heavy-handed tactics that took advantage of the defendant's greater size and wealth. The message was unmistakable: If the plaintiffs persisted in carrying forward the litigation, they would become enmeshed in an expensive and burdensome struggle. But Swartz, unintimidated and determined to sustain a prolonged effort, wasn't about to settle cheaply.

Purofied and Kodak then sued Forest Converting Corporation, the manufacturer of the shell fabric sold to Purofied for its comforter. If Purofied and Kodak were held liable for the dangerous comforter, they wanted Forest Converting to contribute to the award.

Swartz used the discovery process to learn more about the comforter and its manufacture. Under the rules of civil procedure, each side can require its opponents to answer interrogatories, be questioned at a deposition, and produce relevant records and documents. Swartz decided to begin discovery with a set of interrogatories that would elicit information that would help him decide whom to depose and what questions to ask.

The defendants scheduled a deposition of their own, however, before answering Swartz's interrogatories. They wanted to question Linda and Paul Buckley and learn as much as possible about the fire. The deposition was also an opportunity for the defense attorneys to assess what kind of witnesses the plaintiffs would make at trial.

At the deposition, Linda and Paul presented themselves as articulate, sympathetic, and credible individuals. Kodak's attorney questioned Linda closely about the identity of the comforter, hoping to establish that it wasn't made with Kodak fiberfill. But Linda was certain where she bought the comforter and distinctly recalled the Kodak logo on its tag.

The battle began in earnest. Swartz deposed Dr. Charles Mather, chief executive of Kodak's Fiber Development Division. Under cross-examination, Mather conceded that Kodak knew that its fiberfill caused serious burns in its melted form and that this substance would adhere to skin. Nevertheless, no warnings were given consumers.

Swartz sent interrogatories to Witt Langstaff, one of Kodak's top technical troubleshooters, who admitted that the company never tested its comforters for flammability even though it had a fire protection program under which it had tested other products including mattresses, mattress pads, quilted robes, padded bras, rugs, blankets, and bed-spreads.

Later Swartz deposed Langstaff:

"Now with respect to bedding generally," Swartz asked, "you indicated that your company made some efforts to improve the flammability characteristics of different items of bedding prior to January twentieth, 1968, is that correct?"

"Yes," replied Langstaff.

"Why is it important for the flammability characteristics of items of bedding be improved?"

"Much of that work was in response to industry interests. For example, we did considerable work with the Veterans Administration to develop flame resistant pajamas because many of the patients smoked. . . ."

"So that in answer then, one of the reasons is that it is recognized that items of bedding could be exposed to a source of ignition such as people smoking in bed?"

"Yes."

"Would that be one reason it would be important to have items of bedding made safer from the point of view of flammability?"

"Smoking in bed is the source of accidents of this kind. . . ."

". . . I would imagine . . . all items of bedding would be in that category, I suppose, comforters?"

"Not by any stretch of the imagination."

"Is it because of your opinion that people don't smoke in bed when they use comforters that you are able to say not by any stretch of the imagination?"

"Objection," said an opposing attorney. Nevertheless, the witness answered because adjudication of all objections was reserved until trial.

"I am familiar enough with burn injury data," said Langstaff, "to know that thousands . . . have died as a result of mattress fires. I have never heard of anybody dying as a result of a blanket or comforter fire."

"You haven't?" said Swartz. "From the point of view of present investigation, hopefully we can make a product safer before anyone has to die. Don't you think that is a fair standard to apply?"

"Objection," a chorus of four opposing attorneys shouted.

"Am I supposed to answer that?" asked the witness.

"Yes. . . . Go ahead," said Swartz.

"Now I have forgotten the question," Langstaff said. Swartz repeated the question.

"No, I don't like the way the question is phrased . . . ," said Langstaff.

"Can you answer the question?" said Swartz.

"I will have to answer it no as I understand it. I don't understand it very well."

"You have answered no, right?"

"I don't understand the question."

"Would it alter your judgment if we told you that indeed prior to January twentieth, 1968, people were injured in blanket fires, in that kind of a situation?"

A chorus of defense objections was followed by the witness replying, "I would like to see the data."

"Studying the data involving mattresses," said Swartz, "did you take into account that usually mattresses are covered by such things as comforters, and such things as sheets, so that before a mattress ignites, usually other articles ignite first?"

Langstaff conceded that his company hadn't taken that into account.

At a pretrial conference Kodak's attorneys asserted that the company wasn't liable because Swartz couldn't prove how the fire began. Swartz replied that the cause of the fire was irrelevant. His suit was based on how the product performed after it was exposed to fire. "You pick out whatever you want to be the source of ignition and I'll stipulate to it," he offered. "You want it to be a match, we'll make it a match. You want it to be a cigarette lighter or an electrical fire, I'll stipulate to it, because I don't care." The offer only infuriated the defense attorneys.

Swartz then disclosed that he had reached a settlement with Purofied Downs and Forest Converting for $665,000. Since Gorin's had an indemnification agreement that required Purofied Downs to reimburse it for any award against it, Swartz agreed to dismiss the state complaint against Gorin's as part of the settlement. If the case went to trial, Kodak would stand alone.

Through discovery Swartz learned about Kodak's certified fabrics program that allowed vendors of products that incorporated fiberfill to use the Kodak label to promote their products. While Kodak demanded that these vendors meet certain weight and quality standards, no flammability standards or warnings were required.

Swartz also uncovered a memo from Kodak's files dated May 1, 1964—four years before the Buckley tragedy—that established that the company was aware of the flammability of synthetic fibers and knew that each year thousands of children were burned from unsafe fabrics in bedding. Nevertheless, Kodak conducted no tests, issued no warnings, and made no design changes with respect to its comforters.

Swartz amassed so much damning information that Kodak decided it had better settle. The company agreed to pay $750,000 to the Buckleys, which gave the family combined damages of $1.4 million. They used the money to buy a farm in the countryside so the children could grow up alongside creatures who would love them despite their scars.

The Buckley award was the largest ever in a flammable fabrics case and it sent shock waves through the textile industry. Manufacturers worried that they might be liable for other products. Not only did the defendants have to pay $1.4 million in damages, they also incurred $1 million in legal fees and suffered considerable adverse publicity. Manufacturers were distressed to hear that Swartz had twenty-two other flammable fabrics cases pending.

The industry soon moved to embrace flame-retardant fabrics. The Consumer Product Safety Commission promulgated mandatory standards for flame-retardant children's sleepwear and the number of children burned in sleepwear fires declined substantially. But the standards don't cover other children's garments or adult clothing.

While laymen often perceive attorneys to be parasites living off the tragedies of others, lawyers like Ed Swartz perform a public service by publicizing the existence of dangerous products, inducing governmental agencies to protect the public, and eliminating dangerous products simply by making their manufacture uneconomical.

Swartz is unapologetic about the huge fees he earns. Ralph Nader may be his idol, but Nader's frugal life-style doesn't appeal to him. When Swartz speaks before law students, his message is that they can do good and become rich too.

"The biggest danger consumers face in this country," he says, "is the brain drain. Law students are nervous, scared [about earning a living]. . . . I tell them you don't have to sign up with big corporations for fat salaries. You can earn an excellent living representing little people. That's the genius of the contingent fee system. . . . You don't have to sell out to corporate America."

A contingent fee allows an attorney to represent clients for a percentage of the recovery rather than on an hourly basis. Such fees, often one third or more of the total award, have been criticized as excessive, especially when an attorney settles a big lawsuit without a trial.

Swartz is happy to give his clients the choice of retaining him on an hourly basis or on a contingent fee. He says he has never encountered a client, rich or poor, who prefers to pay hourly. Clients recognize the advantages of a contingent fee— they don't pay a cent unless the lawyer wins, and this provides a strong incentive for the lawyer to fight hard. Without contingent fees, Swartz says, you're throwing away the key to the courthouse for people who otherwise couldn't afford to hire an attorney.

Chapter 3

DEADLY
ARROWS

For the sins of your fathers you,
though guiltless, must suffer.

—HORACE

Albuquerque, New Mexico, lies on a high desert plain where rainfall is scarce and the winters are chilly. A few high-rise towers stand surrounded by a sprawl of single-family residences. Stucco facades are common but much of the flavor of the Southwest has been lost with the invasion of generic supermarkets, shopping malls, and fast-food restaurants. A short drive away, however, one can find the unspoiled and rugged beauty of the old West with ancient pueblo villages and crested buttes soaring off desert floors.

At 8:15 A.M. on Friday, April 18, 1986, Kimberly Hunter arrived at Ken Kirkman's four-bedroom house in Albuquerque. The modern white stucco structure sat on a neatly landscaped lot with a yucca tree out front. As Kirkman's secretary, Kimberly worked out of a room set aside for his vending machine business. The house was quiet when she entered, which was no surprise since Kirkman, forty, was supposed to be out of town that day. She assumed that his son Jason, fifteen, was sleeping late, as was his habit since he had been suspended from high school.

She appreciated the tranquil atmosphere because the six-foot three-inch father and his five-foot-eleven son often quarreled. Two weeks earlier, amid one of their fierce shouting matches, she had grabbed her purse and left. That night Ken had called her, apologized, and asked her to return. She refused, agreeing to come back only temporarily until he could find a replacement.

She made a pot of coffee and began her normal business routine of handling phone calls and paperwork. When one of Ken's salesmen dropped by, she typed some correspondence for him. Around noon she left a package for UPS by the front door and walked down the hallway to tell Jason she was leaving for lunch. His bedroom door was ajar and she could see that the room was vacant. Perhaps Jason was in Ken's room, she thought, as she knocked on his door and called Jason. Hearing no response, she entered.

On the bed she saw the sheets held aloft like a tent. The shaft and fletch of an arrow protruded. She approached, lifted the bedcovers and saw a lifeless hand and a pool of blood. Shocked, she rushed out of the room, jumped into her car, drove home, and tried to phone her husband. Unable to reach him, she ran to a neighbor, who tried to calm her and called the police.

When the police entered Ken Kirkman's bedroom, they found his nude body stiff from rigor mortis. An arrow had gone through his right upper arm and pinned him to the bed. A second was lodged in his right shoulder and a third was stuck in his abdomen. His left leg and right hand had been mutilated with a sharp object and his cheek was sliced ragged. There was a gash on his forehead and his left eye had been gouged.

Kirkman's jacket, jeans, and socks lay on the corner of the bed; his underpants were on the floor nearby. The room was neat and orderly without any signs of forced entry or struggle. A window in the house was unlocked but neighbors informed the police that it was kept that way so

Jason could enter. The father refused to give his son a house key on the grounds that the boy would only lose it.

On the carpet in Jason's room was a pentagram with the number 666, a satanic symbol, drawn in red. A second pentagram decorated the closet door with the inscription: "Satan Rules." On the lamp base was a spot of blood and nearby a note that read: "Go and get the money . . . That night kill my dad, if possible use a knife at late night. If Diane is not there get a bow and use that instead. Put him in the garage and lock up the house good. & get my stuff & go to Durango."

Kirkman's new red Corvette was missing. In the garage were two arrows with razor-sharp blades designed for big-game hunting; they were identical to those extracted from Kirkman's body.

Neighbors told police that Ken and Jason argued often and recently had had a violent fight. Ken had been upset that Jason had stolen his car and one of his guns. Jason was furious that his father's girlfriend, Diane, had torn his Satanic Bible in half. That night Jason phoned his mother and vowed, "Somebody's gonna pay for this."

On the basis of the information they had gathered, the police obtained an arrest warrant for Jason and issued a regional bulletin seeking him and the Corvette.

The news media were quick to exploit the story. Headlines proclaimed, DAD'S ARROW DEATH TIED TO SATANISM, and SATAN BIBLE FEUD LINKED TO SLAYING. The police were quoted as saying that Jason should be considered "armed and dangerous." Several reports incorrectly stated that Kirkman's body was found under a satanic symbol.

The murder provided the impetus for a series of news reports about the dangers of teen occultism and Satan worship. According to one psychiatrist, satanism was attractive to teens because they liked the complex rituals and saw the devil as the ultimate rebel. A Christian psychologist stated, "There are supernatural worlds where we are pulled toward good and evil," and advised parents to tell Satan,

"This is my child and you take your hands off." A Los Angeles police detective was quoted as saying that many of the teens attracted to satanism were drug users and fans of "heavy metal" music.

Wanita Kirkman, Jason's mother, was shocked by the murder of her ex-husband. The attorney probating Ken's estate suggested that she retain a criminal defense lawyer to represent Jason. He recommended Bill Parnall, who had recently left the public defender's office after a seven-year stint. Wanita met the soft-spoken attorney and asked him to represent her son.

Tall, dark, and handsome, the thirty-three-year-old Parnall has a full beard and wears cowboy boots with his suits. In Albuquerque he is renowned not for lawyering but for playing a hot lick on his Fender Stratocaster guitar. He performs with two other lawyers in a local country-rock band named Lawyers, Guns, and Money. Parnall plays guitar and harmonica, sings lead vocals, and sounds like a young Johnny Cash. He writes his songs and when he argues before a jury, it's the songwriter as much as the lawyer who is speaking. It's no secret he'd rather be Willie Nelson than William Rehnquist.

Parnall had recently begun a six-month sabbatical from the law to devote himself to music; and unless he became rich and famous in the interim, he planned to open a private practice. But because defending Jason Kirkman was a rare opportunity to bask in the limelight of a highly publicized case and boost his legal practice, he decided to take the case.

Parnall's first step was to send a private investigator to the Kirkman residence to search for clues that someone other than Jason might have killed Ken Kirkman. Afraid that the police might jump to the conclusion that Jason was the culprit without bothering to investigate all leads, he asked his investigator to take fingerprints in the event the police had missed any.

Parnall then called the district attorney's office to determine their position on the case. They told him that they hadn't decided how they would proceed other than intending to transfer the case to district court and try Jason as an adult. In New Mexico, juveniles between fifteen and eighteen years of age can be tried as adults if the children's court determines they aren't amenable to treatment as a juvenile in an existing facility in the state. If Jason was convicted as an adult, the judge would be required to sentence him to life in prison. There would be no suspension of sentence or parole until Jason served thirty years. On the other hand, if Jason was convicted as a juvenile, the maximum sentence he could receive would be two years at the New Mexico Boy's School.

In order for Parnall to block transfer, he would have to establish that if Jason was found guilty, he could be adequately treated at the Boy's School and that two years was enough time to rehabilitate him. Parnall called a psychiatrist and several psychologists to see who was available to evaluate his client and testify on his behalf.

On the morning of April 22, four days after Kirkman's body was discovered, two Nevada police officers patrolling the Las Vegas strip spotted a red Corvette with New Mexico plates in the parking lot of the El Rancho motel. After running a check on the plate, they learned that the car belonged to Ken Kirkman and that a felony hit from Albuquerque was outstanding for his son who was wanted for murder. While one officer watched the car, the other went to the front desk, checked the register, and ascertained that Jason was registered in room 4223. Additional officers were called as backup.

The officers approached room 4223 and attempted to open the door with the motel master key. But the interior dead bolt prevented their entry. Inside, Jason and a friend, Carl Williams, were lying in bed. They heard keys jiggling in the door and assumed the maid was trying to enter. Suddenly the door burst open and cops rushed in with guns drawn, towering over Jason who was clad only in his gym shorts. The policemen turned him on his stomach and handcuffed him.

After informing Jason of his Miranda rights, the officers then asked if he had killed his father. Jason immediately confessed and added that he felt no remorse. He told the police that his father wasn't going to tell him what to do anymore, and he was tired of all his "father's shit." Again the officers advised Jason of his rights and then they asked if he had been driving the Corvette parked outside. Jason admitted that he had and that the car belonged to his father.

At the Clark County Jail Jason was booked on a fugitive murder charge. Carl was taken to the local juvenile home as a runaway. The car was sealed and towed by the Albuquerque Police Department. When it was opened, a compound bow was found in the trunk with a spot of blood on it that matched that of Ken Kirkman.

When Parnall learned that Jason had been apprehended, he flew to Las Vegas. He didn't intend to fight extradition, which under the circumstances would be a futile gesture that would only delay proceedings. He went to meet his client, accompany him home, and ensure that everyone had "a good feeling" about Jason and that the police didn't treat him roughly. He considered it best to get Jason back to New Mexico quickly so he could be near his family and in a juvenile facility away from hardened criminals.

Unlike most lawyers who rely heavily on their analytical skills and aggressive advocacy to win cases, Parnall is always concerned about other people's feelings—those of his client, the prosecution, the police, and the judge. His strategy is to cultivate relationships and try to wrest concessions through friendly persuasion rather than by bludgeoning his opponents. By reining in his ego, respecting his opponent's views, and not polarizing the dispute unnecessarily, he creates an atmosphere conducive to negotiation and compromise. It's the Zen approach to lawyering and it's a good tactic when the prosecution has sufficient evidence for conviction.

When Parnall represents a juvenile, he typically calls the appropriate probation officer to learn the facts of the case and get a fix on the department's views. The officer may express the opinion that the juvenile is running wild and needs to be sent to Boy's School. Parnall will respond that he understands the officer's point of view and concede that perhaps the officer is right, even though Parnall may be thinking, "Over my dead body is this kid going to Boy's School!"

In the following weeks Parnall will build rapport with the officer and pretty soon they will be talking like old friends. Parnall perceives cops, prosecutors, and probation officers as well-intentioned people who, if given the chance, will do the right thing. He will tell them of his client's virtues and try to generate sympathy. Eventually, he may coax his opponent to propose alternatives to incarceration—perhaps placing the juvenile in a group home and giving him therapy. Such a recommendation will carry much more weight at sentencing than if Parnall had proposed it.

Parnall's parents were from Rochester, New York. After World War II, his father, an orthopedic surgeon, and his mother, a professional violinist, decided they wanted a change of climate and moved the family to Albuquerque where they bought a one-hundred-year-old adobe farmhouse on six acres of land in what's known as the South Valley. It's an area in which Spanish families have resided for generations, and is considered the other side of the tracks by Anglos. Parnall grew up a skinny gringo kid surrounded by Hispanics.

He respected his father's integrity and compassion, and admired his mother's musical ability. His father liked to sing operatic arias; and although both parents encouraged him to study music, they were genuinely horrified when he took up rock and roll. The most important childhood influences on him, however, were his maternal grandfather, an uneducated Italian shoemaker who made saddles for the Italian cavalry during World War I, a young Spanish maid who lived across the street, and a large German shepherd dog, Heimrick.

From his grandfather he learned humility; from the maid he learned to appreciate Spanish culture; and from Heimrick, who he claims had the greatest influence, he learned to be both gentle and strong. While the dog was more powerful than any human or beast he encountered, he was a noble creature who never acted maliciously. He would protect young chicks and children, yet wouldn't hesitate to use his great strength when wronged. Parnall tries to lead his life the same way.

He trusts others easily and because he is six feet one, people aren't inclined to take advantage. "I don't have to be tough and mean and suspicious," he says. "I can be open and honest and assume that because I don't mistreat anyone or lie to anyone they will treat me the same way. And a lot of what goes around comes around. Maybe it's karma." He concedes that this approach wouldn't work back East where you have to be a little more aggressive in protecting your interests. But out West, where people smile at strangers, it produces positive results.

In court he doesn't feel the need to lash out when verbally attacked. He will smile and remember Heimrick, who was filled with love and admiration for everything around him and who remained calm, secure in the knowledge that he could rip his opponent's throat out if he needed to.

Divorced, he lives happily with his ex-wife. They have a joint bank account and share everything yet have no plans to remarry. They've been together and separated numerous times since they were teenagers. "We have always gone our own ways and enjoyed other people," he says, "and yet enjoy each other and never figured out how to deal with that."

He likes to hunt, which gives him confidence that he could survive in the wilderness on his own. Walking through the wilderness, he stalks his prey silently with a bow and arrow or an ancient muzzle-loader, forgoing modern arms because they would reduce the challenge. Besides, he wants to be close to his prey since hunting is a metaphysical experience for him. When he shot an eight-hundred-pound elk, he was deeply affected by the intense gaze of the animal as it died.

He once hunted with an Indian from the Deer Clan who needed to kill a deer and relate to it as the animal's spirit departed. "And that stuck in my mind," Parnall says, "and I realized when I was with this animal when he expired that there was that point where his energy or his soul or whatever left, and that had a great effect on me."

Parnall met Jason in the Las Vegas jail. Although Wanita had asked him to represent her son, the decision was ultimately Jason's. The boy took an immediate liking to the attorney, however, and affirmed her choice. Jason was relieved to have someone helping him, and Parnall's warmth and sympathy were welcome.

Jason immediately confessed that he had killed his father. The night of the murder Ken announced he was committing Jason to a group home. Jason pleaded not to be sent away but Ken was adamant.

Jason returned to his father's room later that evening with his bow and arrows, although he only intended to talk to his father. After Jason begged to be allowed to finish the baseball season, Ken responded by throwing a shoe at his son. In a fit of rage, Jason shot an arrow into his father. "I'm gonna hurt you more than you've hurt me," an angry Ken shouted as he tried to raise himself out of bed, whereupon Jason sent two more arrows into him. Then with an arrow in his hand, he gouged his father's face and body, took his money and car keys, and fled.

Satanism played no part in the killing, according to Jason. He had dabbled in the occult with his friends because he thought it was "cool," but he didn't know much about it nor did he believe in devil worship.

Jason explained that, while he and his dad argued frequently, his father had rarely hit him and never seriously injured him. Notwithstanding their fights, Jason loved and admired his father. His complaint was that his dad, who worked long hours and was frequently out of town on business, didn't spend enough time with him.

Parnall concluded that Jason was more neglected than abused and consequently Jason wouldn't be able to claim self-defense. Under New Mexico law self-defense can be claimed only if the defendant at the time of the killing was threatened with great bodily harm or death, was afraid of the apparent danger, and killed the victim out of that fear. Moreover, the defendant must have acted as a reasonable person would have under the circumstances. Using deadly force in response to a non-deadly attack has never been considered reasonable.

Parnall told Jason that he would have to do things he might find objectionable, such as cutting his hair. Parnall wanted Jason to look as young as possible while Jason, like most fifteen-year-olds, wanted to appear adult. Parnall trimmed Jason's hair himself (Parnall cuts his own), hoping the personal attention would strengthen his bond with the boy.

Parnall also encouraged Jason to act more like a juvenile, urging him to smile frequently and to be open and sensitive. He asked him to bare his soul to the psychologists who would be interviewing him. Jason found it difficult to talk about the incident, however, and wasn't the introspective type. Moreover, while Jason was of average intelligence, he was fairly inarticulate.

On Thursday night, April 24, Jason was returned to Albuquerque, and the next day he was arraigned in children's court before Judge John E. Brown. Parnall entered a plea of denial, the equivalent of a not-guilty plea. After moving to transfer the case to district court, the prosecutors asked that Jason be ordered to undergo a psychiatric evaluation and provide a handwriting sample.

Parnall objected to the transfer, and a hearing was

scheduled to argue the issue. As for the psychiatric evaluation, Parnell agreed on three conditions: (1) he could be present; (2) Jason wouldn't be asked about the alleged killing; and (3) any test data collected would be shared with the defense. The court consented. Realizing that he had no basis for objecting to a handwriting sample, Parnall didn't dispute the request.

Shortly thereafter, Parnall filed motions challenging the warrants issued to search the Corvette and the Kirkman house. He wanted to exclude as evidence the bow and Jason's handwritten note. He also moved to suppress the confession Jason gave the police upon his arrest, and asked for a change of venue on the grounds that the news media had made such inflammatory statements that Jason couldn't receive a fair trial in New Mexico.

Although Parnall believed that he was unlikely to win any of these motions, he had a professional obligation to wage a vigorous defense. And even if he lost the motions, he would establish a record that could be the basis for an appeal.

Parnall's argument challenging the warrants relied upon the Fourth Amendment, which guarantees the "right of the people to be secure in their persons, houses, papers and effects, against unreasonable searches and seizures." To ensure that this right is not trampled upon by law enforcement personnel, the Supreme Court has adopted the exclusionary rule, which bars the use of evidence obtained unconstitutionally.

Parnall had Jason testify at the suppression hearing because he wanted to acquaint the judge with his client, hoping that children's court judge Michael Martinez would begin to develop some empathy for Jason. Whatever Jason said during the hearing couldn't be used as evidence against him in a subsequent trial. However, when Jason admitted that he didn't plan to return home after he drove off in his father's car, the judge ruled that Jason had abandoned his father's home and therefore had no standing to challenge the search warrant. Martinez also held that Jason had no standing to contest the search of the Corvette because the car was stolen and Jason didn't have permission to drive it.

As for the motion to suppress Jason's confession upon arrest, Parnall argued that it was given in a coercive setting, considering the boy's tender age and the fact that he didn't have access to the advice of friends or relatives. But the judge concluded that Jason had been properly advised of his rights and knowingly waived them. In regard to the motion for change of venue, Parnall postponed consideration of his request until after the transfer hearing.

Parnall was frankly puzzled by the killing. There must be more to it, he reasoned, because Jason's actions didn't make sense. Patricide is typically committed by children who have been physically or sexually abused, yet Jason said there was no such abuse and claimed to love his father.

Parnall had dealt with many criminals and Jason didn't fit the profile. Murderers are typically antisocial, if not sociopathic, have difficulty relating to others, and have a history of violent behavior. Jason, on the other hand, was a likable and peaceful boy. He made friends easily and participated well in group activities. Other than clashes with his father, he had never been in a fight, not even a schoolyard scuffle. Everyone who knew Jason was shocked by the killing—it seemed completely out of character. Nor did Jason have a drug or alcohol problem, although he occasionally smoked marijuana and drank beer. Parnall began an investigation to try to unravel the mystery.

Wanita and Ken Kirkman grew up in Harrisburg, Pennsylvania. They met in high school when Ken was seventeen, Wanita fourteen. Shortly thereafter Ken left for Williamsport to attend Lycoming College on a basketball scholarship. After he earned a bachelor of science degree in accounting, he and Wanita became reacquainted through church activities and began to date. She was attending the community college in Bucks County and living with her parents.

Wanita's father liked Ken because of his college degree and obvious ambition. Wanita also admired the way Ken drove himself hard, slept little, and worked long hours. She felt certain that he would be a success someday.

After six months of dating they married and rented a house. She dropped out of college and he became a salesman for a Philadelphia printing press manufacturer. The large territory he was assigned took him away from home frequently. Although she was unhappy at being left alone, she was unable to persuade him to give up a job he enjoyed.

Three months later he abruptly announced that he had purchased a house for them in Lake Harmony, in the Pocono Mountains. Not having consulted her about the move, he now simply told her to begin packing. The house was in a desolate area, surrounded by vacation homes that were unoccupied most of the year.

Wanita was employed at a local resort for a time but mostly she stayed home alone. Ken worked longer hours than ever, leaving at four in the morning and returning home late at night. In his free time, he liked to golf, hunt, and fish with his buddies. When he stayed home it was to watch football on television. While he provided well for Wanita's material needs, he all but ignored her emotional needs. Although dissatisfied, she acquiesced and tried to be a good wife, having been taught that women should defer to their husbands.

In 1969 she became pregnant. On the day of Jason's birth, Ken dropped her off at the hospital and then went golfing. That evening he returned to see his newborn son. For each of the next four or five days he visited her briefly. Upon coming home, she found herself completely responsible for cooking, cleaning, and caring for the baby.

Five months after the birth, Ken announced that he was changing careers. He was going into real estate and the family would move to Harrisburg, Pennsylvania and reside temporarily with his mother. Wanita wasn't pleased—she had a cordial but not particularly warm relationship with her mother-in-law. They stayed there for six months until they could afford to buy a house of their own. Once again Ken threw himself into his career, working nights and weekends.

Three years later Wanita gave birth to a second son, Jeff. She hoped to have a girl one day, but Ken, adamantly opposed to additional children, had a vasectomy without consulting her.

Soon thereafter Ken, forced to sell their house because of a bad real estate investment he had made, decided to accept a job with the Xerox Corporation in Harrisburg. He began training while Wanita looked for a place for them to rent.

Ken's new job took him away from home three or four nights a week. A sociable fellow, he was nevertheless intensely competitive and downright unscrupulous in his sales tactics. He quickly became the number one Xerox salesman for the region.

In 1975 the Kirkmans visited Wanita's parents in Albuquerque where they had moved upon retirement. Both Ken and Wanita liked the city and were ready for a change. Upon their return to Pennsylvania, Ken requested a transfer. A year later he flew out and purchased a house for them. The family followed.

Continuing his workaholic ways, Ken soon became the top Xerox salesman in Albuquerque. Wanita ran the household like a single mother except for the fact that she didn't have to worry about money.

When Jason turned six and began to play Little League baseball, Ken became more interested in his sons, spending more time at home on the weekends and buying a travel trailer to take the boys fishing. Wanita was pleased.

Two years later Ken left Xerox for Unicopy and later Savin copiers. The Savin job took him on the road Monday through Friday. His absence was little noticed by the boys, however, who were in school now and were used to their father's being away from home. Wanita kept busy with the PTA, Boy Scouts, and other community activities.

As the children grew older, Ken tried to play more of a role in their upbringing, but Wanita considered his influence counterproductive. He was very lenient with the boys, letting them disregard the rules and responsibilities she had established. Nor did he help them with their homework, which was a serious problem for Jason, who wasn't self-motivated. It was a major endeavor every night to get him to study.

Ken took a job on the side selling machines that measured heart rates. Now on the rare occasions when he was home on weekends, he would spend his time on the phone making sales calls. To occupy herself, Wanita wanted to enroll in the University of New Mexico. Ken objected, saying that she should be home to take care of the children. Wanita thought he feared that she would become too independent if she obtained a college degree. She finally persuaded him to allow her to take one class.

As Wanita was becoming increasingly dissatisfied with her life, she met other couples and she began to see alternatives to the traditional husband-as-monarch type of marriage. Unhappy with Ken's working habits and his seeming disregard for her feelings, she urged him to take a nine-to-five job but he didn't want to be cooped up in an office.

In 1981 Wanita became friendly with Michael Castillo. Ken, who soon became aware of the relationship, confronted her about it. She claimed she and Michael were just friends but took the opportunity to express her dissatisfaction with Ken. Although she said she wanted to save their marriage, Ken refused to listen to her complaints. They fought over dinner and later Ken came into the living room and announced to Jason that he was divorcing his mom. Wanita later told Jason that the problem was that Ken was never home and she wanted to go back to school.

When it became clear her marriage was doomed, Wanita became romantically involved with Michael Castillo. Ken moved out of the house and filed for divorce. Although he continued to pay her bills, he provided nothing extra. Resentful, he tried to make her feel guilty about the breakup.

Ken's erratic attempts to discipline Jason were clumsy and ineffective. When Jason stayed out all night without calling home, Ken grounded him for two weeks. The next day, Ken left town and Jason simply ignored the punishment. Some weeks later Jason skipped school to go skiing. When his father learned of the transgression, he became angry and hit Jason. Half an hour later, Ken acted as if the incident had never occurred; he laughed and carried on with his son, and took him out to dinner.

Ken initiated a system of incentives to induce Jason to improve his schoolwork. If Jason received an A, he would be rewarded with fifty dollars; if he received an F, he would be grounded. Jason thought the system foolish. He believed the only way to resolve their problems was for them to sit down and talk. Ken, however, didn't consider his own behavior part of the problem.

Both father and son complained to Wanita after their disputes. Wanita would resolve to regain custody, but several days later Ken and Jason would say everything was fine. Eventually, Wanita began to discount their complaints, knowing that father and son would soon make up.

In the spring of 1985, Jason was suspended from school because of excessive absences. Ken tried to enroll him in a private school but admission was denied because of Jason's poor grades. Stating that there was little hope for Jason, Ken told Wanita that their son was destined to become a criminal.

In December Ken called Wanita in the middle of the night and told her that Jason had stolen his Corvette and two thousand dollars in cash. Jason had come home and discovered that his father had sold Jason's motorbike without consulting him. Furious, Jason decided to retaliate by taking his father's car. He drove to a friend's house in Albuquerque where the police caught him and brought him to juvenile hall. Although Ken pressed charges, he later dropped them. Within twenty-four hours of his arrest, Jason was released to Wanita. He spent Christmas week at her home and reported regularly to his probation officer.

In January Ken decided to relocate to Albuquerque to expand his business. Jason wanted to stay in Colorado but Ken ignored his wishes. Two days after the move, Ken was infuriated when he discovered that Jason had driven his Corvette a second time. Ken took Jason to Passages, a state-run crisis-intervention home, and left him in their custody. He brought Jason there on a Saturday and promised to return for him the following Monday.

But Ken had no intention of returning for Jason. Instead, he went to the Department of Human Services to file for custody release. There he met with social worker Aza Baxter and talked incessantly about all he had done for his ungrateful son. Baxter quickly realized that Ken was only interested in controlling Jason's behavior, not providing for his needs. She reasoned that Ken had brought on Jason's misbehavior, and that any treatment would have to involve both of them.

After Jason had been at Passages for a week without any word from his dad, Baxter informed Jason that his father had requested a custody release. Jason was shaken; tears welled up in his eyes. He phoned Ken repeatedly, tracked him down at stops on a business trip, and begged to be allowed to come home. Ken refused to reconsider his decision but he did visit Jason several times, bringing him fresh clothes. Twice Ken participated with Jason in counseling sessions with Passages staffer Kay Dunnigan.

During those sessions, Ken spoke about how hard he worked and enumerated the many material things he had provided Jason. Dunnigan queried him about his frequent absences from home and tried to explain that Jason had been rebelling in order to get his attention. Ken became defensive, emphatically stating that it was the quality of time he spent with his son that was important, not the quantity. Jason was docile in Ken's presence; and when he tried to interject his views, Ken would drown him out of the conversation. Even Dunnigan felt intimidated by Ken.

While Jason found living in the group home boring, he got along well with the other residents and staff. Dunnigan considered him a "model kid." He wasn't a streetwise tough but a sensitive boy embarrassed by his crying.

Wanita was surprised to learn that Ken had placed Jason in Passages. She visited her son and participated in his counseling sessions as often as she could. She also drove him to school each day, and after school he came to her house. She was unaware that he continued to cut classes.

Reluctant to regain custody of Jason out of fear that she couldn't control him, Wanita believed a plan needed to be devised to halt his misbehavior and undo the damage Ken had done during the two and a half years Jason had resided with him. Moreover, she didn't really have room in her small house for him nor was she able to afford the extra expense of supporting him. Jason felt that his mother bore a grudge because he had left her. Wanita's dilemma became moot, however, once Ken announced that under no condition would he relinquish custody to her, claiming it would be too much of a burden for her.

Jason remained at Passages for two weeks, the maximum stay allowed, and then was placed in a second crisis-intervention house, New Day. Baxter enrolled him in another high school. She found him to be a friendly and likable boy amenable to treatment. She suggested that Ken hire Jason as his assistant for the summer so that they could travel together. Jason loved the idea.

Baxter convened a meeting with Ken, Wanita, Jeff, and Jason to discuss family relations. They tried to establish what the house rules would be upon Jason's return to his father's home. This led to a discussion of values, with Wanita stating that her foremost value was honesty. Jason blurted out his hurt and resentment that Ken lied to him when placing him in Passages. Jason's emotional outburst made Ken uncomfortable.

After Jason had been away for a month, Ken abruptly retrieved him, saying that New Day was a bad environment for the boy. He told Jason that he was on the waiting list for Hogares, a long-term residential placement program; and if he misbehaved again, he would be sent there.

Ken continued to travel frequently, often going away for weeks at a time. During these trips, Jason would regularly visit his mother. Although she tried to persuade him to attend school, he continued to cut classes and was eventually expelled. He spent increasing amounts of time with dropouts, drug users, and heavy metal music fans and watching music videos that portrayed bizarre and violent behavior.

Jason wanted to study engineering but Ken told him it would be too much work for him. He suggested that Jason work in his company but that didn't interest Jason, who felt that his dad never considered what he wanted. He expected his father would commit him to Hogares for several years, and was frightened at the prospect. His anger and frustration mounted, and with Ken gone so much of the time, Jason stopped thinking of him as his father and began to see him as an enemy.

In March Ken decided to take Jason, Jeff, and Ken's girlfriend and daughter on a short trip to California. The night before they left, a depressed Jason called his mom and said he was a failure and didn't know what he was going to do. A long silence followed. Wanita rushed over to the house and found the phone off the hook and Jason staring into space with a distant look on his face, as if he were on drugs. The next day, Ken told her Jason was fine and they departed for California.

Ken and Jason quarreled throughout the trip, disagreeing over which restaurants to eat in and which motels to stay at. Jason perceived that his father was constantly nagging him, recounting instances of past misconduct and lecturing him. Nor did Jason get along with his brother. At one point an exasperated Ken pulled the car over to the side of the road and threatened to leave Jason in the middle of the desert. By the time the group arrived in Las Vegas on the return trip, Jason, who wanted some time by himself, made the rounds of the casinos alone. But even this aggravated Ken, who scolded him for deserting his brother and girlfriend's daughter.

When they returned home, Ken told Jason to get a job. Jason, who was only fifteen, was willing, but when Ken wouldn't drive him to any interviews, the idea was dropped. The next morning Ken chastised Jason for sleeping late and threw a shoe at him. They argued and Ken punched his son in the mouth, causing profuse bleeding. For the first time, Jason struck back, hitting his father with a guitar. Ken backed off, and without a word walked away.

Wanita, increasingly concerned about Ken and Jason's relationship, began to attend "Tough Love" meetings in an effort to learn new ways of dealing with her son's behavior. The organization believes that adolescents must be taught that misbehavior won't be tolerated. Parents are urged to punish a child by reducing his privileges and, in extreme cases, locking him or her out of the house—although the child is always welcome to spend the night at the home of another Tough Love parent.

After Ken told Wanita that Jason had stolen his gun, Wanita urged Ken to get rid of his guns, put a lock on his bedroom door, and stop giving Jason money. Scornful of the Tough Love approach, Ken refused to attend their meetings. Wanita tried to persuade Ken and Jason to seek counseling, but Ken insisted that Jason was the only one who needed help. Later that day, Ken told Wanita that everything was fine. But that evening, a furious Jason told Wanita that Ken's girlfriend, at Ken's urging, had torn his Satanic Bible in half.

Wanita was eventually able to persuade Ken and Jason to attend a private session with a Tough Love counselor but the encounter accomplished little. Since there was no discussion of why Ken worked such long hours and spent so little time at home, Jason perceived the meeting as merely an attempt to find a way to get him to clean his room and behave.

On April 17, Ken told Jason that he was being sent to Hogares. Jason begged not to be sent away and in the ensuing argument he killed his dad. At the time of the murder, Jason was in such an unthinking rage that he didn't consider the consequences of his act. He jumped into his father's Corvette and drove off at high speed, swerving on the highway from lane to lane. At one point he pulled to the side of the road and another driver stopped to inquire if he was all right, thinking perhaps Jason was drunk. But Jason wasn't drunk, he was emotionally distraught and unaccustomed to driving on highways.

About an hour after the killing, when Jason's anger had subsided and the gravity of what he had done began to sink in, he realized he was in a lot of trouble. He expected to be caught, not having much money and knowing that a fifteen-year-old driving a brand-new Corvette is likely to attract police attention. Feeling a compelling need to get away from Albuquerque, he drove to Durango and picked up his friend Carl, who agreed to travel with him to California. Jason didn't tell Carl about the murder or that he was a fugitive. They stayed up all night in Las Vegas and then drove on to Los Angeles.

The traffic in Los Angeles so frightened Jason that he avoided driving. They stayed at a hotel in West Los Angeles for three days and then drove back to Las Vegas where they checked into a motel. The next morning the police broke in and arrested them.

The more Parnall learned about Ken Kirkman, the more sympathy he felt for Jason. But bad parenting and an occasional beating is not a defense for murder. Parnall suspected that Ken might have sexually abused Jason; he advised him that the killing might be justifiable self-defense under those circumstances. Jason denied the existence of any sexual abuse, however, and continued to speak highly of his father, often referring to him in the present tense, as if he were still alive.

The psychiatrist and psychologists Parnall had retained produced a mixed bag of conclusions. They regarded the murder as an isolated and idiosyncratic incident, the result of accumulated rage and frustration arising from Jason's long-term relationship with his father, and agreed that Jason was not likely ever to repeat the act. While Jason responded to family conflicts with greater emotional intensity than the average teenager, he dealt with outsiders in a more aloof manner. Although they agreed that Jason's problems were treatable, they thought he would need more than the two years available to him at the Boy's School.

Especially disappointing to Parnall was the psychology experts' refusal to support Parnall's contention that the killing was done without deliberation (making it second-degree murder). They considered that the note Jason wrote outlining the murder and the rational manner in which he escaped were strong evidence to the contrary. Parnall, on the other hand, believed Jason's explanation that the list had been written in a flight of fantasy several weeks beforehand, and that he had completely forgotten about it by the time of the murder. According to Parnall, Jason only realized the gravity of what he had done an hour or more after the killing.

Because the psychologists' findings were problematical, Parnall didn't ask them for full reports. Instead, he had them write letters stating their belief that Jason wasn't a danger to himself or others, and giving their estimate of how long he would require treatment.

Parnall talked to Ken's sister, Jason's aunt, and was pleased to hear her say that she didn't seek vengeance for her brother's death; and she hoped Jason would be given treatment and not just locked away. Parnall asked her to write him a letter reiterating her feelings, intending to present it to the prosecutors and judge. When the letter arrived, however, Parnall was disappointed to read that the aunt considered a fair sentence would be twenty-five to fifty years—a term longer than that sought by the prosecution. The letter was useless.

Wanita spoke to Janet, Ken's ex-girlfriend, hoping she might testify for Jason. Although she liked Jason, she made some unflattering remarks about him, and Parnall decided it would be best not to put her on the stand.

Parnall's frustration mounted. He had represented more than two thousand juveniles as a public defender and he had often been able to obtain a break for them. But now it seemed that every avenue was blocked. He couldn't even attack the father to generate sympathy for the son because Jason remained protective of his dad's reputation.

Parnall wrote an impassioned letter to Jason outlining their options. Although he made it clear that the decision was Jason's, Parnall expressed the opinion that if the case went to trial Jason would be convicted of first-degree murder. On the other hand, if Jason accepted the plea offered, the maximum sentence he could receive would be twenty-four years. And knowing Judge Martinez, Parnall reasoned it unlikely Jason would get the maximum. Parnall predicted a twelve-year sentence, which meant that with time off for good behavior, Jason could be out of prison in six years.

Jason's last chance to help himself would be during his upcoming interview with the state's psychologist. Parnall concluded his letter by urging Jason to do his best:

I want to help you in any way I can and will keep fighting for a better deal, but it looks as though this is the deal we will get and nothing better. All the little tricks I have tried have not done the job. They may have helped us, but I don't know how much. All that is left to help or hurt us is your interview with Jamie Franklin, so I am begging you to show him your most sensitive side. His opinion will make the difference between a good sentence and a very bad one. He is a nice guy and he may help us. Try your best to be a *kid* with him and tell him about how you feel inside. I have spent a great deal of the money I have been given on this case for experts to see you. One of my reasons was to get you used to opening up to strangers about your feelings. Now is the time to show me I didn't waste that money. It is very important to me that you show your remorse to Jamie Franklin. I care about you and that is the only way I can really help you. You have to help me too. If you don't open up and spill your feelings now to Jamie, I am afraid our case is lost . . . You will have two hours to save this case during the next interview. You can't just tell him you are sorry. You have to mean it and show him that you mean it. You have to break down when you talk about it or he will say you don't care. Then no one will know how you really felt about your dad and he will have died for nothing. If you don't open up your feelings to Jamie there will be two victims in this case—your father and *you*. Don't do that to me. I don't want to let you down, but you have to help or you might as well not have a lawyer at all.

Parnall met with Jason the morning of the interview to try to open him up emotionally, hoping the attitude might carry over. With Jason's consent, Parnall observed the interview through a one-way mirror.

After speaking to Jason and administering a battery of tests, Franklin wrote up a report that concluded that Jason was an immature and alienated boy with an "anxious, aimless, poorly governed personality." Such persons, wrote Franklin, were likely to alternate between periods of impulsive acting out and periods of guilt and self-deprecation.

Franklin felt that Jason was naively unmindful of the consequences of violence and given to act out his anger in aggressive ways. Perhaps most ominous was his belief that Jason's social values were similar to those of street gang members and that there was a likelihood of recidivism. While Franklin thought Jason was treatable, he stated that at least four to five years of therapy would be needed before one could predict whether Jason could be rehabilitated.

In considering whether or not to strike a plea bargain, Parnall recognized that the evidence against Jason was highly incriminating. Jason's note laid out a plan to kill his father, a plan Jason appeared to have followed. This was strong evidence of premeditation. Furthermore, a friend of Jason's, Ron Martinez, told the police of a conversation he had had with Jason three weeks before the killing in which Jason spoke of his intention to lure his father into the garage, kill him, and then dump his body in the junkyard. Ron claimed that Jason phoned him the evening of the murder and said he was going to kill his father because Ken intended to place him in a group home. At the time, Ron didn't take the threat seriously.

Wanita had mentioned to the police her conversation with Jason in which he expressed great anger that his Satanic Bible had been torn and vowed that someone would pay for it. Jason told Parnall that he was merely demanding to be reimbursed the $4.95 cost of the book. Finally, there was Jason's confession to the police that he had killed his father and felt no remorse.

Although Parnall considered that the deal offered by the prosecution, which would subject Jason to a potential twenty-four-year jail term, was better than the mandatory thirty-year-sentence that Jason would probably get if the case went to trial, he was dissatisfied, feeling the plea was unfair because it was identical to the one recently offered a boy who had brutally raped and murdered a seventy-eight-year-old woman (the judge sentenced him to the full twenty-four years). Certainly, Jason deserved a better deal than that. But the prosecutors were adamant. They knew they had a first-degree murder conviction. Parnall knew it too. The offer was open until the transfer hearing scheduled for August 15.

In the meantime Parnall lobbied prosecutors, probation officials, state psychologists, and anyone else he thought he could soften up. He worked on reporters and was pleased to see them reiterate his sentiment that Jason had been subjected to great emotional abuse and that no satanic worship was involved. Through Parnall's efforts, the media had become more sympathetic toward Jason—even their pictures showed him in a better light. Nevertheless, the only concession he could wrest from the DA was to allow his client to plead to one second-degree crime, murder, and a bunch of lesser crimes totaling twenty-four years, rather than plead to two aggravated second-degree crimes (murder and armed robbery).

Parnall assumed the judge would view these lesser crimes (unaggravated armed robbery, auto theft, possession of a stolen credit card, tampering with evidence, possession of drug paraphernalia [a marijuana pipe], and damage to property [soiling the carpet] as insignificant since they were really part and parcel of the murder. Moreover, some of these charges were clearly unsupported by the evidence. Armed robbery, for instance, requires the use of force to steal—Jason didn't kill his father for money; the theft was an afterthought. Consequently, Parnall was hoping the judge would run the sentences for these minor crimes concurrently.

In a prehearing conference Judge Martinez indicated that if the prognosis for treatment was good, he wasn't disposed to give Jason a long sentence. But if it was bad, he would give him the maximum time allowed to keep him locked away from society.

Realizing that no better offer would be forthcoming, Jason and Parnall decided to accept the deal. Parnall then turned his energies toward influencing the sentence. He had Jason write a letter:

Dear Judge Martinez:

I think, for the first time, I understand how much I loved my dad. If I didn't love him I don't think I would have done what I did. I wanted him to be around more, and not be away on trips all the time. Sometimes he would leave someone there to watch me when I was alone, but most of the time he would tell my mom that he was leaving someone there to watch me and he never did. He would just leave on business and leave me all alone. He would lie to me and my mom and brother Jeff. He told us several times that he would pick us up after skiing which he never did, and we would have to hitchhike home. He did that sort of thing so much that I felt he didn't care.

We set down some rules to help him and I [*sic*] both to follow but he would never follow them. It hurt me that he wouldn't believe how important it was to me for us to be closer. Even though I thought about hurting him before, I had put it out of my mind until that night when he told me I could not even live with him, and would have to live in a group home. It was like his final sign that he would not work on our problems. I tried to talk to him about our problems but he just threw a shoe at me and cussed me out. It was like I had finally lost everything. I really do care for him, especially now, seeing what I did to his future life. I really miss him and I'm sorry for what I did. I realize that doesn't help now but I wish I could have a chance to handle the problem differently, now that I have thought about it. I still don't really understand how I could have wanted to hurt him.

I just don't react that way. I know I have a lot of work to do and I need to get a lot of help to understand what really happened between us. I hope I can someday. I know it's hard to believe, after what I did, that I miss my dad now but I do, more every day.

Jason Kirkman

Parnall called the National Center on Institutions and Alternatives (NCIA), an organization that promotes alternatives to traditional incarceration, and asked them to review the case and recommend a sentence. Their report portrayed Jason as a troubled youth unable to withstand much stress, who became locked in a twisted and sick relationship with a father who provided little affection, trust, or discipline.

While the report concluded that Jason's actions weren't justified and that he deserved to be punished, it cited as mitigating circumstances Jason's young age and the lack of any criminal record. The report noted the absence of any research indicating that imprisonment could deter crimes of passion, and mentioned that defendants without prior offenses who murder out of passion have the lowest rate of recidivism.

The report suggested two sentencing options. The first was to incarcerate Jason for eight years with the initial year to be spent at either the Mount Airy Psychiatric Center in Denver or the Menninger Foundation in Topeka, Kansas. The cost would be from $160,000 to $180,000 a year. The second option was to incarcerate Jason for a period of up to twelve years in one of several medium- or minimal-security correctional facilities where he would receive psychological treatment.

Under either option, the report recommended parole conditions requiring Jason to complete his high school

serve his time in a New Mexico prison. The judge requested that the Corrections Department provide therapy, but the recommendation wasn't binding.

In 1987 there were an estimated 2.25 million reports of child abuse in the United States. About 140,000 children are brought into court annually on the ground that they are being neglected or abused, according to the last survey, which was conducted in 1972. Rarely are children taken away from their parents. Even when the parents are clearly ill-equipped to raise children, courts are loath to intervene. The feeling of most jurists is that the child is usually better off with his or her parents than being placed in an institution or in a succession of foster homes.

Although child abuse occurs in families of all income levels, poor parents are more often taken into court. Class and cultural bias may influence intervention decisions, and abuse is more likely to be detected in poor families because welfare workers observe their domestic lives. In an affluent setting, abuse can be difficult to detect—the children are well-nourished and nicely clothed. And even when there are indications of abuse, the problem is often handled with discretion by the family's physician.

State intervention in the parent-child relationship can be traced to the sixteenth century when bands of beggars roamed England terrorizing towns and villages. As the number of poor multiplied, Parliament enacted remedial legislation. The old and disabled were sheltered in tax-supported hospitals and almshouses. Those who were fit to work were required to do so or were imprisoned. The children of the poor were apprenticed. Eventually, many were shipped to the American Colonies or impressed into the merchant marine.

Although the Elizabethan treatment of poor children seems harsh by today's standards, the system was not designed so much to discriminate against the poor but rather to reduce costs by having children pay for part of their care through their own labor. Moreover, apprentices learned useful skills and good work habits in an era when there was no public education. Indeed, the program was considered humanitarian in that it put poor children on a more equal footing with upper-class children who were often sent away to other families to receive training.

But the apprenticeship system never fulfilled its promise. As a result, more repressive measures were passed and workhouses were established.

While neglect proceedings were originally an outgrowth of society's concern for the welfare of poor children, gradually the focus expanded to protect children of all classes—and to include other forms of abuse, such as commercial exploitation and exposure to immorality. The state increasingly became the arbiter of acceptable parenting, with worrisome implications.

In 1975, for instance, a white Alabama man complained to police that his ex-girlfriend might be neglecting their son. There were no signs of child abuse, but the woman was white and she was living with a black man in a black neighborhood. There had been no prior complaints of child neglect and the boy was well-clothed, clean, and in good physical condition. Nevertheless, the police forcibly removed the boy from his mother and took him to a shelter. The judge who issued the order justified his decision on the ground that it would be unhealthy for a white child to live in an all-black neighborhood.

The woman challenged Alabama's child neglect law. In reviewing the case, a federal district court in *Roe* v. *Conn* stated that Americans' fundamental right to family integrity is protected under the Fourteenth Amendment to the United States Constitution. The court said the Alabama statute was unconstitutionally vague because it didn't define when a home was "unfit" or "improper," Moreover, the statute was unconstitutional because it failed to provide the mother with an opportunity to refute the charges against her before the child was taken away. The government can remove a child, the court said, only when he is subjected to real physical or emotional harm and less drastic measures, such as counseling, would be unavailing.

In most child abuse cases, however, judges haven't been officious meddlers but reluctant intervenors. Consider, for example, the case of Rubin Almeyda, born in March 1977 to Ralph Almeyda and Lourdes Delgado. Soon after the child's birth the New York Bureau of Child Welfare removed him from his parents because of doubt that they could create a good home for him. Both parents were twenty years old and indigent; and Lourdes, who had polio as a child, was crippled. She was described by a psychiatrist as a "severely disturbed, irrational and angry young woman whose behavior has been extremely self-destructive." She became easily enraged, threw tantrums, and had been diagnosed as having a borderline personality with paranoid features. The father suffered from depression and had been violently assaulting his mother for years.

Nevertheless, a psychologist retained by the New York Legal Aid Society, which represented the baby's interest, and a psychologist who worked for the family court, found no evidence to indicate that the parents would harm their child. Even a caseworker who had expressed doubts about the parents' ability to make sound judgments conceded that they appeared to be warm and loving. Consequently, family court judge Kathryn A. MacDonald ruled that the Bureau of Child Welfare had not proven conclusively that the child was in imminent danger and ordered him returned to his parents. Arrangements were made for a caseworker to visit the family regularly.

Three months after the baby was given to his parents, his bruised body was dead upon arrival at Columbia Presbyterian Medical Center in New York City. Every rib in his body had been broken several times. His skull had been fractured. His father had burned his buttocks and feet by placing his son into a hot, empty pot on the stove. Ralph Almeyda was promptly arrested for murder.

During the baby's short lifetime there were indications

of abuse. Lourdes had seen Ralph bang the baby against the wall and punch him but she didn't report the incidents because she felt she could control her husband. Ralph's mother was afraid to report him for child abuse because she feared he would assault her. The caseworker never noticed the baby's bruises because the mother kept him clothed during visits and the caseworker didn't want to seem too intrusive.

Unfortunately, the tragic death of children like Rubin Almeyda is an all too common occurrence. According to the National Committee for Prevention of Child Abuse, there were 1,132 child abuse fatalities in the United States during 1987. "Within the courts, there is a 1930s thinking that tells us the first goal is always maintenance of family," according to Dr. Judianne Densen-Gerber, an expert in child abuse. "It shouldn't be. The first goal should be the life and security of the child . . . The second attitude that has to change is that children are the 'property' of their parents and that unless we can demonstrate damage, children should always remain with their parents."

Indeed, the law allows parents great discretion in raising their children, permitting them to administer corporal punishment that would be considered assault and battery in any other context. Courts consider parenting decisions to be matters within the sole jurisdiction of "domestic government." In 1886 the North Carolina Supreme Court in *State v. Jones* expressed the prevailing view:

> If, whenever parental authority is used in chastising them [children], it could be a subject of judicial inquiry whether the punishment was cruel and excessive—that is, beyond the demerits of the disobedience or misconduct, and the father himself exposed to a criminal prosecution at the instance of the child, in defending himself from which he would be compelled to lift the curtain from the scenes of home life, and exhibit a long series of acts of subordination, disobedience and ill-doing—it would open the door to a flood of irreparable evils far transcending that to be remedied by a public prosecution.

The court ruled that the father could be held criminally responsible only if he inflicted permanent injury on the child, or if the punishment was malicious and not for the purpose of correcting the child's behavior.

However, studies show a strong correlation between severe corporal punishment administered to children and their development into violent juvenile delinquents. Among violent inmates of the California State Prison at San Quentin, for instance, 100 percent of them had experienced extreme violence between the ages of one and ten, according to a paper presented at the 1976 California State Psychological Convention. A study by a New York University psychiatrist of fourteen juveniles on death row found that nine of them had suffered serious head injuries during childhood and almost all had been brutally beaten and abused.

In light of this evidence, the current trend is to hold parents liable for excessive corporal punishment even if they mean well. Parents today are justified in using force upon their children only if the degree of force is reasonable under the circumstances and it is administered for the purpose of maintaining discipline or safeguarding the child's welfare.

Moreover, child abuse is no longer defined merely in terms of physical punishment. Emotional abuse and parental neglect are now well-accepted grounds for removing a child from the home. Judges recognize that young children who are underdeveloped mentally, physically, and emotionally may be suffering from "psychosocial dwarfism" or "deprivational dwarfism," a condition brought about by a lack of kissing, holding, hugging, and emotional interaction with other human beings. Some courts have even taken away children from their parents on the grounds of potential neglect. In *In re East* the court took a newborn infant away from a sixteen-year-old sexually promiscuous mother who had no visible means of support.

But courts usually remove only very young children on the grounds of emotional abuse, although the same abuse can have a devastating effect on adolescents. "People tend to think that emotional abuse is less serious than physical or sexual abuse," says Paul Mones, an attorney who specializes in parricide cases, "but the most insidious part of physical and sexual abuse is the emotional component. The scars of psychological abuse run very, very deep and they last much longer than sexual penetration or a blow to the head."

Mones continues: "The common pattern in these cases is extremely demeaning comments where the parent eviscerates the soul of the child. If I say to an adult, 'You lousy fink I don't want to see you again in my house,' the adult will respond by telling me to screw off. If I say that to a twenty-eight-year-old son, he will say, 'Dad, this is the end of our relationship.' But if you take a forming personality, especially during prepubescent years [the impact is more severe] . . . These kids are looking for acceptance. Their father becomes their role model. Parents take on mythic qualities, they become Zeus. The kid doesn't have any touchstones and when the father repeatedly treats him terribly, it has a dehumanizing effect . . . the kid loves this person who is terrible to him. They end up loving their tormentor."

Mones says such children are helpless. "He can't go to his mother because his mother knows what is going on and isn't doing anything for him. His friends know and they are either afraid of the father or unwilling to help. Teachers are ineffective. And cops never believe kids. So when you take out all the spokes of the wheel, it crushes the hub. So before the kid is crushed—which is suicide—he takes the only action he can to get out. They run away from home or kill their parent."

Although the law has long recognized self-defense in the face of physical or sexual assault, the courts have been reluctant to embrace self-defense against emotional abuse. "It's a subject that is so totally misunderstood by the legal community, it's as if they ignore it," says Mones. "Most judges and lawyers don't understand the case because the kid wasn't hit and for some reason that belittles the importance of the abuse . . . [yet] one of the greatest tortures you can [dispense] . . . is psychological torture."

Ironically, courts seem more sympathetic toward abused wives who kill their husbands than abused children who kill a parent. In several recent cases, judges and juries broadly interpreted the self-defense and legal insanity doctrines to acquit sympathetic defendants who were victims of what is known as the battered wife syndrome.

In 1977, for instance, Francine Hughes, a Michigan mother of four, was charged with first-degree murder of her husband. During their thirteen-year marriage, she was repeatedly subject to physical abuse. Claiming she was desperate and was unable to obtain help from relatives or law enforcement authorities, she poured gasoline under the bed of her sleeping husband and set it afire. He died of smoke inhalation and Mrs. Hughes then turned herself in to the police. After a trial, the jury found her not guilty by reason of insanity. Two weeks later she was found sane and released after a one-hour interview.

In 1977 another Michigan woman, Mrs. Sharon McNerney, mother of three, pleaded self-defense to charges of second-degree murder of her husband of twenty-four years. She shot him although he was unarmed, claiming she believed he would follow through on his threat to kill her. She testified that she had been beaten about once a month during the marriage and that her husband had been briefly jailed for shooting at her. She was acquitted.

Wanda Carr of Redding, California, pleaded not guilty by reason of insanity after killing her husband of twenty-two years. One night she removed a loaded weapon from her closet, pointed it at her husband, woke him, and asked that they talk. When he moved toward her, she shot him. The prosecutor reduced the charge from murder to manslaughter and conceded after her acquittal that he didn't care whether he won or lost the case. The judge was reported to have said, "I don't think she had a viable alternative. This was a classic case in the sense of a long period of abuse and harassment. . . . It was serious protracted mental and physical abuse."

In many of these cases the women became so demoralized and degraded by their inability to predict or control their husband's violent behavior that they sank into a state of psychological paralysis. They were without job skills or financial wherewithal to leave the relationship, and low self-esteem led them to believe they deserved the beatings. Frequently they didn't confide in friends or family out of a sense of shame and humiliation, as well as fear of reprisal by their husbands.

Adolescents who commit patricide also tend to fit a pattern. They are typically white middle-class boys without much of a criminal history. According to Mones: "If they were delinquents, their crimes were usually status offenses like running away from home, being truant in school, or committing minor acts of vandalism. Often the son appears to have a buddy relationship with the father, like two guys living together. The kid has no boundary identification. He doesn't know where the man stops and the father begins. There is competition between the two and when the father tries to act parental, the kid gets all confused. These kids are in a state of inextricable confusion. And nobody helps them.

"When they kill, the parent is in a vulnerable position . . . sleeping or they have their back turned. And the kid usually uses an overabundance of force. Their rage just comes out . . . Many of these kids [afterward] still think the parent is alive . . . because [the parent] . . . is so real and so omnipresent and lives on in their minds.

In all the cases Mones has studied, if the child didn't enter into a plea bargain, he was convicted upon trial. Not once was self-defense or insanity used successfully. Part of the problem is that children often don't inform their attorneys about instances of physical and sexual abuse. "The child wants to protect his dad," says Mones. "Or the kid forgets. It's a natural blocking mechanism for him not to want to remember, so there is a sort of amnesia." But almost always, Mones emphasizes, there was a lot more abuse than meets the eye.

Jason was incarcerated in the Central New Mexico Correctional Facility in Los Lunas, about fifteen miles south of Albuquerque. He was the first juvenile in the medium-security facility and when he arrived he worried that other inmates might prey on him. He was given his own cell and so far no one has bothered him.

He expects to be out of prison by the time he is twenty-two, which makes him feel he can still lead a full life. He is more motivated than before, studying hard so that he can realize his ambition of becoming an engineer. He has already obtained his high school equivalency degree, which places him ahead of his classmates in high school. In another year and a half, he hopes, he'll be permitted to attend college. Although he'll have to return to prison every night, his days won't be much different from those of an ordinary student.

He has a girlfriend, Karen, nineteen, two years older than he. They met after she read about his case in the newspaper and wrote him a sympathetic letter. She visits three times a week. He finds the relationship very comforting and hopes it will continue beyond prison. In the meantime, he worries about her working nights at a convenience store, afraid she might be robbed.

Finding prison boring, he tries to keep busy attending classes, building model airplanes and cars, playing basketball, and listening to music. He speaks to his mother every day by phone.

He feels a great deal of remorse over the killing but doesn't like to talk about it. When inmates ask him what he is in prison for, his response is "Man, I don't care what you're in here for, there's no reason why you should care why I'm in here. We're all in the same place, why don't you make the best of it."

He receives little therapy. Once a week he participates in a session with his mother but he doesn't find the sessions helpful and has little rapport with the therapist. She asks him to do "weird" things like pet animals. "I have a hard time with these psychologists," he says. "Sometimes they are more whacked out than the [patients]." Parnall feels Jason would do better with a male therapist but the prison authorities have ignored his request.

Parnall had planned to take time off after the Kirkman case to devote himself to his music. But when a sixteen-year-old boy was accused of killing a friend during a game of Russian roulette at a drinking party, Parnall once again laid aside his guitar and headed for the courtroom.

Chapter 4

THE
HALLUCINATING
KIDNAPPER

> *To be an effective criminal defense
> counsel, an attorney must be pre-
> pared to be demanding, outrageous,
> irreverent, blasphemous, a rogue, a
> renegade and a hated, isolated and
> lonely person. . . . Few love a
> spokesman for the despised and the
> damned.*
>
> —CLARENCE DARROW

Minnesotans are quiet, reserved, and, most of all, sensible people. The state was first to restrict smoking in public places; noise barriers have been erected alongside highways; heated skywalks link downtown buildings. About the only time irrationality surfaces is on "Crazy Days," when merchants move their goods onto the sidewalks and slash prices.

Garrison Keillor likes to poke fun at Minnesotans who live in the mythical town of Lake Woebegon. Their real-life counterparts accept the ribbing with good humor. People here aren't pretentious or flashy; they're just decent, hardworking, and neighborly. Bizarre crimes are rare, which was why everyone was shocked when they heard the news that a Minnesotan had kidnapped his former algebra teacher and imprisoned her as a sex slave for seven weeks.

The abduction occurred on May 16, 1980, in a parking lot in Roseville, a suburb of St. Paul. Inside Carmen's Beauty Salon sat Barbara Lund, thirty-six, a slender, bespectacled woman with a lively personality and a ready smile. A wholesome-looking midwesterner who made few concessions to glamour, she wore her hair short and dressed simply. She was waiting while her daughter Ann, eight, had her hair cut. The family was busy preparing for their imminent return to the Philippines, where Barbara and her husband Harvey had been Baptist missionaries for three years. They were on furlough, visiting congregations in the Midwest to report on their work.*

Behind a line of trees waited Ming Sen Shiue, twenty-nine. Of Chinese ancestry, he was solidly built, weighed 175 pounds and was five feet seven inches tall. He had brown eyes, black hair, and a round face with just enough whiskers on his upper lip and chin to form the faint outline of a mustache and goatee. He was dressed in a loose-fitting dark brown leather jacket, brown corduroy pants, and leather gloves, and wore dark glasses.

At 4:30 P.M., Barbara and Ann left the beauty salon. As Barbara was about to open the passenger door of her light green 1973 Ford LTD, Ming suddenly appeared, pushed a gun into Ann's side and said, "I need a ride."

Ming climbed in the front seat with them and directed Barbara through rush-hour traffic. He had her turn and change direction frequently; either he was uncertain of his way or was checking to see if anyone was following. Barbara was frightened and confused but maintained her composure. She calmly asked if there was a problem and offered

---

* The names of members of the "Lund" family have been changed to protect their privacy. Everything else is factual.

her assistance. Ming wouldn't respond. After she mentioned that they were expected home for supper and would be missed if they didn't arrive on time, Ming told her to keep quiet and drive?

At one point while they were on an interstate highway, a police car pulled behind them. Ming glanced back nervously and warned Barbara not to try anything funny because he had a gun at her daughter's side. Dismissing all thoughts of escape, Barbara did nothing to alert the police car, which soon turned off in another direction.

Ming directed Barbara to drive onto a dirt road in a wooded area. He asked her to turn the car around, and in the process the rear wheels spun furiously as they became immersed in sand. An agitated Ming demanded that she extricate the vehicle. After some maneuvering, she did. He then had her turn off the ignition.

Ming told Barbara and Ann that he was going to bind their hands and put them in the trunk. Barbara was afraid they would suffocate but Ming assured them they would not. After tying their hands with rope, he had them climb into the trunk where he bound their feet.

Barbara and Ann were uncomfortable lying on their stomachs in a hot and dusty trunk, jostled about over bumpy roads. Barbara tried to comfort her frightened daughter, leading her in prayer, as she began to work loose the ropes around her daughter's hands. After twenty-five minutes, Ming stopped the car in Hazelnut Park, about one-quarter mile from Carmen's Beauty Salon. Opening the trunk, he noticed that Barbara had untied Ann's hands. "What will I do with you now?" he exploded. "I can't trust you." He tied their ropes tighter and taped their hands. Then he unfastened the spare tire and placed it on top of them to make it more difficult for them to maneuver.

As Ming worked on his captives, a young boy who had been playing in the park approached, curious to see what Ming was doing. He offered an innocent hello. A startled Ming shouted, "Hey, you," and grabbed the boy and threw him in the trunk. A playmate of the boy, standing forty or fifty feet away, witnessed the incident and ran home to tell his mother. As Ming sped off, Barbara learned that the boy's name was Jason Wilkman, and he was six years old.

Jason, frightened, began to cry. Barbara tried to calm him, saying that Jesus was looking after them. Jason was concerned that he would miss a visit the next day to his grandparents. Ann mentioned that she also was supposed to visit her grandparents tomorrow.

It was dusk when the car stopped. Ming removed Jason and a jack handle from the trunk; Barbara and Ann never saw the boy again. Ming later told Barbara that he took Jason into the woods, cautioned him never to talk about what he had seen, and let him go.

After another short drive, Ming once again stopped the car. Barbara and Ann had begun to sweat and found it difficult to breathe. They believed they might have been abandoned and left to die. Barbara cautioned her daughter not to exert herself in order to conserve air.

Meanwhile, Barbara's husband, Harvey, was becoming increasingly agitated about the absence of his wife and daughter. He had expected them to return home by 6:00 P.M. for dinner. Barbara's sister, Sandra, had been invited to join them; and when they failed to appear, Harvey and Sandra ate by themselves before Sandra left for a meeting.

At 8:00 P.M., Harvey tried to reach Sylvia Bird, the hairdresser who had cut Ann's hair, but she was out for the evening. Worried, Sandra later called Harvey, who bundled his son, Steven, five, in some warm clothes and drove the route to Carmen's Beauty Salon to see if Barbara might have become stranded. But there was no sign of his wife and daughter or their car. Harvey returned home, gave Steven a shower, and put him to bed. Finally he reached Sylvia Bird, who informed him that Barbara and Ann had left the beauty parlor at four-thirty that afternoon. Harvey called the sheriff's office to report their disappearance.

Ming, meanwhile, picked up a van and returned for his

captives, whom he blindfolded and transferred to the van. When Barbara expressed concern that her car might be stolen, Ming assured her the doors were locked and he had the keys.

Barbara complained that their hands were red, swollen, and losing feeling. Fearing that her hands might be permanently damaged and she would be unable to play the piano again, she asked that their bonds be loosened, as well as that they be allowed to go to a bathroom. In response, Ming brought them to a stereo repair shop that was closed for the evening, where he removed their bonds and allowed them to use the toilet. After Barbara had cleaned up her daughter, who had already wet her pants, Ming gave them some fruit juice before retying and blindfolding them, although not as tightly as before.

It was after midnight when Ming led his blindfolded captives into his home in Roseville. Although he untied their hands and feet, he restrained them by binding their elbows to their torsos. After removing Barbara's watch, rings, and glasses, he placed mother and daughter in a closet that was bare except for a rug, two pillows, a couple of blankets, and an ice cream bucket for them to use as a chamber pot. The closet was barely wide enough for Barbara and Ann to lie down side by side, and Barbara was unable to stretch out. Ming removed the inside doorknob, locked the door, and propped a chair against it.

The next morning Ming allowed his prisoners to visit the bathroom. Whenever he let them out, however, he would first blindfold them. He later gave them some canned stew and Kool-Aid to consume in the closet.

That afternoon Ming instructed Barbara to write a letter to her husband, wording it to appear as if she and Ann had left of their own accord, and planned to return home in time to catch their scheduled flight to the Philippines. Ming promised to release them by then.

Under Ming's direction, Barbara redrafted the letter until he was satisfied. He then had her copy it onto a fresh

"No, no, just never," she replied.

"That is real. That happens," he said.

Blaming Barbara for all the disappointments in his life, Ming said, "I want things that I could never have. . . . I want a good job, can't have that, respect, can't have that."

Barbara said he could still attend college but Ming replied that no one would hire a thirty-four-year-old graduate. Besides, life is not just work, he wanted a family too.

He told her that he didn't care what happened to him, that he would just as soon go out in a blaze of glory, in one big fight. "That's what I've been trained for, okay? The Army beats that into your head, you know."

Barbara tried to reason with him and spoke of religion. "I'm not a holy person and that's why I needed Jesus Christ because I was a very sinful person. Everybody is sinful."

"Yes, but do you do the things I do?"

". . . I don't think God has a scale of sins, that kidnapping is worse than lying." Barbara tried to explain her religious beliefs but Ming wasn't interested.

"See, to me you are just being self-righteous," he said. "You are demonstrating what you believe as [*sic*] a moral superiority. Which is fine. I'm not arguing with you . . . [but] why didn't you think of this fifteen years ago?"

He had been stalking her for two months, he revealed, and had attempted to break into her apartment on three occasions. Barbara remembered that one morning her husband had noticed that the glass on the patio door had been shattered, and marks on the exterior casing indicated an attempted break-in. Several weeks later, awaking at 4:00 A.M. after hearing a scraping noise, she walked into the dining room and saw a man trying to break in through the window. As she hurried back to the bedroom, she tripped over a packing box. She woke her husband who went into the dining room, shouted at the man, and then called the sheriff.

Ming also disclosed that he had broken into her husband's parents' home in Duluth under the mistaken belief that Barbara lived there. He bound Barbara's in-laws but didn't rob or harm them. Barbara recalled her in-laws telling her about the bizarre incident.

By the third hour of their conversation Ming began to remove items of her clothing. She begged him to leave her alone.

"You obviously don't realize you're dealing with somebody that is determined," he said. "I'm not gonna stop until I get it done. Do you understand? . . . This is nothing compared to what I've been through. Like I say, you will be suffering a little bit of degradation right now."

He tried to persuade her to submit to him. She begged him to refrain, saying, "God says that a husband and wife should be one flesh and that wife shall not have any other person." Ming wasn't deterred. Finally, Barbara said she would rather he hit her than rape her.

"I can understand that," Ming said. "But I prefer that you don't have, I don't leave any marks on you. I know you'll probably have emotional scars, but see, that's the beauty of it. You will have the same feeling that I have and that's where, ah, ah, [I] even things up."

Ming warned her that she could make it easy or difficult, but the act would be done. Barbara reasoned that if she screamed, she would upset her daughter and she feared Ming might hurt her. Over the next half hour he repeatedly penetrated her as she lay blindfolded, bound, and helpless. She tried to console herself by praying silently.

Ming then let Barbara put her clothes on and visit the bathroom to clean herself while he stood by the door. After she was returned to the closet, Ann asked if she was all right; Barbara said yes, she was okay.

The pattern was repeated over the following weeks. Ming would keep Ann, or "Annie" as he affectionately called her, in the closet watching television while he took her mother to the living room for the videotaped rape sessions, some of which lasted three hours.

*   *   *

The Ramsey County Sheriff's Office was frankly baffled by the case. On Friday night they received a report that Jason Wilkman had been abducted and that Barbara and Ann were missing. Lieutenant William Sass was in charge of the investigation and by Saturday morning he felt the incidents might be linked. Jason's playmate had described the kidnapper as Oriental, and Sass knew that the Lunds had recently returned from missionary work in the Philippines. He figured that the kidnapper's motive might be political.

The Lund car was soon found, locked with the keys removed. Sass considered this odd behavior—when criminals abandon cars they usually leave them unlocked with the keys in the ignition. With the arrival of Barbara's letter, Sass knew that at least she and Ann were alive, although the absence of any mention of Jason concerned him.

The day after the abduction, the FBI was asked for assistance. Up to forty agents worked on the case alongside some sixty local law enforcement officers and some three hundred civilian volunteers who combed the crime scene for clues. When the story of the kidnappings broke, Sass was inundated with fifty to sixty leads a day, none of which proved useful.

Although Barbara and Ann Lund were always blindfolded or locked in the closet, Barbara discovered their location. A blanket on the top shelf of the closet fell down; attached was a dry-cleaning tag with a North Hamline Avenue address on it. Barbara had Ann memorize the address; in the event Ann was freed first, she could lead the police back to her mother.

On the first Monday after their capture, Ming warned his captives not to make any noise because a man lived in the basement. Before leaving, he locked them in the closet and they assumed he was going to work. After loosening their gags, they were able to talk; Barbara told Ann Bible stories and they prayed together.

Some time later, they heard a door opening and closing

downstairs. They beat on the closet door with their feet, hoping to attract attention. Since they didn't know Morse code, they rapped out series of three knocks, hoping someone would recognize it as an SOS plea for help. Receiving no response, they pounded out the theme song from *Dragnet*. But their efforts were to no avail. When Ming returned he said he thought he heard pounding. "What pounding?" they replied.

Several days later Barbara asked Ming if they could wash their clothes, pointing out that they had been wearing the same items since their capture and could hardly stand their own body odor any longer. Ming agreed and let Ann and Barbara wear some of his clothes until theirs dried. Meanwhile, Ming took Barbara into the living room and became angry when she didn't respond to his advances. He fastened a rope to her ankle, ran it around her neck, and tied it to her other ankle. Then he pulled the rope tight so her knees were held aloft. In this uncomfortable position, Ming repeatedly raped her for more than an hour. Finally, her clothes were dry and she was permitted to dress.

Although Barbara and Ann spent most of their captivity locked in a closet, on Sunday, May 25, Ming took them for a drive. After blindfolding them, he put them in large cardboard boxes, which he dragged to his van. Then he took them out into the countryside, stopping near a sod farm in a remote wooded area where he let his captives enjoy the fresh air while keeping their arms tied and their feet loosely bound.

On June 3, Ming expressed concern about all the publicity their absence had generated. He was disturbed that law enforcement agencies were reportedly conducting an extensive search for Barbara and Ann. Consequently, he told them that he wouldn't be able to release them as he had promised. Ming instructed Barbara to write a second letter to her husband. The second letter read:

Dear Harvey,

Ann and I are well, and we hope to see you soon. I realize that the apartment will have to be vacated soon so I am asking that when you do have to move, please stay in the Metropolitan area so that we can contact you. It would be good to leave a forwarding address and telephone number where you can be reached with the seminary office as well as the Minnesota Baptist Conference, our local churches such as Calgary, Central, Brookdale, my sister Ruth and any other mutual friends you can think of. Because of the large amount of police activity and media publicity connected with the first week of our so-called disappearance, we could not carry out the plan stated in our first letter, therefore do not involve the authorities: Police, Sheriff, FBI, et cetera when you receive this letter as it is very important that you know our contact must be kept confidential, private and personal otherwise you may not hear from us again. So please keep everybody else out of this.

If you comply with the contents of this letter, we will be contacting you soon regarding the arrangements of our eventual return.

Contrary to what the authorities and media may have implied, this is not a kidnapping situation so there is no ransom money involved. All we want to do is come home quietly without publicity or further investigation.

We love you and Steve and miss you so. Please continue to trust in the Lord as we are.

Love,
Barbara and Ann

The following day, Ming made affectionate overtures to Barbara and became angry when she didn't respond. "Have you ever watched anybody die by suffocation?" he asked. "It takes four or five minutes. . . . You are going to see your daughter die by suffocation if you will not cooperate." Barbara tried to explain that she believed in the Bible and felt his requests were wrong. This so enraged Ming that he stormed out of the room. Barbara rushed to the door and tried to lock it, but Ming returned quickly with a large plastic bag in hand. He opened the closet door and said to Ann, "Do you like to play with plastic bags?"

She had never played with a plastic bag, Ann replied. "Here, I'm going to put this over your head," Ming said, and he did so, telling Barbara, "You will watch and you will see that the bag will just contract and the air will be used up." Ann, frightened, said, "Mama, what's going on? What's the matter? What does he want?" Barbara said, "Annie, he wants me to sin, to do something that is not right." Ann replied, "Mama, don't sin," and then she asked, "Ming, what do you want my mama to do?" He said, "She knows what she has to do."

Ann became uncomfortable and pleaded, "Mama, can't you please do what he wants?" Barbara told her daughter to trust in Jesus and she began to pray. Watching her daughter perspire, Barbara tried to walk to the closet to remove the bag. But Ming blocked her. The bag was collapsing and clinging tightly to Ann. When she couldn't stand the sight any longer, she went over to Ming and kissed him on the cheek. "That's not good enough," he said. So Barbara kissed him on the lips, indicating that she would do whatever he wanted.

Ming removed the bag from Ann and let Barbara bring her into the bathroom to wash off the sweat-soaked girl. He said that as punishment for trying to lock him out of the room Barbara wouldn't be allowed to sleep in the closet with her daughter that night. Then he put Ann in the closet and took Barbara to the living room, telling her to remove her clothes.

The rape session began and Barbara cooperated. She kissed Ming, put her arms around him, put her legs up when he asked her to, and moved her body as he instructed. After letting her dress, he demanded that she lie down on the bed and sleep with him. Barbara and Ann slept fitfully that night, and Ming eventually relented and let Barbara rejoin Ann in the closet.

The next morning Ming told Barbara he wanted to use up the remainder of his videotape. He brought her into the living room and raped her again. Barbara asked why he was recording these sessions; he explained that should his anger reoccur, he wanted to be able to look at the tapes and recall that he had had his revenge. He also reasoned they would be highly embarrassing to her and would deter her from reporting him to the police.

As the weeks passed, Ming allowed Barbara and Ann more freedom to move about the house. By padlocking chains around their waists, which he attached to cables running between door hinges, he effectively prevented their escape.

In the evenings, the three of them would play board games. One day Ming rented a Winnebago and took his "family" on a trip to Chicago. It was the happiest period of his life. Barbara and Ann, however, lived in fear, and the rapes continued. They prayed daily for God to show them a way to escape.

But there was little opportunity for escape. Once the doorbell rang while Barbara and Ann were in the kitchen preparing a meal. Ming told the caller, "I am in the shower, come back later." When the caller persisted, an angry Ming slammed the door and threatened to call the police—which Ann and Barbara found ironically amusing.

Barbara tried to smuggle out a note to the man who lived downstairs asking him to call the sheriff's office. She planned to slip the note into his food, which he stored in the same refrigerator they used. One day she deduced that a new carton of milk belonged to him. She stashed a note in her bra as she waited for an opportunity to visit the refrigerator. That evening, however, Ming warned her that he would kill them both if they tried to escape. Then he became affectionate. Frightened that he would undress her and discover the note, she excused herself, went to the bathroom, and flushed the note down the toilet. But the paper floated, and she had to retrieve it and bury it in the wastebasket.

On the Fourth of July, Ming took them out to a restaurant and then to Como Park to see the fireworks at the state fairgrounds. Barbara's hope that someone would recognize her and alert the police was unfulfilled, and she was afraid to flee into the crowd lest Ming be armed and start shooting.

On July 7, Ming mentioned that the owner of the house would be visiting in August and they would have to move out temporarily. He spoke about taking a long-term lease on a motor home. Disconsolate, Barbara confided to her daughter, "It doesn't sound as though he's ever going to release us."

Shortly thereafter Ming decided to chain the Lunds to a different door, which restricted their movement and meant they could no longer reach the bathroom on their own. After Ming left for work, and while Ann was watching Popeye on television, Barbara walked over to the new door hinge and tried to dislodge the hinge pin with her bare hands. Miraculously it slipped out.

Trembling with excitement, she told Ann. But her daughter feared Ming was playing a trick on them—that he had only pretended to leave and was lying in wait for them. "Mama, don't do it," the little girl pleaded. Barbara replaced the hinge pin temporarily in an unsuccessful attempt to calm her daughter. Finally, she slapped her. "Annie, if God has given us this way to escape we have to take it," she said. "Mama, you try to check and see if he is here," Ann begged.

Barbara went to the bedroom door, opened it, and didn't hear any sounds. Returning, she removed the hinge pin, went into the kitchen, and phoned the sheriff's office. Barbara identified herself, gave her location, and asked that officers be sent quickly—but warned them to approach with caution because Ming was armed. "Is Jason with you?" Barbara was asked. "Haven't you found him yet?" she replied. She was devastated by the question, realizing that Ming must have killed the boy. Mother and daughter grabbed their toothbrushes and some belongings and reinserted the pin in the door.

The wait seemed interminable although the police arrived within minutes. Barbara and Ann, having decided it would be best not to remain inside in case Ming returned, hid behind a car parked in the yard. They were contemplating moving to a better hiding place when two squad cars pulled into the driveway.

Barbara and Ann rushed into one of the cars and the deputies and FBI agents took them safely away. After Barbara gave them the license plate number of Ming's van, the deputies called it in to headquarters and found that the van belonged to Sound Equipment Services, a stereo store. An FBI agent asked Barbara if Ming had transported them across state lines, and when she replied yes, he called Assistant U.S. Attorney Thorwald Anderson, who authorized Ming's arrest.

At about six-thirty that evening two FBI agents and a St. Paul police detective walked into Ming's electronic repair shop. Although he repeatedly denied knowing Barbara Lund or anything about her kidnapping, he was arrested and taken to the Ramsey County Adult Detention Center in St. Paul.

The next day Ming's house was searched and twenty guns, assorted ammunition, videotapes of the rape sessions, Barbara's purse, and Ann's note pad and crayons were found. Ming was brought to federal court and charged with kidnapping. Bond was set at one million dollars. In state court he was later charged with the abduction of Jason Wilkman.

After Ming's mother and stepfather learned of their son's arrest, they called their family lawyer. He recommended that they retain Ron Meshbesher, one of Minneapolis's preeminent criminal defense attorneys, to defend their son.

Ron Meshbesher, aged forty-seven, is slightly built, with a thick head of gray hair and a neatly trimmed salt-and-pepper beard. He has a reputation for winning difficult cases.

He won an acquittal for a doctor accused of raping a

fourteen-year-old girl in a hospital. "She was a nice little girl," according to the mild-mannered attorney, "but I don't know . . . [the doctor] claimed he didn't do it."

Representing Dave Forbes, a Boston Bruin hockey player accused of felonious assault after hitting an opposing player in the eye with a hockey stick during a Bruin-Minnesota North Star game, Meshbesher got the charges dismissed after a hung jury.

He defended Duane Bicek, thirty-five, who was accused of murdering his wife and twenty-month-old daughter to collect $270,000 in life insurance. The victims died when fifty pounds of explosives stored in the family car detonated. Bicek claimed the explosion was an accident that occurred when he tried to jump-start the car with his pickup truck. Meshbesher persuaded the jury that his client was merely negligent, and they convicted him of the lesser offense of manslaughter, which carried a six-year sentence.

Once Meshbesher defended a group of blacks involved in a confrontation with police. During the highly publicized trial, Meshbesher accused several officers of prejudice. Soon thereafter he began to get anonymous phone calls denouncing him as a "nigger lover." His wife was phoned during the day and told, "Your husband is fucking one of his nigger prostitutes in his office right now." Thousands of dollars' worth of hors d'oeuvres and dozens of pizzas mysteriously arrived at his home, followed by a truckload of sand dumped in his driveway. Then a hearse arrived to pick up his body.

Interestingly, he received the most hate mail and the greatest number of angry phone calls when he defended a man accused of cruelty to horses. The owner lived in Florida during the winter and had hired a local man to care for his herd. The employee apparently pocketed the money and fled. The public was outraged after watching news broadcasts showing emaciated horses lying dead in snow-covered fields. "It's a funny thing," said Meshbesher, "that people were more irate that I had the audacity to defend this SOB than I ever got representing a murderer or a rapist."

Not only has Meshbesher endured the public's wrath, but he also has had to contend with ungrateful clients. "Many have unrealistic expectations. They expect me to be a miracle worker. And I have to . . . tell some that they've got a losing case, perhaps we better negotiate and make the best deal we can. But most people don't want to hear that and a lot of them insist on going to trial despite my insistence that they plead guilty.

"Even if I get them what I think is a pretty good deal— they'll only do five years instead of going to prison for twenty—after they're in prison awhile they talk to other people and think perhaps I sold them down the river. Many of these people are paranoid. And sometimes people who I've worked the hardest for show very little appreciation afterwards, become highly critical . . . they'll charge me with malpractice or claim I charged them too much. . . . So I am not only fighting the system but I have to cover my own ass with my own clients and treat them as though they are potential adversaries."

Several years ago Meshbesher represented an Iranian exchange student who was accused of illegally purchasing and possessing a firearm. The student claimed he didn't realize that his actions were illegal, which technically wasn't a defense. Nevertheless, he insisted on going to trial, perhaps because he faced deportation if guilty.

At trial, the student insisted on testifying and claimed he didn't understand that he couldn't buy the gun and that he didn't intend to violate the law. He said the questionnaire he filled out at the time of purchase was ambiguous and a trap. Much to Meshbesher's surprise, the jury acquitted his client.

"Now, get rid of all your damn guns," Meshbesher told the student. "You can't have a gun, do you understand?" Meshbesher knew his client understood, because he spoke English fluently and was no dummy. The student later refused to pay Meshbesher the balance of his fee. "He came from a completely different culture," according to Mesh-besher, "and couldn't quite understand how an innocent person like him had to pay to get a lawyer to get him acquitted. And he called me one day very angry and refused to pay me and threatened me in no uncertain terms. He said he would take care of me if I persisted in going after him for the money. . . . The conversation scared me because I knew the guy had a fetish with guns and a violent streak in his personality . . . so I stopped billing him—it wasn't worth it to me.

"Within a year I got a call from his wife who wanted me to visit her husband in jail. He had been arrested for murder. He killed a law student and his wife living next door. They had an argument over Iranian [politics] . . . and he shot them. I said, 'Lady, you've got to be kidding.' I wasn't going to represent him. Several months later I found out that he committed suicide awaiting trial."

Meshbesher wanted to be a lawyer ever since he was five. The desire was planted by his father, Nate, a salesman who had longed to join the profession himself but his parents couldn't afford to send all their children to college, so older brother Si went to law school while Nate dropped out of high school to work in the family bottling company. During the Depression the company failed, and Nate took a job in the liquor business and later became a fluorescent lighting salesman. Nate's idolization of his older brother, who was a fairly successful lawyer, made a deep impression on Ron.

Ron had an excellent relationship with his father, who adored his children and enjoyed their company. The gregarious, rambunctious, and fun-loving father would take nine-year-old Ron and younger brother Ken traveling with him in the summer. He nicknamed his companions Cyclone and Dynamite; they would sit in the car and read comics while he made sales calls. To induce them to accompany him, he taught them how to drive, seating them on phone books so they could peer over the wheel.

"A lot of criminal behavior is genetic . . . some of it is based on conditioning. I mean where a person is brought up will determine much of their future life. Why do you think so many black people are in trouble today? Well, I don't think they're just born criminals. Maybe some have a criminal gene, but when you grow up in a ghetto and you have single-parent households, and you don't have love and support or education and you see prejudice wherever you turn, you're bound to get bitter. What are you gonna do? You're gonna lash out against society.

"The worst son of a bitch, and I've hated some of my clients, has a spark of some good. And sometimes, to my amazement, I find myself liking somebody I started out disliking—after dealing with them and seeing their human side, even though some of them should never get out of prison . . . they belong in prison."

Fellow attorneys admire Meshbesher for his thorough preparation, aggressive tactics, and effective cross-examination. In a survey of Hennepin County trial lawyers, he was voted best criminal defense attorney and best at questioning witnesses. He rarely asks a question to which he doesn't already know the answer, and on the infrequent occasion when he is surprised by a damaging revelation, he is shrewd enough not to react and let on to the jury that he has been hurt.

In one case he was confronted by a hostile witness who had refused to testify at a deposition, asserting his Fifth Amendment right not to incriminate himself. When trial commenced, however, the witness spoke freely, claiming that he had only taken the Fifth at the behest of his attorney. The unexpected development would have thrown many attorneys, but Meshbesher dealt with it cleverly.

"You told your attorney all about everything you did?" asked Meshbesher.

"Yes," replied the witness.

"Didn't leave anything out?"

"No."

"You're sure?"

"Yes."

"Your attorney was also a good friend?"

"Yes."

"You trusted him?"

"Yes."

"Told him everything, told him the truth?"

"Yes."

"And after you told him the truth he advised you to take the Fifth?"

"Yes," said the witness.

"No further questions," said Meshbesher, leaving the implication with the jury that the man must have been guilty otherwise his attorney friend wouldn't have advised him to remain silent.

Meshbesher is especially adept at generating sympathy for his clients. When he was defending a teenager accused of stealing a car, he had the boy cut his hair and hang his head between his knees for the duration of the trial. After the forewoman announced his acquittal, she strode up and shook her finger at the boy and made him promise not to do it again.

His most celebrated defense was of Kenneth Callahan, a man accused of kidnapping Virginia Piper, the wife of a wealthy investment broker. A million-dollar ransom was paid to several masked kidnappers before she was released, unharmed.

The FBI was determined to catch the culprits who had made off with the largest unrecovered ransom in Bureau history. Up to 250 agents were deployed at a cost of more than ten million dollars. After nearly five years of investigation, with time under the statute of limitations about to expire, the Bureau indicted Callahan and Donald Larson. A key piece of evidence against them was a fingerprint on a scrap of paper torn from a brown shopping bag.

At trial Meshbesher discredited witnesses for the prosecution by showing that they were criminals encouraged to testify by FBI promises of reduced sentences. The defense rested its case on a Friday. Over the weekend, Meshbesher was finally able to locate Lynda Billstrom, an important witness he had been seeking. Billstrom agreed to testify that her late husband and his friends had committed the crime. She admitted she had lied to the FBI in providing an alibi for her husband.

The following Monday when the trial resumed, Meshbesher strode into court with Billstrom and asked that he be allowed to reopen his case. The judge refused. The case went to the jury, and after a deadlock lasting several days, they found the defendants guilty. Meshbesher appealed the verdict and won a reversal on the grounds that he should have been allowed to put Billstrom on the stand.

At the second trial, Meshbesher produced another revelation: The fingerprint evidence gathered by the FBI had apparently been doctored. It was an embarrassing disclosure for a government agency proud of its reputation for integrity. The defendants were acquitted and the victory added to Meshbesher's luster.

As one of the top criminal defense attorneys in the Midwest, Meshbesher has been able to build a lucrative practice. His firm includes his brother Ken, eight other partners, and eleven associates. They handle both civil and criminal matters. Meshbesher draws a six-figure salary and is surrounded with the accoutrements of success. The firm owns its office building, which has an exercise room and sauna in the basement and a sun deck on the roof. Meshbesher drives a silver Cadillac and lives in an elegant condominium in downtown Minneapolis.

He has three daughters, is twice divorced, and recently married for the third time. He attributes the failed marriages to his long working hours. Without hobbies, he puts his fervor into his work, feeling that there is nothing quite as exciting as hearing the jury announce, "Not guilty."

His courtroom exploits have made him a local celebrity.

He enjoys the prerogatives of fame, which in Minnesota amount to the privilege of not having to wait for a table in top restaurants. While his reputation can be intimidating, once people get to know him, they tend to like him. Outside of court, he is a quiet and personable fellow.

He does relish publicity and will sometimes take cases that pay little but bring him media attention—which, in turn, attracts other clients. Ming, however, was able to pay him a healthy fee. This defendant was a successful businessman with frugal habits—his net worth was close to $250,000.

Ken Meshbesher, aged forty-four, conducted the first interviews with Ming, because Ron was home recuperating from neuritis in his leg. Ken initially believed Ming's explanations that Barbara Lund loved him. At Ken's suggestion, the two brothers quickly arranged to view Ming's videotapes, which they expected would exonerate their new client. But when they played the tapes, they were shocked by what they saw.

The Meshbeshers also discovered that Ming was never a prisoner of war, hadn't served in the armed forces, and had never lost a scholarship on account of bad grades. He had been a student of Barbara's but she had given him a grade of B, one of two Bs he received in the ninth grade. The grade did little, if any, harm to his record since he earned straight As from tenth to twelfth grade and graduated first in a class of 503 students. Indeed, his classmates voted him Most Likely to Succeed. After graduation, he attended the University of Minnesota but dropped out several years later to devote himself full-time to his burgeoning electronic repair business.

Ron felt the videotapes and Barbara's expected testimony made it virtually impossible for him to obtain an acquittal. The only possible justification would lie in a plea of insanity—a difficult defense, which he considered a last resort.

Ron broached the idea to Ming, who resisted, refusing to admit that he was mentally ill. Realizing that mentally ill people are unwilling to acknowledge their condition, Ron wasn't surprised by Ming's protestations.

His difficulty in persuading his client was compounded by Ming's distrust of his attorneys, which caused him to maintain a stoic demeanor in their presence. Only once did he become animated—when Ron asked him about a problem he was experiencing with his stereo, Ming quickly suggested several solutions.

After Ron explained to Ming that they had no choice but to plead insanity, Ming agreed to cooperate in the defense, although he continued to assert that Barbara loved him.

Meshbesher decided to retain Dr. James Stephans, a psychiatrist, as a consultant on the case. An expert in his field, Stephans had testified extensively for both prosecution and defense, and had evaluated more than one thousand subjects in commitment hearings as a court-appointed psychiatrist. A graduate of Harvard Medical School, he had served eighteen months in Vietnam as a neurosurgeon before returning to Minnesota to begin a psychiatric residency. As a professor at the University of Minnesota, he taught forensic psychiatry, the application of psychiatric principles to legal disputes.

Stephans interviewed Ming and administered a battery of psychological tests. He also spoke to Ming's relatives and associates, examined his school records and the police reports, viewed the videotapes, and read his diary, trying to determine whether Ming suffered from a mere personality disorder or a more serious psychotic illness in which he had lost touch with reality.

Stephans concluded that Ming suffered from schizophrenia, a psychotic ailment characterized by delusions and a split personality. Ming's schizophrenia was of the paranoid variety in which two kinds of delusions are common: feelings of persecution ("Someone is following me") and feelings of grandiosity ("I am Napoleon").

Stephans told Meshbesher that there was no longer any

scientific doubt that schizophrenia was a biochemical abnormality of the body, just as diabetes was. The cause of the disease had been narrowed down to a group of six to twelve neurotransmitters, chemicals that relay impulses from one nerve to another.

As with diabetes, there is a genetic predisposition to schizophrenia. Nonetheless, most people who have a genetic history of the disease never develop it. Nobody has adequately explained why, although some scientists believe stress triggers its onset.

The first sign of schizophrenia is typically an emotional disturbance during adolescence. Symptoms frequently disappear until the person is in his twenties, when he starts to say crazy things and his life begins to deteriorate—often accompanied by dropping out of school or losing a job.

The disease progresses in stages, beginning with a vivid fantasy life. For instance, the schizophrenic may imagine he is President of the United States. In the next stage of the disease, however, the schizophrenic comes to believe he really is President and he proclaims his belief to others. At this point family and friends usually intervene, and if treatment with antipsychotic medication is begun the symptoms of the disease can often be alleviated.

Without treatment, the schizophrenic begins to act upon his delusions, sometimes becoming a danger to himself and others. In the final stages of the disease, the schizophrenic becomes so incoherent and disorganized that he can't care for himself. He may aimlessly wander the streets—unkempt, malnourished, and homeless.

Ming's life history supported the diagnosis of schizophrenia. His father was largely absent from the home until Ming was eight. At that time, the family emigrated from Taiwan, leaving friends and family to settle in a foreign land, although Ming appeared to adapt well and had a normal relationship with his father.

When Ming was eleven his father succumbed to cancer. Soon thereafter Ming began setting fires in apartment houses by pushing lit newspapers under doorways. The

Roseville Fire Department apprehended him and a juvenile court judge placed him on probation on condition he receive therapy at the Child Psychiatry Clinic at the University of Minnesota.

The doctors there concluded that Ming was severely disturbed. For example, he was abnormally curious about his mother's genitals and cut out the crotch of her pajamas so he could sneak into her room late at night with a flashlight to look at her private parts.

After nine months of psychotherapy, Ming's probation was terminated, notwithstanding the vigorous objection of the director of the Child Psychiatry Clinic, an objection that somehow was not communicated to the juvenile court.

According to Stephans, Ming fell in love with Barbara Lund when she was his algebra teacher. On one occasion, she stayed after class with him to discuss a theory about squares that he had developed and of which he was very proud. He interpreted her actions as an expression of love.

Similarly, when Barbara stopped in the hallway to chat with him and when they happened to cross paths on the University of Minnesota campus, Ming regarded these chance encounters as proof that Barbara and he were destined to live their lives together.

In the tenth grade, Ming experienced a striking personality change and became a classic overachiever. His grades shot up from Bs and Cs to straight As despite his participation in such extracurricular activities as football, baseball, wrestling, and track. He won numerous scientific prizes, including a National Science Foundation Award for an exhibit he made involving semiconductors. Stephans explained that this type of dramatic life change sometimes occurs as schizophrenia progresses.

After graduation Ming attended the Institute of Technology at the University of Minnesota. Although he was a scholarship student, his grades were mediocre, mostly Cs. For someone who had shown such promise, his performance undoubtedly caused him humiliation and a loss of face, especially since his parents were high achievers—

his mother taught mathematics and his father had been an expert in the field of forestry. Ming's grades fell further during his second year of college, culminating in a D in calculus.

Stephans postulated that Ming's academic performance deteriorated because his disease left him unable to think clearly and concentrate. It was during this time, said Stephans, that Ming began to hallucinate. He would sense a flash and feel pressure inside his head. He would see images and hear commentary about his thoughts and actions as if he were watching television. Although he couldn't recognize the male voice that spoke to him, he didn't consider the experience abnormal.

Ming saw images of himself having sexual relations with a variety of screen actresses. Frequently, they would seduce him. Sometimes he was the reluctant male seduced by older, mother-type figures. Once he saw himself having relations with the mother of a girlfriend.

Stephans was convinced that Ming's hallucinations were genuine. The psychiatrist noted that Ming even mentioned the flashes and pressures inside his head while talking to Barbara—a scene recorded on videotape.

The hallucinations would last hours, sometimes days, keeping Ming in a constant state of tension. At first he masturbated to obtain relief but that brought only a short respite. When he discovered that writing about his hallucinations eased the pressure, he scribbled furiously and produced a massive volume of material. His writings described the exploits of a character named Ming.

Barbara Lund's name suddenly appeared and reappeared with increasing frequency in Ming's diaries, until she eclipsed all the glamorous movie actresses who had dominated Ming's hallucinations.

The typical schizophrenic reveals his or her illness to others by talking about their crazy beliefs; but Ming never spoke about his delusions, he expressed them in writing. And when he began acting upon his delusions, he was guarded and withdrawn in his behavior. Consequently, his illness went undetected by friends and relatives who might have encouraged him to seek treatment.

In 1972 he went canoeing and camping with a friend for several days near Duluth. After bidding his friend farewell, Ming drove about the area until morning, when he stopped at a restaurant. Over breakfast he hallucinated and became obsessed with finding Barbara. He knew she was originally from the region and searched for her in a local phone book. Finding what he believed was her husband's name, he drove to the corresponding address. He entered the house with a loaded .22-caliber rifle in hand and encountered Barbara's in-laws. After forcing them to lie on the floor, he searched the house for Barbara and then left without harming anyone.

The obsession continued. In April 1980 he read a notice that she and her husband had returned from the Philippines. Believing that she was in love with him and that all he had to do was to see her and they would have a happy, fulfilled life together, he made at least three attempts to break into her house. The most bizarre attempt was when he gained entry into their basement and tried to drill up through the floorboards into her bedroom.

After listening to Stephans, Meshbesher realized that Ming was the most troubled individual he had ever encountered. If anyone deserved to be acquitted on the grounds of insanity, it was Ming. Proving insanity, however, would be another matter.

Insanity has long been recognized as a legitimate defense. In 1582 legal scholar William Lambard stated, "If a man or a natural fool, or a lunatic in the time of his lunacy, or a child who apparently has no knowledge of good or evil do kill a man, this is no felonious act . . . for they cannot be said to have any understanding will." In 1724, the "wild beast" test was enunciated, which held that a defendant who didn't know what he was doing—like a wild beast—should be exculpated.

The dominant standard used to determine legal insanity was articulated in 1843 by English judges in the trial of Daniel M'Naghten. In that case, the defendant had suffered from delusions that caused him to believe that Sir Robert Peel, the prime minister of England, was persecuting him. M'Naghten arrived in London with the intent of assassinating Peel. His plan would have succeeded except that, unknown to him, Queen Victoria was out of town at the time and Peel decided to ride in her carriage rather than his own. As a result, M'Naghten mistakenly shot and killed Edward Drummond, Peel's secretary.

After a lengthy trial, the jury found M'Naghten not guilty by reason of insanity. The queen was displeased with the verdict, for England was in a state of social upheaval at the time and there had been three attempts on her life and one attempt to kill the prince consort. In an extraordinary request, she summoned the House of Lords to question the fifteen judges of the common law courts about the verdict.

In a tense atmosphere, the judges explained that "to establish a defense on the grounds of insanity, it must be clearly proved that, at the time of the committing of the act, the party accused was laboring under such a defect of reason, from disease of the mind, as not to know the nature and quality of the act he was doing, or if he did know it that he did not know he was doing what was wrong." This principle became known as the right/wrong test or the M'Naghten rule.

Thus, if a madman believes he is squeezing lemons when he is strangling a person, he clearly doesn't understand the nature of his act and he can't be held criminally liable. Even if the accused understood he was strangling a person, he might be excused if he didn't understand it was wrong— perhaps he was suffering from a delusion that made him believe that he had to kill in order to save the planet. In such a case, he would have a valid defense if the jury interpreted "wrong" in a moral rather than strictly legal sense. The M'Naghten judges, however, never explained how they construed "wrong," and in the United States the issue has never been definitively resolved.

The M'Naghten judges also said that defendants who were influenced in part by a delusion, but were otherwise sane, should be judged as if the delusion were real. Thus, if a defendant's delusion makes him believe someone is about to shoot him and, as a result, he kills his supposed attacker in self-defense, insanity could be asserted. On the other hand, if the defendant was suffering from a delusion that someone had defamed his reputation and consequently killed that person, insanity wouldn't be a valid plea, because even if the delusion was true, killing to uphold one's reputation isn't recognized as a defense.

The M'Naghten rule has been supplemented in some jurisdictions with the "irresistible impulse" test, which exonerates a defendant whose mental disease prevents him from controlling his conduct. Thus, even if the defendant knew what he was doing, and understood his actions were wrong, he could be excused from charges of theft or arson if he was suffering from compulsive behavior such as kleptomania or pyromania.

For a while the District of Columbia followed the so-called Durham rule, which stated that an accused wasn't criminally responsible if his unlawful act was a product of a mental disease or a mental defect. Although the rule was praised by psychiatrists because it broadened the permitted area of inquiry, others claimed that its basis was so broad that it provided insufficient guidance to juries. The rule has little influence today.

The formulation for insanity offered by the American Law Institute (ALI) in its Model Penal Code states that a defendant isn't criminally responsible for his actions if, at the time of his conduct and as a result of mental disease or defect, he lacked substantial capacity either to appreciate the criminality of his conduct or to conform his conduct to the requirements of law. This rule has been praised as being more realistic because complete impairment of cognitive capacity and self-control isn't required. By 1982 every federal court of appeals and about half the states had adopted the ALI test.

The Model Penal Code specifically excludes from the definition of mental disease or defect an abnormality manifested only by repeated criminal or antisocial conduct. This provision excludes psychopaths, who are in touch with reality and are only abnormal in their flagrant disregard for society's mores. Without this provision, criminals could claim that the very fact that they committed a crime was evidence of insanity. Some psychiatrists, however, subscribe to the view that psychopaths should be allowed to plead the defense because they're suffering from a mental disease. This school notes that headway has been made treating psychopaths and consequently it's more appropriate to commit them to hospitals than to imprison them in jails from which they may well be released back into society as sick and dangerous as before.

No matter which test of insanity is used, the underlying rationale for distinguishing between the mad and the bad is the same. An essential element of criminal conduct is a guilty mind, or mens rea. The issue is not simply whether the accused did or didn't violate the law but whether he did so voluntarily and intentionally. Thus, a plea of insanity is just another way of claiming that the defendant didn't act purposefully. Furthermore, punishment won't rehabilitate him or deter others from committing similar crimes.

Laymen tend to be skeptical of psychiatric theory because of the feeling it is being used to free defendants who should be held responsible for their behavior. When Dan White was tried for killing Mayor George Moscone and City Supervisor Harvey Milk of San Francisco, a psychiatrist testified that White's diet of candy, cupcakes, and Cokes aggravated a chemical imbalance in his brain. This so-called "Twinkie defense" was successful in reducing a charge of murder to manslaughter; the verdict prompted howls of outrage among the citizenry.

Insanity is rarely invoked as a defense. About 95 percent of criminal cases are plea-bargained; of those cases that go to trial an insanity defense is raised in only 1 to 2 percent of them—even though 15 to 20 percent of the prison population have problems that call for psychiatric treatment.

Attorneys are reluctant to use the defense because it is ordinarily effective only when the defendant has no criminal record. When sanity is at issue, the prosecution is permitted to delve into the defendant's past conduct, including any prior arrests, convictions, and antisocial behavior. Such evidence is otherwise inadmissible in a criminal trial because it can be highly prejudicial as well as irrelevant to the question whether the defendant committed the crime he is charged with.

An insanity defense is also rare because, unlike other defenses, which, if successful, result in acquittal, a defendant who convinces a jury he is insane is almost always committed to a mental institution. If the crime is minor the defendant may prefer a short and definite prison stay to an indefinite confinement in a hospital.

Since Ming had been accused of both federal and state crimes, the insanity defense would have to be asserted in two trials. Meshbesher was pleased that the federal prosecution was scheduled first because the federal courts had adopted the Model Penal Code definition of insanity, while the M'Naghten rule prevailed in Minnesota courts. In federal court, Meshbesher would only have to show that as a result of mental disease, Ming lacked the substantial capacity either to appreciate the criminality of his conduct or to conform his conduct to the law. More important, the burden would be on the prosecution to prove Ming sane.

But Meshbesher realized that, no matter which insanity test was used, juries tend to be skeptical of the plea, especially sensible Minnesotans. He expected the prosecutors would attempt to demonstrate Ming's sanity by presenting evidence that he had acted with premeditation and had carefully carried out his plan.

The stakes were high. If the jury agreed with the defense, Ming could be treated with antipsychotic drugs and possibly rehabilitated, although it was unlikely he would be released quickly because of the public outcry that would surely erupt. On the other hand, if Ming was found guilty of kidnapping he could be incarcerated for life.

In August Ming took a bolt from a piece of furniture in the recreation area and scraped the putty from around his fourth-floor cell window. It was a futile attempt at escape since the building's design prevented removal of the window, which was made of half-inch polycarbonate, a substance strong enough to withstand the blow of a ten-pound sledgehammer. Furthermore, if the window was removed or broken, an alarm would have immediately sounded. Since Ming's actions never had a serious chance of success, he was not charged with attempting to escape. He was, however, moved to a maximum security area of the Ramsey County Jail and confined to his cell.

Ming was carefully watched because he was a celebrity. The kidnapping was one of the hottest regional stories of the year and the papers and television stations thoroughly reported every development. Reporters competed for tidbits of information.

The day after his arrest, two editors of the *Minneapolis Star* sent Ming a mailgram, flattering him by commenting that he had a reputation as a "brilliant young man from an exceptional family," and expressing skepticism over the FBI's claims. The newsmen asked for an opportunity to interview Ming in order to get his side of the story. Ming turned the mailgram over to Meshbesher who refused to permit any interviews.

As befitting a high-profile case, Thomas Berg, thirty-nine, the United States attorney for the district, decided he would personally try it. While Berg had tried civil cases, he had never prosecuted a criminal case before his appointment as U.S. attorney—and had tried only three since then. Consequently, he asked Thor Anderson, forty-two, a veteran assistant United States attorney and the office expert on kidnapping, to join him.

Both prosecutors were slender, clean-cut men. Berg was the snappier dresser, with horn-rimmed glasses and an Ivy League wardrobe. Anderson was balding and his suits and ties looked as though they were selected one evening at Sears during a power outage.

Berg, a Democrat appointed to his post by President Jimmy Carter upon the recommendation of Berg's friend Vice President Walter Mondale, had served in the Minnesota state legislature for eight years until he retired to devote more time to his family. Anderson, a Republican, had also served in the state legislature before becoming a prosecutor.

When he first heard of the Lund kidnapping, Berg wondered why Barbara hadn't been able to escape sooner. But after interviewing Barbara and her husband at their house—with the kids running under the sprinkler—he realized that Barbara and Ann were bona fide victims and he could understand why this frail-looking missionary woman was afraid of Ming.

Judge Edward J. Devitt, sixty-nine, was assigned to try the case. A statuesque man with a head of white hair, he looked as if he had been ordered straight from central casting. Although he was charming and compassionate outside of court, he maintained a tight rein over proceedings before him. He treated attorneys with courtesy and had such an excellent rapport with jurors that lawyers were loath to quarrel with him for fear of alienating the jury.

Meshbesher knew Devitt well—he had tried the Piper kidnapping case before him. After Meshbesher lost the trial, he successfully appealed Devitt's ruling—one of the few times Devitt had been overruled—and won an acquittal on retrial. Meshbesher considered Devitt intelligent and gracious and recalled that he had taken prosecutor Anderson and himself out to dinner while the Piper jury deliberated.

*   *   *

People lined up three hours early to obtain seats for the trial. From the first day, the courtroom was packed with reporters and thrill seekers anxious to learn the sordid details of the victims' captivity. Unusually tight security was in place; every person entering the courtroom had to pass through a metal detector.

The jury was composed of nine men and three women of varying ages, most of whom had children: an account auditor, a sales rep, an owner of a bowling alley, a carpenter, two factory workers, a housewife, a widow, an electrical engineer, a disabled railroad worker, a physical therapist, and a retired truck driver. It was a group without much formal education, many of whom lived in the suburbs around St. Paul.

Ming, dressed in a checked sport coat, gray shirt, and black slacks, listened impassively as Thor Anderson began his opening statement, explaining how the kidnapping had been accomplished, how Ming had abused his captives, and how Barbara and her daughter had managed to escape.

When Meshbesher made his opening statement, he didn't challenge Anderson's account of what had transpired. "This is perhaps the most difficult case I have ever been involved in," Meshbesher conceded, "and it's not going to be a pleasant task for you folks to listen to the evidence. What the Defendant did to Mrs. Lund was despicable. It is inexcusable. I cannot minimize it to any extent, and please don't interpret anything I say as an attempt on my part to minimize this horrible deed. It was indeed horrible, and it was the act of an insane mind."

Meshbesher explained that Ming had been a deeply troubled boy with a history of emotional problems. He recounted how Ming had set fires along his paper route and how he was required to seek psychiatric care as a condition of probation. Meshbesher said that the psychiatrists considered Ming's behavior an indication that he was severely disturbed and needed continuing therapy.

"Somehow the probation officer had a personality conflict with the social worker at the University Hospital," he explained, "and did not convey the message in those terms to the Ramsey County Juvenile Court, and at a hearing in Ramsey County in September 1965, the boy was discharged from probation and his treatment at the university stopped.

"When the psychiatrist who was treating him found out about this, he wrote a stinging letter to the juvenile court in Ramsey County saying that this boy was disturbed, and he seriously needs our help. 'Why have you discharged him?' [he asked.]

"The juvenile court judge responded that he wasn't aware that they felt that strongly about his disturbance. He apologized to the psychiatrist and said that if he had known of it he would not have been discharged from probation.

"Yes, that bureaucratic slip-up, if you want to call it that, started this boy down his road of perversion and caused him to become so mentally ill that he continued his perverse thinking up until May of 1980 without interjection of further psychiatric care and treatment."

Meshbesher spoke of Ming's delusions and hallucinations, and his obsession with Barbara Lund. He asked the jurors to keep an open mind. "I am confident after you hear all of the testimony and this man's life history and his emotional problems that you will concur that there is only one verdict to be rendered in this case and that is a verdict of not guilty—not because the man did not do the act, the kidnapping itself, because the man did not have the intent, because of his terrible mental illness that overpowered him and caused him to lose the ability most of us have to control our behavior and act in accordance with rules and regulations."

Barbara Lund entered the courtroom, her head erect. As she walked to the stand, Ming jumped out of his chair and strode toward her, exclaiming, "Why? Why?" Berg instinctively blocked Ming's path and deputies quickly moved to restrain him. "Bitch," Ming spat out as he was forced back to his seat. After taking a ten-minute recess, the judge decided to adjourn until the afternoon.

Meshbesher wasn't sure what the jury made of the outburst. Ming's behavior certainly confirmed his delusion; on the other hand, the jury might perceive him as a dangerous man who should be imprisoned. Ming told Meshbesher that he hadn't intended to harm Barbara; he merely wanted to know why she was cooperating with the prosecutors. He still believed she loved him.

When the proceedings resumed, Barbara testified in a forthright manner without displaying any rancor toward Ming. Occasionally she would smile, and she maintained her composure even while describing acts of rape before sixteen jurors, ten reporters, and nearly one hundred spectators. Her courage and mettle made her an especially sympathetic witness.

Under Berg's questioning, she recounted her trip to Chicago with Ming. He rented a Winnebago with a bathroom, sink, stove, and refrigerator. She and Ann were restrained with bicycle chains fitted around their waists and secured to a cable anchored to a pipe underneath the stove. He warned them that if they broke the pipe, they would asphyxiate themselves.

"Do you remember whether or not Mr. Shiue mentioned any legal consequences of the fact that he left Minnesota with you?" Berg asked.

"Yes," Barbara replied. "He said that he was taking a risk by taking us out of the state. He said that made it a federal crime and that would add, I think he said five years onto his prison sentence, if he were ever caught."

"When did he say that?"

"That was before we left for the trip."

"Did he say how he knew that?"

". . . he said that he had been going to the library and reading up on kidnapping cases so that he wouldn't make the same mistakes that other kidnappers had made."

". . . did he make any statements to you about the possibility of escape?"

"He warned us continually not to try to escape, that as long as we did not try to escape he would give us—he could trust us more, give us a little more freedom, but if we tried to escape it would be very rough, and he would have to tie us again as he had done in the early days of our captivity."

Whenever Ming pulled into a gas station he had Barbara and Ann draw the drapes and lie down. He would fill the tank himself. Barbara considered shouting for help but she didn't know whether an attendant would hear or respond. Moreover, she feared Ming's reaction; she was unsure whether he was armed.

At one point Ming took her and Ann on a shopping expedition. A description of their clothing had been widely reported by the news media, and he wanted it replaced. He drove to a shopping center and parked the Winnebago in an isolated spot. With Ann locked inside, he took Barbara into Sears, J. C. Penney's, and several smaller stores, always staying by her side except when she entered a dressing room.

In one dressing room, Barbara encountered a sales clerk with another customer. Tempted to ask for help, Barbara wondered how the clerk would react. If the clerk even looked at Ming oddly, he might panic, run to the motor home, and flee with Ann. She decided she couldn't take that chance.

Barbara purchased a house dress and underwear for herself and some new clothes for her daughter, paying for the merchandise with a fifty-dollar traveler's check from her purse.

Ming next took his newly attired captives to a K mart store. Once again Barbara considered escape, but she hesitated, not knowing if the bulge in Ming's pocket was a wallet or a gun. He had warned her that if they fled there would be a gun battle and that they and innocent passersby would be killed. Barbara decided that she would have to be satisfied for the moment with some toothbrushes, deodorant, and a pad of paper and crayons for her daughter. This time Ming paid for the purchases.

Ming allowed Barbara to make a phone call to find out where her husband was. He pulled the Winnebago into an alley adjacent to a gas station in Evanston and he escorted her to the phone, warning her not to identify herself. She looked up the number for the Baptist General Conference as Ming inserted several coins.

While Barbara talked on the phone, a pickup truck pulled into the alley behind the Winnebago. The occupants of the truck shouted at Ming and Barbara to move their vehicle, which was blocking the alley. Ming asked them to be patient as he tried to monitor Barbara's phone conversation. Meanwhile, Barbara reached Paul Pierson, a Baptist executive, and asked him how she could reach the Reverend Harvey Lund.

Pierson asked who was calling; Barbara said she was a friend of the family. "Just a minute," Pierson said as he began looking for the address. By this time, the occupants of the pickup were irately yelling at Ming, distracting him. Barbara whispered, "Paul, it's me, Barbara." But Pierson didn't respond. Ming refocused his attention on Barbara just as Pierson came back on the line. He gave her a phone number, which she wrote down. Seeing that her husband's number had changed, Barbara asked if the Reverend Lund had moved. Pierson informed her that his address remained unchanged.

"Do you know what has happened?" Pierson asked, and then he proceeded to recount how the reverend's wife and daughter had been kidnapped and their whereabouts were unknown. Barbara expressed her concern and said she would hope and pray for their return. Ming was becoming impatient, so Barbara thanked Pierson and hung up.

They returned to the Winnebago but not before a young man parked his car in front of it, blocking its path. Ming sat quietly in the driver's seat for a minute and then walked over to a house the man had entered. Ming began shouting and the man replied that the alley was private property and that he was sick and tired of people driving into it every day.

Ming replied that he didn't park there every day, he was

from out of town. An argument ensued and quickly escalated. Ming threatened to blow the man's head off. At this point a friend of the man intervened and tried to pacify Ming, who demanded an apology. Eventually, the car was moved and Ming drove off.

Ming then took Barbara and Ann to a favorite restaurant of his for dinner. Although the restaurant was crowded with patrons, Barbara didn't dare escape, fearing that Ming might pull out a gun and start shooting.

Back in the Winnebago, Barbara saw a man running, looking over his shoulder as if he was fleeing the scene of a crime. Barbara asked Ming if he believed the man had committed a crime. Ming said yes. "Why?" asked Barbara. Ming laughed and said, "It takes one to know one."

"Did you laugh at that remark?" Berg asked.

"Yes, we did. And then we got into the Winnebago and . . . he started the motor and we were just pulling out when three or four squad cars pulled up . . . confirming our suspicion that indeed a crime had been committed." Despite the proximity of the police, Barbara once again decided not to try to escape or call for help.

After they returned home, Ming allowed his captives greater freedom. They could sleep outside the closet and twice a day they were taken to the kitchen so Barbara could prepare meals.

One night Ming lay down beside Barbara and became affectionate. When she didn't respond, Ming grew angry and asked if she was rejecting him.

"What do you expect at three o'clock in the morning," Barbara said. The next day, Ming returned Barbara to the closet and brought her and Ann a small bowl of leftover gravy, a piece of hard bread, and some water for breakfast. He was going to take Ann to work with him, he announced, while Barbara remained in the closet.

Before he left, Barbara took him aside and asked what was the matter. He mentioned her rejection of him the previous night. She explained that her daughter was awake and reminded him that she had asked that her daughter never witness their sexual relations—a request he had agreed to.

"Well . . . that helped a little," Barbara testified, "but I was made to stay in the . . . dark closet without anything to do during that time. . . . Then he came back from work . . . he gave us some supper and then he put Annie in the closet with the TV, and he told me that I would have to take a bath with him and show him that I really was not rejecting him."

"What happened then?" asked Berg.

"So then we went into the bathroom, and I had to put water in the tub and take off my clothes and get into the bathtub, and he also took off his clothes and got into the bathtub, and he made me wash him and he attempted to rape me in the bathtub, and then finally after doing that awhile, he had me get out of the tub and then took me into the bedroom and continued to rape me."

Berg asked Barbara what happened on June 20, the day Barbara turned thirty-seven years old. She explained that when Ming came home from work he removed Ann from the closet and took her aside to confer with her. After dinner they brought out a birthday cake. Ann gave her mother gifts she had made from yarn, and Ming gave her a book of articles compiled from *Reader's Digest*.

After completing his examination of Barbara, Berg introduced Ming's videotapes into evidence. One monitor faced the judge, the other the jury; the audio was supplied through headsets. Many spectators departed, disappointed that they would not be able to view the tapes.

The prosecution used Ming's own videocassette recorder—which had been seized as evidence—to play the tapes. The first tape showed Ming explaining to a bound and blindfolded Barbara why he had kidnapped her.

When the videocassette machine malfunctioned, the judge called a recess while an FBI technician struggled to repair it. Ming mumbled something and an FBI agent asked him if he knew what was wrong with the machine. Ming said yes and promptly fixed it. The jury was brought back and the presentation continued.

Tapes covering the time up to the first rape were shown. The prosecution chose not to show the actual rapes because they didn't want to embarrass Barbara and they considered her testimony sufficient proof.

Meshbesher was gentle and respectful in his cross-examination. He asked Barbara whether she had ever told Ming, "We love you?" She admitted that she had.

"And did he ever respond to you in some way that you got the impression that he took your remark as meaning that you loved him in a romantic sense?" asked Meshbesher.

"No. I don't think he ever took it that way because I explained very clearly that for one thing the Bible says love your enemies, and I told him very frankly that at that time he had become our enemy . . . it was very clear that we had no such feelings for him: that I loved my husband in that way, and that I could not give myself to any other person."

Meshbesher's other attempts to elicit helpful testimony also failed. He kept his cross-examination brief; in light of the terrible ordeal she had been through, hostile questions would only make him appear callous.

Thor Anderson next called Richard Thorson, twenty-nine, to the stand. Thorson, assistant manager of Ming's electronic's repair company, had worked for him for four years.

Thorson testified that his employer was a superb repairman who managed his business competently and conversed lucidly with his employees and customers. Even after his arrest, Ming displayed considerable acumen when negotiating the sale of his business to Thorson.

On cross-examination, Meshbesher elicited from Thorson a description of Ming as a lonely, isolated, and sexually frustrated individual whose working hours became increasingly erratic. Ming was a perfectionist who didn't brook any arguments from his employees. After his store had been broken into several times, Ming began to sleep there. One night three burglars broke in and attacked him. Ming shot two of them. One died.

"And later on did he ever discuss with you how he felt after the shooting and the killing . . . ?" Meshbesher asked.

"Yes, he did . . . he found it hard to accept having killed another human being."

"Did he ever tell you that he suffered from nightmares as a result of that?"

"Yes, he did. . . ."

Thorson recounted his reaction to Ming's arrest. He was so incredulous that he laughed upon hearing the charges against Ming.

". . . Did you ever tell anyone that Ming was the last person on earth that you would suspect of having done that?" asked Meshbesher.

"Yes, I did."

"In fact, in dealings with his customers, he was scrupulously honest, was he not?"

"In about ninety-nine percent of the time, yes."

With her hair in pigtails and dressed in a red jumper, Ann Lund took the stand. Berg gently asked about the kidnapping and had her describe her effort to escape. She explained that while she was locked in the Winnebago alone, some boys passed by. She shouted through a closed window that she had been kidnapped. But they ignored her plea, apparently thinking she was engaged in a prank.

Ann's appearance in court brought a rare show of emotion to Ming's face. He smiled at her and as she walked off the stand he said, "Hi, Annie." She didn't reply.

The government rested its case and Meshbesher called Mei Dickerman, Ming's mother, to the stand. She explained that after she remarried in 1973, she moved to Virginia to live with her new husband. Her sons Ming and Ronald continued to reside at her house on North Hamline, and she would periodically visit them.

During a visit four years earlier, she'd had a strange encounter with Ming. She was in bed reading a book when he came into her room. He said he was very cold and lay down next to her.

"I put my hands between his hand," Mei said. "He put his foot to my foot so I warm him up, quite a while like a half hour, and I think it warm him up pretty good so I said, 'Well, now you can go to bed. I want to go to sleep.'"

"I like to sleep here because you are warm," Ming said.

"You are not a baby. I warm you up so you now can go to your own bed to sleep," she replied.

"I have done nothing, you know. I just want to stay here."

"You are twenty-six years old. You are not a baby. So you can't. . . . You have to go to your own bed." Mei offered her son a hot-water bottle, which he declined.

"Now, did his relationship . . . with you change after that incident?" asked Meshbesher.

"Yes. . . . He never kiss me again or hug again," Mei said.

Next, Meshbesher put Ronald Sen Shiue, twenty-one, Ming's brother, on the stand. Ron lived in the basement apartment of the North Hamline house; Ming permitted him upstairs only to use the kitchen.

Ron explained that Ming always demanded respect and obedience from his younger brothers. He acted more like their master and demanded that they meet him at the door when he came home from school, carry his books, take off his shoes and socks, bring him a change of clothes, and serve him. On one occasion Ming punished five-year-old Ron by placing him in an oven and turning the gas on and off. As Ron and his brother Charles grew older, their relationship with Ming deteriorated further. They argued and fought and eventually became estranged and avoided contact with their older brother.

"Now, was there any time in May or June of 1979 that you in fact talked with your brother outside the home where he seemed to be much friendlier?" asked Meshbesher.

"Yes. One occasion I was at Appelbaum's shopping and Ming was there also, and he came up to me and started talking to me like we were very close, and he asked me what

I was doing there and what I had been doing that day and things like that, and really surprised me because normally he would just ignore me totally."

". . . In other words, you would pass on the street and he wouldn't even acknowledge your presence?"

"Yes."

Meshbesher asked Ron about the day Ming brought home a Winnebago van. Ron said he was surprised when Ming offered to give him a look inside. "He seemed strange because he is being pretty nice to me," Ron said. "I decided to take the opportunity to ask him if I could borrow his van to go fishing . . . he said yes. And he asked me if I had any bicycle chains or cables or locks or anything he could borrow to lock the van up and I said I did. So I gave them to him."

Meshbesher's star witness was Dr. Stephans. The attorney had the psychiatrist recite his credentials and note that he had testified many times for both prosecution and defense. This was the first time Stephans had testified for Meshbesher.

Stephans attempted to explain Ming's motivation. On the day of the kidnapping, said Stephans, Ming was cruising about Barbara's neighborhood when suddenly she appeared in a car coming around the corner. It was the first time he had seen her since high school; a flash shot through his head and a voice commanded him: "This is your chance. Go find her. Go after her." He followed her in a frenzy and later abducted Barbara and her daughter.

Ming told Stephans that nothing short of being shot could have stopped him from pursuing Barbara. If a policeman had been sitting beside him, it wouldn't have mattered. "Now, when you first talked with him in the jail, did he tell you that he was mentally ill?" asked Meshbesher.

"No, he didn't," said Stephans. "He denied it absolutely." Stephans said he asked Ming to tell him what had happened and Ming replied that everything was perfectly normal until July 7 when fifteen FBI men arrested him. He claimed the preceding weeks were the happiest days of his life. He described an idyllic existence with Barbara and Ann.

"Did he tell you those tapes would help his case, bear out that she consented to these sexual acts?" asked Meshbesher.

"Yes . . . he was confident this would all be proved that he was right. That this was a mutual love relationship . . . a happy family. . . ."

"And were there any things that happened that you know of now from listening to Mrs. Lund's testimony . . . that could cause a person who was not thinking straight to believe perhaps that it was a consensual relationship?"

"Yes. I think so. And these I want to emphasize are not in any way implying I am criticizing anything that Mrs. Lund or her daughter did. I admire them very highly. I think they handled the situation in absolutely the best way they could. . . . [But] things that were said were distorted as a result of Ming's mental illness, not because of anything she did or said.

"For example, she would say in a religious sense, we love you . . . but he took it to mean again that she was expressing her love for him."

Stephans recounted his experience viewing the tapes with Ming. Ming sat rigidly immobile in a trance. When Stephans touched him on the shoulder, Ming was startled and appeared to suddenly return to reality. He said, "I am confused. I can't believe that was me. I would never do a thing like that. I would never humiliate her. I have experienced humiliation. It's terrible. I wouldn't do that to anyone." Stephans believed Ming's response was genuine.

Meshbesher asked Stephans about Ming's sexual experiences. Stephans said Ming fantasized a great deal about sex but only dated two girls during high school. His experiences were limited to a little kissing and petting. He had never had intercourse with anyone before he raped Barbara Lund.

"Now, we know that he was never in the Army and never

in Vietnam and never a prisoner of war," said Meshbesher. "Did you ever ask him why he said that?"

"Yes. . . . He didn't know. He didn't recall saying all that. He was a bit confused by the whole thing."

"Now, there is evidence here," said Meshbesher, "that the defendant went to some great lengths to make sure that there were no fingerprints on any of the items he handled and particularly the letters that were sent to the Lund family and the pictures that little Annie drew. How does he fit into the scheme of things with his delusional feelings that what he was doing there was a happy thing and this woman loved him?"

"Well, it doesn't fit in very well in any rational, logical, sane way of trying to figure it out. It's insane. It's crazy. It's psychotic . . . and he did some very crazy things in the process.

"He was attempting to cover his tracks sometimes. Other times he was just flagrantly the opposite. Videotaping himself there which is as positive identification as you can get, and videotaping himself in the scene of a crime . . . this is not any rational, sane criminal who is methodically going about concealing a crime. It's a psychotic charade of it. . . . In my years of experience I have never encountered anything quite like this," replied Stephans. "This, in my opinion, is the craziest, most insane behavior I have run across."

Thor Anderson had encountered Stephans before. The prosecutor considered the doctor a glib, I'm-okay-you're-okay sort of showman who belonged on the Johnny Carson show, not in a court of law. A year earlier, Stephans had gotten a girl off a murder charge on the grounds of insanity and had become the great hope of defense lawyers. Anderson was determined to cut the doctor down to size.

Anderson first brought out that a psychiatric diagnosis is in the nature of an opinion and not a scientific fact that can be conclusively established. And it can be difficult to define a mental illness. Anderson noted that in 1973 the

American Psychiatric Association reversed itself and by a vote of its members decided that homosexuality would no longer be considered a mental disease. Stephans admitted the reversal made the profession appear inconsistent.

"Even assuming for argument that the defendant did suffer from paranoid schizophrenia," Anderson said, "the question would be whether he was in a psychotic state when the crime was committed?"

Yes, the witness replied.

". . . So what we really need to know in order to decide if he was really insane, as the law defines it, is to know what his thoughts are while the crime is being committed?"

"Yes . . ."

Anderson elicited the fact that the only way for a psychiatrist to know a patient's thoughts is to ask him, and that Ming claimed amnesia for much of the time he held Barbara and Ann in captivity. Moreover, Ming refused to take Sodium Amytal, which might have helped his recollection.

"Now, what delusion do you believe Mr. Shiue had as it relates to your diagnosis in this case?" asked Anderson.

"Well, he had more than one, Counsel. . . . He had a delusional love relationship with Mrs. Barbara Lund which he felt was a mutual or reciprocal love. He had delusions of grandiosity, delusions of being sort of superman, certainly within the sexual area. . . ."

". . . Okay. And is it your view that when he kidnapped Mrs. Lund, he held the delusion that he loved her and she loved him?"

"Yes. That was his delusion."

According to Stephans, Ming was driving his van when he happened to encounter Barbara driving. "There was a moment of shock. There was the realization that this was Mrs. Lund . . . then the words started telling him: Follow her. Follow her. . . ."

"And he thought when this voice said follow her, follow her, that when he did so and she recognized him she would love him?"

"That was his hope. . . ."

"... So thinking ... she loved him, he kidnapped her at gunpoint, right?"

"That's possible if those are the facts, yes."

"And had with him ropes and tapes to tie her, didn't he?"

"Yes. I asked him about that, of course. ... He had twine, pieces of twine, he said, and pieces of tape that he always carried in his pockets to patch up the packages that he was going to be mailing back through UPS that afternoon."

"He told you that?"

"That's what he told me."

"I suppose he was going to wrap the gun up and send it, is that what he told you?"

"I don't find that very funny, Counsel, no. I am not saying that at all. I am not being humorous. ..."

"... And while he had her tied up and blindfolded, he was under the delusion that she loved him and found it necessary to tie her up?"

"That's absolutely correct."

"That is not consistent either with reality or with the delusion, is it?"

"It's not consistent with sane, logical reasoning. It's insane—psychotic. ..."

"Well, if you don't want someone to get away, why is it insane to tie them up? Doesn't that achieve your purpose? Isn't that in fact a logical thing to do if you don't want someone to get away as opposed to an insane thing?"

"Certainly that would be quite logical. That's not inconsistent."

"So that's not crazy—insane, tying her up?"

"It's not—what you are doing is mixing up parts that are within his circumscribed delusion with parts that are outside. This has no validity in my way of thinking. ..."

"... what significance do you attach to the fact that in your opinion Mr. Shiue would have kidnapped Mrs. Lund even if there was a policeman in the front seat?"

"The significance is that ... he did not fully appreciate the nature of what he was doing and that it was wrong. He did not have the capacity, substantial capacity to control his behavior so as to conform with the law."

"Even if a policeman would have seen him he would have done it?"

"That is what he told me, yes."

". . . This delusion or this psychosis was so strong in your opinion that it forced him to commit the crime even if he risked discovery?"

"That's correct."

"But in fact when discovery became possible he tried to avoid it, didn't he?"

"To some extent he did, yes."

"He encountered Ann, which according to the delusion, he didn't expect, is that right?"

"I don't know if that's part of the delusion. He told me that he saw the one person in the car and saw nobody else."

"Come on now, he doesn't have a delusion he is in love with Ann?"

"I see no logical question [*sic*] between my answer and your comment, Counselor."

"No. I'm saying his delusion was about Barbara, not about Ann, right?"

"That's right. Yes."

"So when he saw Ann, he did not have any delusion or hallucination or anything eating at him that made him want to kidnap her. Is that right?"

"That's right. . . ."

"So since a person can be partly in touch with reality, his kidnapping of Ann was not the result of a mental illness, was it—just his kidnapping of Barbara?"

"Well, my point is that at the time Ann had not been part of the delusion, yes. Subsequently Annie did become part of the delusion, became part of the delusional family."

"But at the moment he kidnapped her, she wasn't part of his delusion, was she?"

"I suppose it's possible to look at it that way."

"I didn't ask you which way it's possible to look at it. I asked you was she in the delusion or wasn't she?"

"I'm trying to answer your questions."

"Is it yes or is it no?"

"Could you repeat the question?"

"Was Ann part of the love delusion that Ming Shiue had prior to the kidnapping?"

"No. I think I answered that no, Counselor, before."

"All right. But Ann was there and he had to kidnap her so she wouldn't run away and tell there had been a kidnapping, didn't he?"

"He put her in the car with Mrs. Lund, yes."

"He had to do it or he would have been caught, isn't that the fact?"

"I suppose that's correct, yes."

"All right. And so in fact there was a policeman there in the person of Ann, and he took Ann to avoid being caught?"

"Well, that's exactly, of course, what I'm saying. He carried this out in spite of the presence of another person."

Anderson questioned Stephans about Ming's alleged hallucinations. Stephans conceded that the results of Ming's EEG and CAT scan were normal and that Ming's biochemistry had not been checked for abnormalities because tests for schizophrenia weren't clinically available yet.

". . . Now, you aren't really arguing," the prosecutor asked, "that he didn't appreciate the wrongfulness of his acts?"

"Yes, Counselor, I am."

"You watched those videotapes, didn't you?"

"Yes, I did."

"And he tells Mrs. Lund he realizes he's wrong, doesn't he?"

"Yes. . . ."

". . . you said . . . he realized it was illegal?"

"That's correct."

"But that isn't what he said, is it, in the tapes? He said he thought it was wrong, didn't he?"

"Well, my impression is he was referring to it as being wrong in a legal sense."

"That's your impression of what he was referring to, but that's not what he said, is it?

"That's my opinion, Counselor."

Anderson asked if Ming's ability to manipulate and adjust his videotape camera was a symptom of being psychotic.

"No," answered the psychiatrist. "He seemed to be functioning quite well in that area. Generally with the electronics area in general he functioned reasonably well with his electronic repairs."

"Do you consider these sex acts also were caused by his mental illness?"

"Yes."

"Now, he was able to restrain himself sexually during this three-hour conversation with her that we first watched, wasn't he, while he talked with her, wasn't he?"

"Yes. Counselor, during that time he was very involved with part of the delusional system that if he could sort of coax her to recall him that the flood of her love would come pouring back."

"In other words, while he did that he was able to restrain his criminal instincts?"

"Oh, yes. I don't—"

"He was able to restrain himself sexually during two menstrual periods, wasn't he?"

"I recall one, Counselor. There may be a second."

"She testified to two. He was able to restrain his sexual instincts while traveling to Chicago in this van for a week while he didn't have any privacy, wasn't he?"

"Yes. . . ."

". . . Just before he went to Chicago, he had a lucid conversation with his brother Ron about lending him the van. Is this a symptom of being in psychosis?"

". . . people in psychosis can carry on lucid conversations, yes."

In rebuttal, Meshbesher lobbed some easy pitches to his witness to give him a chance to more fully explain himself. He asked Dr. Stephans to explain the difference between sociopathic criminals and people who are mentally ill.

"Criminal instincts in criminals manifest themselves in many ways," the doctor said. "They are not just criminal in one particular direction. Mr. Shiue is noted for his honesty. He was noted for reliability and integrity by his customers and employees.

"Other than a very bizarre fire-setting incident that was part of the mental illness, as far as I know, there is no other criminal record. This is not a person with criminal instincts. . . ."

". . . Now, if he were just kidnapping Barbara Lund to satisfy a sexual drive, would he have been able to kidnap other women to satisfy that drive as well?"

"Certainly."

"Why did he pick on Barbara Lund and keep her in his mind for eight solid years?"

"In my opinion because he was suffering from a psychotic mental illness and was insane."

"And would no other woman have done the same to satisfy him?"

"No other woman could have done the same. . . ."

". . . Now, did you ask him about the fact that he had a gun with him the day of the kidnapping?"

"Yes, I did."

"What did he tell you?"

". . . He said he had carried a gun every day except a few days when he forgot to ever since his store had been robbed."

". . . Now, there was some mention in cross-examination about the Sodium Amytal test. Was there a reason why that test wasn't given?"

"Yes."

"What was it?"

"Initially this test had been planned, and he had agreed to it. In the interim the neurological evaluation was carried out which included, as I stated, a brain wave test and a computerized X-ray scan, and I carefully informed him of the procedures there and what would happen. I didn't know, and this was my fault, I guess, I didn't know that they would do what is called an enhanced CAT scan, which is a second part of the CAT scan . . . which involved injecting intravenously a chemical, a type of dye that shows up on the X ray. He had a rather violent reaction to this chemical as he had had one several years earlier at a different hospital when a different diagnostic X-ray-type study was done; and he became very ill, vomited, was very sick, and at that point he decided he did not want any further injection of any type of chemicals.

"Now, this I can appreciate, and in my opinion the Amytal interview would have been of some value, but in a way it would have been like frosting on the cake since we already had in beautiful detail, on videotape, a very clear picture of what this man's mental status was during this first week when he had a psychotic amnesia, and at best, all the Amytal interview would do would be to repeat and allow him to recall those events that are beautifully, I think, displayed and portrayed in the videotape.

"So in my opinion this was a reasonable decision on his part to decline the Amytal interview. . . ."

"Were you aware that he had almost a phobia for use of chemicals including aspirin?" asked Meshbesher.

"Yes. I was. I had investigated this thoroughly not only with him but with other people who knew him, and he did not use chemicals of any kind. He did not smoke. He did not use alcohol. He even strongly resisted the use of aspirin for headaches."

The jury adjourned to begin their deliberations. Although Meshbesher realized he had been waging an uphill battle, he believed there was a fifty-fifty chance of an acquittal.

After a day of deliberation, the jury returned to the courtroom. As he waited for the verdict to be read, Meshbesher could hear his heart thumping. He hoped for the

words "not guilty," but over the years he had learned to steel himself against disappointment.

The jury found Ming guilty. Meshbesher wasn't sure if he was more sorry for himself or his client. While his ego felt a personal defeat, he empathized with Ming because the man had no insight into his problem. Meshbesher considered his client sick and believed a jury comprised of psychiatrists would have come to a different conclusion.

Six-year-old Jason Wilkman remained missing five months after his abduction. Everyone assumed the boy was dead. Ming repeatedly denied any knowledge of his whereabouts.

Meshbesher sympathized with Jason's parents and would have liked Ming to tell authorities where to search for the boy's body, but, as Ming's attorney, he was obliged to tell him that if the body was discovered, he was likely to be charged with murder. Meshbesher was certain Ming knew the boy's whereabouts. Yet Ming wouldn't confide in his attorney although all their conversations were privileged and couldn't be disclosed to others.

Then Ed Abas, chief United States probation officer, showed Ming his presentencing report and Meshbesher told him that his cooperation might improve it. Ming withheld his assistance, however, until two concrete concessions were offered: The state prosecutors agreed not to charge him with more than second-degree murder, and Abas agreed to recommend that he be imprisoned at a medium-security facility in nearby Oxford, Wisconsin.

Although Ming wouldn't confess to killing Jason, he agreed to take authorities to a wildlife refuge where he said he released the boy. But Ming had trouble fixing the exact location, saying he was uncertain because the twilight sun had been in his eyes.

An intensive search of the area was mounted by the sheriff's office, assisted by twenty-five volunteers. Jason's parents purchased black tennis shoes, a blue plaid shirt, and corduroy pants, the exact clothes that he wore the day of the

abduction, in order to assist the searchers. A two-acre corn-field surrounded by birch, pine, and poplar trees was combed, as a state highway patrol helicopter hovered over-head.

After Ming spent three days at the site, one of the searchers spotted some cloth similar to the clothing Jason had worn. Upon further investigation, Jason's badly de-composed body was found under a pile of sticks. The county medical examiner inspected the remains and con-cluded the skull had been split open. An autopsy was per-formed, and the medical examiner concluded that Jason was hit with a blunt instrument, which authorities specu-lated was the L-shaped lug wrench Ming had removed from the trunk of Barbara Lund's car.

Ming was sentenced for kidnapping the Lunds the day after Jason Wilkman's body was discovered. Devitt was known as a tough sentencer, especially for violent crimes. Neverthe-less, Meshbesher pled for leniency:

"I feel . . . because of the horrendous nature of the crime, that it was impossible for untrained laypeople to set aside their emotional reactions, whether they be conscious or unconscious, and decide this case strictly upon the law and the psychiatric testimony. . . ."

". . . I only hope that the Court in sentencing will bear in mind that this man is mentally ill. He showed a spark of genius in his early years. He was selected as most likely to succeed by his classmates. He was respected and well liked. Obviously something had to go wrong someplace. The seeds of his misdeeds were probably sown early in life and they exposed themselves when he was but fourteen or fifteen years old.

"For the Court here to mete out punishment is a difficult task. It's difficult for the Court to punish someone whose remorse is already greater than their misdeeds. And I know that from talking to the Defendant, he will live with what he has done for the rest of his life. . . ."

The judge turned to Ming and asked, "You want to say anything at all?"

"No," Ming replied.

The judge sentenced Ming to life, recommending that he be incarcerated in the United States prison at Oxford, Wisconsin, and that he not be eligible for parole until he had served thirty years. Under federal law, a life sentence was considered a thirty-year term for parole purposes and prisoners could be paroled after completing one third, despite the judge's recommendation.

After the trial, Twin Cities television station KSTP petitioned the court for copies of Ming's videotapes, citing the recent Abscam decision as precedent. In that case an appeals court ruled that the three television networks could broadcast an FBI videotape of a congressman taking a bribe. KSTP asserted that once Ming's tapes were shown in court they became a matter of public record and should be available for inspection and reproduction. WCCO, another local television station, joined in the request.

The stations' petition was opposed by an unusual alliance of prosecutors, defense attorneys, and Barbara Lund's attorney. She personally wrote Judge Devitt saying, "I am deeply disturbed by this request which appears to me to be an attempt to sensationalize the human tragedy which has happened." She noted that the videotapes were made without her consent, that they violated her right to privacy, and that to allow them to be broadcast would only exacerbate the damage.

The stations took pains to point out that they weren't requesting the tapes of the rapes. They were asking only for the first three hours of tapes, those that were shown in court. Under questioning by Judge Devitt, counsel for KSTP stated that the station hadn't yet decided what, if anything, it would do after receiving the tapes, but it wanted the material on the principle that anything used in a trial should be accessible to the public.

Judge Devitt was troubled by the request. He noted that court decisions have long held that the news media have no greater right to such information than the public at large. Consequently, he wondered, should he grant the request, whether he would also be obliged to make the tapes available to anyone else who might want them, such as a pornographer seeking to mass-market them.

Thom Berg expressed the prosecutors' concern for protecting their witness. He said that if the tapes were made available they would have a more difficult time getting victims of crime to testify in future trials. Barbara Lund did everything that any prosecutor anywhere could ever ask, Berg said. "Her conduct showed her to be a real credit to our society, and I submit that society should now not go against her wishes and allow the tapes to be spread all over TV screens all over our state and I suspect very possibly the nation. I think that the effect of this would be to play into the hands of the defendant in the crime. You recall his testimony on the tapes was the purpose of it was to degrade Mrs. Lund, to have her feel ashamed. The publication of this evidence, Your Honor, on TV screens would have exactly that effect."

Minnesotans were outraged by the stations' request. Angry letters appeared in the local papers. "It staggers the imagination to read that KSTP and WCCO are so desperate for news that they have to go after tapes showing the torture and degradation of kidnap victims," one woman wrote, adding, "This is not news, this is voyeurism." Another writer complained that the stations wanted the tapes only to achieve higher ratings. "Victims of these heinous crimes must be protected from such shabby sensationalistic journalism," she opined. Even newspaper editors who were normally allies of their broadcast brethren condemned the request.

Devitt denied the petition, stating that there was no public interest to be served by releasing tapes that depicted the humiliating and degrading circumstances of Barbara

New Mexico juvenile defense attorney William Parnall and client Jason Kirkman
*Copyright © 1987 by Al Cabral/*Albuquerque Journal

Lawyer for the homeless Nancy Mintie
Ardon Alger

Product liability lawyer Ed Swartz
Mark Litwak

Alaska lawyer Robert H. Wagstaff
Mark Litwak

Criminal defense lawyer Phillip
Weidner at home
Mark Litwak

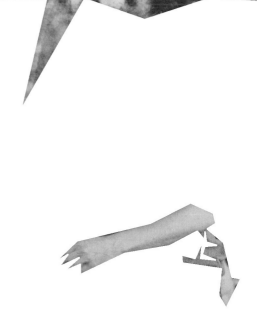

Environmental attorney Eric Smith on
the Yukon River near Tanana, Alaska
Mark Litwak

Defendant Ming Sen Shiue
Minneapolis-St. Paul Star Tribune

Minneapolis criminal defense lawyer
Ronald Meshbesher   *Mark Litwak*

U.S. Attorney Thomas Berg
Mark Litwak

Consumer activist and attorney Ralph Nader
Mark Litwak

Public interest attorney Alan Morrison
Beverly Orr

Left to right, Mafia prosecutors Gil Childers, Michael Chertoff, and John Savarese
Kings County District Attorney's Office/Matthew Barcia

Lund's imprisonment. KSTP announced it would appeal the decision but never did.

Ming was tried in state court for kidnapping and killing Jason Wilkman. Meshbesher considered the trial unnecessary since Ming had already been sentenced to life in prison. He offered to plead his client guilty to second-degree murder if the prosecution would agree to run the state sentence concurrently with Ming's federal sentence. The Anoka County attorney declined.

A new jury was impaneled and Barbara Lund testified again. While Meshbesher was cross-examining her, Ming suddenly pulled out a two-and-a-half-inch pocket knife hidden in his waistband, bolted from his chair, leaped over the counsel table, and dashed twenty-five feet to the witness stand before three stunned deputies could react. "Oh, my God," Barbara cried as Ming grabbed her in a bear hug and put the knife to her throat.

The twelve jurors and two alternates jumped out of their seats and cowered in the far end of the jury box; one broke into tears. Ming warned everyone to stand back or he would kill them, but three deputies jumped him and tried to pull him off Barbara. As they struggled, he slashed her throat. With the help of two more deputies, Ming was dragged to the floor as spectators shouted, "Get him, get him." Ming was forcibly removed from the courtroom as Judge Robert Bakke ordered the courtroom emptied and proceedings adjourned. Meshbesher was so shaken he was trembling.

Barbara, her neck dripping with blood, was taken to the ladies' room. Although frightened, she didn't make a big fuss. When informed that an ambulance had been called, she asked if she could go by car instead. At the hospital, sixty-two stitches were required to close a four-inch gash on her neck.

The next day Meshbesher met with Ming and asked him why he had attacked Barbara. Ming said he didn't intend to ing him as a con man out to make money off Ming, noting that Green had a prior robbery conviction.

Judge Bakke sentenced Ming to forty years. Under Minnesota law Ming would have to serve a minimum of twenty-six years before he would be eligible for parole. Anoka County assistant attorney, Michael Roith, publicly denounced the sentence because it ran concurrently with Ming's thirty-year federal sentence. It was possible, said Roith, that Ming wouldn't serve any additional time for killing Jason. Meshbesher reiterated his opinion that the second trial was unnecessary, and the newspapers noted that the two trials had cost taxpayers more than $450,000.

Bakke fiercely defended the propriety of his sentence, explaining that it was contrary to judicial practice to run sentences consecutively for crimes committed at the same time. Moreover, Ming was eligible for parole on his federal sentence in ten years and if past practice was any guide, he was likely to serve less than his full thirty years. If he was released before serving twenty-six years, he would be transferred to state prison to finish his state term.

Ming was sent to the U.S. Medical Center for Federal Prisoners at Springfield, Missouri, for psychiatric evaluation and then was imprisoned in Leavenworth penitentiary in Kansas. He was upset about being held in Leavenworth but his courtroom attack on Barbara had convinced the Bureau of Prisons that he was too dangerous to be kept in less than a maximum-security prison.

Meshbesher lost his appeals of Ming's federal and state convictions. Ming was never prosecuted for the courtroom assault on Barbara.

Meshbesher believes Ming was genuinely insane. But the crimes were so brutal, he says, that the jury was simply unwilling to forgive him. According to Meshbesher, Minnesotans are reluctant to accept the defense and insanity acquittals are rare.

After both trials had concluded, Harvey and Barbara Lund spoke to the news media. She appeared to have survived the ordeal remarkably well and asserted that she hadn't suffered any lasting emotional damage. "It's not my place to be bitter," she said. "That only destroys a person."

She declined offers of counseling. "Harvey and I had talked about all that had happened right away, and we just felt the Lord's strength and the Lord's peace and have never felt ourselves falling apart over it. . . . Our faith in God and His strength in us was all we needed."

Ann didn't adjust quite as easily. Being locked in a closet for most of the summer was a traumatic experience. Moreover, upon her return to school, classmates teased and ridiculed her about her mother's sexual relations with Ming.

The family returned to the Philippines and resumed their missionary work. They visited the Twin Cities area several times on furlough and stayed in touch with Thor Anderson, who has remained a federal prosecutor. U.S. Attorney Thomas Berg resigned from his post after Ronald Reagan became President. He now practices law with a prestigious Minneapolis firm.

Ming has not tolerated prison well. "He does what we call 'hard time,' " said Anderson, "resenting imprisonment, fighting it and never getting used to it. I don't think he'll ever adjust to it and he is facing a lot of time and is an unlikely candidate for [early] parole." Anderson says Ming has attempted suicide and tried to contract for the murder of Devitt and Anderson.

After eight years in prison Ming is still obsessively in love with Barbara. "My impression is that if he got out today," said Anderson, "he would try to kidnap her again."

In 1982, John W. Hinckley, Jr., was tried in a District of Columbia courtroom for attempting to assassinate Ronald

Reagan. Several persons, including the President, were wounded. The defendant was clearly a troubled youth. His professed motivation for the assassination was to impress a movie actress he admired.

The jury had been instructed that they should acquit the defendant if there was a reasonable doubt as to his sanity under the more liberal Model Penal Code approach (excusing the defendant if he lacked substantial capacity either to appreciate the criminality of his conduct or to conform his conduct to the law). While juries often disregard such instructions and follow their common sense, this jury faithfully followed its mandate and shocked the nation with a verdict of not guilty by reason of insanity. The resulting outcry focused renewed attention on the insanity defense and spurred efforts to change or abolish it.

The American Psychiatric Association (APA) advocated restricting the defense by scrapping the Model Penal Code approach in favor of a modernized wording of the old M'Naghten rule (right/wrong test). The association recognized that psychiatrists were not able to reliably determine if a person could control his or her behavior. Consequently, under the APA proposal, a defendant's inability to control his or her conduct would no longer support an insanity plea. Only those persons who were unable to appreciate the wrongfulness of their criminal acts would be excused.

The American Bar Association also recommended eliminating the defense for those who claimed they couldn't control their behavior. The American Medical Association advocated outright abolition of the insanity defense and replacing it with a statute that would provide for acquittal only when the defendant, as a result of mental disease, lacked the mens rea, or guilty mind, required as an element of the crime.

President Reagan subsequently signed the Insanity Defense Reform Act of 1984. The act severely restricts the insanity defense in federal cases, allowing it only when the defendant, as a result of mental disease, is unable to appreciate the wrongfulness of his act. Moreover, the new law places the burden of proving insanity on the defendant. And defendants found not guilty by reason of insanity are automatically committed for up to forty days for mental examination, followed by a commitment hearing to determine whether they are presently insane. If the defendant caused bodily injury or serious damage to property, he has the burden of proving by clear and convincing evidence that his release won't create a substantial risk of harm to others.

Chapter 5

In the
Wilds of
Alaska

Absolute freedom mocks at justice.
Absolute justice denies freedom.
—Albert Camus

In the "Magic Moose" case, attorney Robert H. Wagstaff challenged Alaska's game law, which prohibited taking moose out of season, arguing that the law unconstitutionally abridged the religious beliefs of Athabascan Indians. His client, he said, needed to kill a moose for a funeral potlatch feast, which the Athabascans believe is the last meal shared with the departed. Songs of eulogy are sung, and native foods such as moose, bear, caribou, porcupine, duck, and berry dishes are served to help the deceased on his journey. Wagstaff convinced the Alaska Supreme Court that moose was an essential ingredient of the ceremony, the equivalent of the wine and wafer in Christianity, and the court struck down the law.

After reading the decision, I decided to visit Alaska to learn more about the practice of law in the least populated part of America. In 1958 Alaska became the forty-ninth state. Its 586,000 square miles comprise a landmass greater than two thirds of the continental United States. It has 80 percent of the United States' shoreline and within its borders are three million lakes, ten thousand rivers and streams, seven mountain ranges, and the tallest mountain on the North American continent, Mount McKinley. The area is largely unsettled, with only one fifth of the land accessible by road and many of the tiny outposts reachable only by plane.

When I arrived in Anchorage the hotels were completely booked, so I rented a room in a private residence. Many Alaskans lodge visitors because they both enjoy the company and like the extra income. My hosts were Paul W. Waggoner and his family, who live in a beautiful lakeside home within walking distance of downtown.

Coincidentally, Waggoner is an attorney who defends insurance companies. Having just returned from a trial in the bush, he told me that it is difficult to predict what kind of argument will appeal to a Native American jury. The case he was handling involved two Anglos fighting over the title to a piece of property. Since natives don't believe in private property, their participation gave new meaning to the term "disinterested jury." Waggoner likened the trial to having a Buddhist adjudicate a theological dispute between two Catholics.

On my first morning in Anchorage, I telephoned Robert Wagstaff to arrange a meeting. He picked me up in a beautifully reconditioned, dark purple 1948 Hudson. Although he was president of the Alaska Bar Association, he didn't look like an establishment type. He was short and stocky, had a full beard, and was dressed in blue corduroys and a plaid flannel shirt. When he appeared before the United States Supreme Court, the clerk told him that he had the longest hair of anyone who had argued there in the past century.

He offered to take me for a spin in his plane, an amphibious Cessna 185 mounted on pontoons with retractable wheels, one of several planes he shares with his wife, a stunt pilot.

Wagstaff was raised in Kansas. Although his father and grandfather were lawyers, initially he didn't intend to follow in their footsteps. But after graduating from Dartmouth College, he enrolled in law school at the University of Kansas, mostly as a preferable alternative to being drafted. Two of his happiest memories of law school and his early career are his third year when he began working with prisoners at Leavenworth Federal Penitentiary and his clerkship for Missouri Circuit Court judge Richard Koenigsdorf, who inspired him to become a trial lawyer. But he disliked working for a top law firm in Kansas City. "That was a valuable experience," he said, "because it taught me what I did not want to do."

Anxious to explore the world, Wagstaff considered moving to South America. A friend who had worked there and was now in Alaska enticed him north, explaining that Alaska was a frontier community with a lot of opportunity for a young lawyer. The state also attracted him because he enjoyed the outdoors and loved flying.

Wagstaff moved to Fairbanks, where he worked as an assistant district attorney for several years before moving to Anchorage to join a law firm and later establish his own practice.

Wagstaff's first years in Alaska were exciting because of the state supreme court's expansive view of civil liberties. In *State v. Browder* (1971), Wagstaff represented Richard Browder, a member of the Brothers motorcycle gang. Dressed in denim overalls and a leather vest, Browder had entered a courtroom with an unloaded shotgun broken open at the breach, handed some keys to a friend, and departed. Fifteen minutes later a bailiff had hauled him back before the judge who summarily held him in contempt for entering a courtroom with a gun and sentenced him to six months in jail.

tentially dangerous parolee into an isolated community without police or parole officers, it may reasonably be expected to take some action to protect the residents."

Although Wagstaff continues to bring potentially precedent-setting cases, he laments that Alaskan courts have grown conservative and are less open to new ideas and less often on the cutting edge of legal developments. After oil was discovered, a lot of money poured into the state, office buildings were erected, and the pioneering attitude gave way to an outlook more protective of the status quo.

I arranged to meet attorney Phillip Weidner, who had a reputation as both a top criminal defense lawyer and a colorful character. I wasn't disappointed. With his long scraggly beard, purple corduroy shirt, gray pants, and cowboy boots, he looked like a rugged nineteenth-century frontiersman. Prosecutors spooked by his penetrating eyes and cunning tactics have nicknamed him Rasputin.

Weidner is an extraordinarily tenacious individual who leaves no stone unturned in defense of a client. He is known for filing fifty pretrial motions, contesting every point strenuously, and resisting any attempt to limit his argument. His thoroughness often exasperates prosecutors and judges, and he sometimes prevails by simply wearing his opponents down.

"He is brilliant and more intelligent than almost any judge he comes in contact with," says one lawyer, "so he is constantly in battles with judges. He's probably got the most courtroom contempt citations of any attorney. The district attorneys don't quite tremble [in his presence] but they know when they're opposing him they're going to have to work twenty-four hours a day, seven days a week."

Prosecutors accuse Weidner of trying to free his clients by disparaging the judicial system. He often turns the tables on them, impugning their integrity. "I've never seen Phil not accuse the prosecution of doing fifty million rotten things during a trial," said Laurie Otto, a former deputy prosecutor with the Anchorage District Attorney's Office. As one former colleague put it, "When the going gets ugly, Phil Weidner gets interested."

Weidner's reputation for contentiousness arises primarily from his ongoing battles with several judges. Judge Ralph Moody removed him from a case despite the client's objections. Weidner had the decision overturned on the grounds that his client had been deprived of counsel of his choice. In another case, Judge Moody fined Weidner for filing frivolous motions, a ruling that was also reversed on appeal.

Weidner has also fought with Judge Justin Ripley, a former prosecutor who had frequently tangled with Weidner. Ripley recently fined Weidner $4,650 for ten counts of contempt. Weidner appealed and $3,900 of the fine was affirmed. Weidner plans to appeal to the Alaska Supreme Court.

While Weidner can be tough-minded, he is soft-spoken and polite before juries. "I think whenever you lose your temper in the courtroom, huff and puff, slam around, yell and scream, you just lose points," he said. "Nobody likes it really . . . I've cross-examined young children that claim they've been sexually abused [and asked them] about some pretty intimate details. If you're polite, you can do that. But if you're not, it doesn't matter what you're trying to say . . . you're losing . . . [an eminent attorney once told me] 'Cross-examination doesn't have to be cross.'"

He feels that Alaskan juries are earthy, open-minded, and tolerant. "A person may disagree with you one hundred eighty degrees, but still treat you like a human being." In one case Weidner defended a twenty-one-year-old who had attempted to hold up a restaurant. When the proprietor pulled a gun and began shooting, Weidner's client threw down his gun and tried to retreat. Running into a room without an exit, he tried to surrender but the restaurant owner seemed intent on killing him. In the ensuing struggle, the boy grabbed the gun and shot and killed the man.

"That's the kind of case that anywhere but Alaska you wouldn't have a chance on," said Weidner. "[But] people here still understand the basic right of self-defense." The case ended in a hung jury and Weidner then pleaded his client guilty to a reduced charge of manslaughter. The boy, who did seven years, is now on parole and doing well.

Weidner makes a specialty of seemingly hopeless causes. He defended a fellow attorney who hadn't filed income tax returns for five years. In a psychiatric defense, he contended his client had a mental block against the date April 15, and since that day didn't exist for him, he wasn't guilty of willfully failing to file his returns. Weidner noted that his client hadn't filed returns for two years in which he was owed a refund. Remarkably, the jury acquitted the defendant.

Weidner grew up in Illinois, the son of immigrants. His family was persecuted during World War I because of their German heritage and their pacifist, antimilitary views. His father, a self-educated man and a freethinker, worked as a farmer and labor organizer and during the Depression he rode the rails as a hobo. With the outbreak of World War II, he was drafted into the Coast Guard, where he was repeatedly transferred for insubordination. He simply refused to take orders. After he was banished to a quasi-concentration camp for incorrigibles in Kodiak, Alaska, authorities tried to break his will with hard work. Instead, he fomented revolution among the inmates and was exiled to Attu, a remote island where he spent the remainder of the war hunting and fishing.

Weidner shares his father's stubbornness and his pacifist leanings. "If I was in my own home and I had to defend my children, I would defend them to the death. Or myself. I'm not that much of a pacifist. But I would not go to war. . . . I disapprove of organized war."

Indeed, he disapproves of organized government, claiming to be an anarchist. He says he doesn't want or need the state's protection. "I'll protect my own home. I have firearms," he said, glancing at a revolver resting in a holster hanging on the wall. Although his house has an alarm system but no door locks, his garden is protected by an electrified fence to keep moose away from his vegetables.

When pressed, he concedes that the state may perform a legitimate function protecting the weak and disabled. But he doesn't believe prosecuting people accomplishes much good. "I believe in karma," he explained. "Those people [who do wrong] end up creating their own justice. They often get killed by someone else's hand, sometimes they get killed in car wrecks, they commit suicide . . . there's a divine justice and I think a lot of the job of a defense attorney is minimizing the damage that the courts do in complex situations."

A charter member of the Lionel Model Train Club, he is a man of eclectic interests who enjoys fishing, gardening, composing poetry, and shooting firearms. He designed his magnificent log home made of timbers from a Seattle pier and white oak from Tennessee and served as his own general foreman.

Divorced, Weidner shares custody of his seventeen-year-old daughter and eleven-year-old son. He also cares for several dogs he rescued from the pound, including a malamute named Gandalf after the character in J.R.R. Tolkien's fantasy novel *The Hobbit*.

As a student at the Massachusetts Institute of Technology, Weidner studied math, physics, and engineering. A participant in anti-Vietnam War demonstrations, he was tear-gassed by the Chicago police during the riots outside the 1968 Democratic National Convention. Unlike many of his friends who became dropouts during this tumultuous era, he chose to go on to Harvard Law School, feeling that lawyers could make a difference. Upon graduation he moved to Alaska, intrigued by stories of his father's experiences there, and accepted a clerking position with then-Alaska Supreme Court justice Robert Boochever.

One of Weidner's more unusual cases occurred when his sixty-five-year-old father was arrested in Illinois for selling firearms without a license. The FBI surrounded his house and then dragged him off in handcuffs. After Weidner phoned the United States Attorney's Office in Chicago to learn the charges, he explained to the prosecutors that his father had a heart condition and was without his medication; and he persuaded them to have the police drive him home. He then arranged for a local defense attorney to represent his father, but on the eve of the trial the attorney had a nervous breakdown and decided to abandon his practice and move to California.

The conservative judge nevertheless insisted that the trial proceed. His father told Weidner to stay out of the dispute and let him take his chances. But Weidner refused to allow his father to be convicted of a federal offense that carried a five-year sentence. He rushed to the airport for a night flight and during a stopover in Seattle he called the judge to say he was on the way. Arriving in Chicago, he went to the courtroom without having slept and proceeded to pick a jury and try the case over the next five days.

Weidner conceded that his father had sold three guns over a six-month period. He argued, however, that his father wasn't dealing firearms but merely liquidating part of his private collection because of ill health and his concern that the guns could be stolen. Weidner established that the guns were sold at less than their fair market value. "What kind of businessman," he asked, "what kind of dealer, is going to be selling things at those kinds of discounts?" Weidner also impeached the agents' testimony with their own notes.

Weidner recounts the conclusion of the story with great relish. The U.S. Attorney's Office had a 98 percent conviction rate and when the prosecutor came to hear the verdict, he was wearing a carnation in his lapel and champagne had already been ordered for a postverdict celebration. He was flabbergasted when the jury returned an acquittal after only twenty minutes of deliberations.

Weidner's most famous case was his defense of John Kenneth Peel, a twenty-eight-year-old boat hand accused of mass murder. The boyish-looking Peel, who was married and had a five-year-old son, was arrested two years after the killings.

The case against Peel was built entirely on circumstantial evidence. Five adults and one child had been discovered aboard the charred remains of the *Investor*, a luxury fishing boat found floating off the Alaskan coast. Unable to produce a motive, a weapon, or any physical evidence linking Peel with the crime, the prosecutor relied entirely upon several eyewitnesses who claimed they saw Peel operating the *Investor's* skiff during the time the mother ship was ablaze.

The star witness was Larry Demmert, a longtime friend of Peel's, who testified that he had seen someone he believed to be Peel aboard the boat the night of the murders. Demmert had waited two years, however, before reporting the incident to authorities. Then he equivocated on key portions of his story, claiming his memory had been affected by heavy doses of Valium.

From the outset Weidner was convinced of Peel's innocence. The young man had no criminal record except for one arrest for driving while intoxicated. His family and community were solidly behind him. Friends put up their homes and farms to secure a one-million-dollar bond for his release. Weidner agreed to represent him even though Peel's family had little money to pay him.

Two trials were necessary before acquittal. In the first, Weidner presented a character defense, contending that his client wasn't the type of person who would commit such a heinous crime. Numerous friends and associates testified to his good habits and nonviolent nature. Throughout the trial, Weidner hectored the prosecutors, charging them with ineptitude and misconduct. They, in turn, accused him of playing to the media. A series of nasty confrontations ensued, punctuated by the prosecutors' angry outbursts and repeated objections.

In his closing argument Weidner read a poem that he had composed for the trial. It began:

"Twelve good persons. Tried and true.
Let your minds and hearts unite.
Help us in this hour of need.
All we ask. Do what is right.
Justice lives within your being.
Just as freedom finds her spark
From your love of truth and seeing.
From allegiance to the heart."

After hearing 150 witnesses over six months, the jury retired to deliberate. Six days later the forewoman announced a hopeless deadlock, and a mistrial was declared.
Although most of the jurors leaned toward acquittal, the
prosecutors decided to retry the case.

The second trial began in January 1988. After the prosecution rested, Weidner declined to call any witnesses for
the defense. He contended that the prosecution simply
hadn't met its burden of proof and consequently there was
no need to present a defense, a bold move that was highly
criticized at the time. The jury retired to deliberate and
several days later returned a verdict of not guilty. Weidner's
move was then promptly hailed as "brilliant."

The case was the longest and most expensive criminal
proceeding in Alaskan history. The two trials spanned six
years and cost $3 million. Weidner says he spent about sixty
thousand dollars of his own money on expenses and is now
struggling to stave off bankruptcy. But he doesn't regret
taking the case, admitting that he enjoys a good fight,
especially on behalf of someone in great need.

For the future, he would like to develop more of an
international practice. "Just as beauty is in the eye of the
beholder, so is terrorism," he says. "I mean some people
who are labeled terrorists are freedom fighters. . . . I don't
approve of the murder and mayhem that terrorists commit,
but I don't approve of repression and retaliation [either]."
He objects to the way the British courts, for instance, treat
the IRA, suspending their rights. "I don't think the end
justifies the means."

He regrets the shortness of life because there are so many things he would like to do. He dreams of finding time to sculpt, design innovative buildings, and open a fishing resort in tropical Belize. He would also like to live in the Alaskan bush for a year.

I flew north to Fairbanks to interview Eric Smith, an environmental/public interest attorney from Anchorage, whom I had arranged to accompany to Tanana, an Athabascan village on the Yukon River, deep in the interior of Alaska. He was touring native villages on behalf of the Rural Alaska Community Action Program (RurAL CAP), a private nonprofit, antipoverty group. Tanana, accessible only by small plane, boat, or dogsled, was sufficiently remote, he said, for me to get a feel for native life.

At the airport I met Smith, aged thirty-four. Tall and lanky with an unruly head of hair, a full beard, and wire-rim glasses, he looked like a 1960s activist. He was accompanied by Vernita Cassidy, RurAL CAP's community development director. An Eskimo, she was dressed in green shirt, white pants, and a baseball cap.

Before we boarded the Cessna 207 to Tanana, passengers were asked how much they weighed. I became concerned, for the flight was full and people have a tendency to lie about these matters. Nor was I reassured to see the plane door secured with tape. Nevertheless, I squeezed in behind a young native girl wearing sunglasses and listening to a Walkman stereo. The pilot was a young man wearing earplugs.

We landed on a gravel airstrip and were met by Irene Nicholia, a woman of native and Russian heritage who looked as if she was in her late twenties. After throwing our gear in the back of her pickup truck, she gave us as quick tour of the village. The buildings were generally one- and two-story log homes, weather-beaten and somewhat ramshackle. We passed St. James Episcopal Church, which had

195

a bell tower and was constructed with logs and a sheet metal roof. Some of the newer buildings were made from cut lumber.

The Athabascans, cousins of the Apache and Navajo Indians of the Southwest, settled the great interior of Alaska, living along waterways where they could hunt, fish, and trap. Once a year they would come to Tanana for a festival, "Nuchalahoya," and trade goods. Most of Tanana's five hundred residents are descendants of the Indians and early Russian settlers, but there are also recent immigrants who came here seeking a simpler life.

The villagers derive 30 to 40 percent of their food and shelter from local resources. Although some nearby settlements depend on fishing and hunting for up to 80 percent of their livelihood, few natives choose to completely forsake modern conveniences and often adapt the best of Western civilization to their traditional life-style. When Smith visited the village of Rampart, he was served moosehead soup made with a Campbell soup starter kit.

In Tanana itself, cars, motorboats, phones, and electric appliances were ubiquitous. A large satellite dish sat next to the community center, and many people spoke fluent English. The prices at the local store were a bit steep (everything has to be brought in by barge or plane) but the selection was as varied as in any 7-11 store in the lower forty-eight states, with current newspapers, magazines, books, and videocassettes available.

Irene invited Eric, Vernita, and me to dinner. She removed a large salmon from the freezer and had her younger brother hacksaw off several thick salmon steaks.

After the meal, Irene and her friends took us fishing. Although it was 11:00 P.M., there was plenty of daylight because the sun never completely disappears over the horizon in summer. We returned to the village at 2:00 A.M. in dusk to sleep in an empty house reserved for guests.

The next morning, Smith waited forty minutes to begin his workshop. He wasn't offended by the villagers' tardiness, or by the fact that only eight people attended the meeting, which had been called to give villagers an opportunity to question Smith about proposed amendments to the Alaska Native Claims Settlement Act.

The act was passed in 1971 to settle whatever aboriginal rights natives might have had to Alaskan land. The natives claimed hunting and fishing rights to vast tracts based on their historical use. When Alaska was sold to the United States by Russia in 1867, the Tlingit Indians of southeast Alaska immediately protested, contending that the Russians couldn't sell what they didn't own. The Tlingit and other native groups eventually pressed their case and in 1959 the U.S. Court of Claims finally ruled in their favor, stating that aboriginal title hadn't been extinguished. Thirty years after filing suit, the Tlingit were awarded $7.5 million.

But other native claims went unsettled until after oil was discovered on Alaska's North Slope in 1968. Then the oil industry pressed for a resolution, lest litigation by native groups delay construction of the nine-hundred-mile pipeline planned from Prudhoe Bay to the Gulf of Alaska.

In response, Congress passed legislation extinguishing all aboriginal claims, in exchange for which the natives were given $962.5 million and title to forty-four million acres of land. The Native Claims Settlement Act was hailed at the time as the most generous settlement ever made with Native Americans. The money and land, however, weren't given to native tribes; nor were reservations created. Instead, Congress gave the money and land to thirteen regional corporations and about two hundred village corporations controlled by natives.

All natives living at the date the law was enacted were entitled to receive stock in these corporations. In order to give the corporations time to get their business affairs in order, stockholders were prohibited from selling shares for twenty years and the corporations were exempt from taxation for twenty years.

The money has now been distributed and largely spent. Some of the native corporations used their money wisely but many dissipated their inheritance on consultants, lawyers, and bad investments. According to Smith, the natives on the boards of directors of these companies were inexperienced in business affairs. "Some of them have gotten very sophisticated," he said, "but for the most part it's like any other small enterprise—when you have people who have never dealt with these things before, they get taken advantage of.

"The act took a communal society and imposed a capitalist model on top of it, so you had a lot of people who didn't really understand what it was to be a shareholder." Moreover, the native corporations' desire to make profits encouraged development that often interfered with subsistence living. Gold mining dredges, for instance, discharge dirty wastewater containing arsenic, which destroy fish habitat. "So every shareholder became schizophrenic," said Smith. "Because on the one hand they are supposed to make money, on the other hand they want to continue their traditional culture. The corporate setting pulled them in two directions." He noted that while $962.5 million is a lot of money, the sum was divided among more than two hundred corporations, for an average of less than $5 million, which is not a great sum to be spent over twenty years.

With that period coming to an end in 1991, many natives are worried about having their land taxed and fear they will lose control of native corporations when restrictions on selling stock end. The stockholders, by and large, are land rich but cash poor, and many might be tempted to sell their seemingly useless stock certificates.

In an attempt to protect native interests, a series of amendments have been proposed to the Native Claims Settlement Act that would exempt undeveloped native lands from taxation and would continue the restrictions on the transfer of stock unless a majority of the corporation shareholders vote otherwise. Smith didn't take a position on the proposals; his role was merely to explain their ramifications. Because English was a second language for many of his listeners and because they weren't familiar with such

Western concepts as corporations, he spoke in simple language and tried to describe complex ideas visually.

While Smith was unfailingly polite and patient, he didn't always understand the nuances of native culture. A day earlier, for instance, he committed a faux pas during a visit to the village of Beaver. He was informally chatting with an elder about a liquor ordinance when Vernita walked into the room. Smith momentarily turned to tell her where her fishing rod was located; and when he turned back, the elder refused to continue the conversation. Smith later learned that the elder was offended by the interruption, which he considered extremely impolite. After Smith learned the nature of his blunder, he apologized; and the elder gave him a lecture on manners before forgiving him.

Nothing in Smith's upbringing in affluent Westchester, New York, prepared him for life among the natives of Alaska. His father was the president of an investment firm; his mother gave up writing to devote herself to raising her children. Their home was bordered by a forest and a stream and playing in the nearby woods kindled Smith's interest in the environment.

At Swarthmore College, he majored in philosophy and political science. After graduation he was unable to obtain a job with an environmental group and decided to seek an advanced degree to make himself more marketable. He was accepted by Yale Law School and after graduating joined the Environmental Protection Agency's Office of General Counsel. He was assigned to the Air Division and successfully represented the agency in several suits challenging EPA regulations.

He enjoyed his work during the Carter administration but became disenchanted under Ronald Reagan. His frustration peaked during a Christmas visit with his family when his grandmother read an article in *The New York Times* about Reagan's proposed amendments to the Clean Air Act, a story leaked to the press. Grandmother asked her grandson if he knew about the controversy. Smith said yes, in fact he had drafted a portion of the proposal. Grandmother was very proud, but Smith's mother interjected that the proposal was nothing to be proud of. In his heart, Smith knew his mother was right and he resolved to leave the agency.

He was hired as executive director of Trustees of Alaska, a small public interest law firm specializing in natural resource issues, where he felt his work was important because he had an opportunity to save Alaska from the fate of those states that hadn't had the foresight to protect their land from toxic dumps and other sources of pollution.

Smith also liked the job because it enabled him to exert considerable influence on environmental matters. Since Alaska has so few residents, the news media were anxious to interview him, and state officials were readily accessible. Furthermore, for someone whose favorite activities are hiking, cross-country skiing, fishing, and photography, the state was paradise. He was fascinated visiting villages and learning about native problems firsthand. Although his salary was only $30,000 or so, he could afford a car and to live in a rented house in the mountains only a half hour from downtown Anchorage.

Fund-raising was the only aspect of his job he disliked. The group had an annual budget of $140,000, raised from foundations, private donations, and court-awarded attorney fees. Because the organization was continually strapped for cash, he once filed two suits against the state for enacting unconstitutional laws. The easy victories earned his group $40,000 in attorney fees.

After four and a half years with Trustees for Alaska, Smith grew tired of the constant struggle to raise funds. He now works three quarters of the time for RurAL CAP, for which he serves as general counsel, as well as working on subsistence and tribal government issues. The remainder of his time is devoted to such clients as the National Resources Defense Council, the Trustees for Alaska, and the Kodiak Audubon Society.

One of his projects has been an attempt to get the Alaska Board of Game to modify its hunting regulations to accommodate native culture. The concept of a hunting season is foreign to natives who have traditionally taken game when it was available and needed, and only took as much as they could use. Per-person bag limits seem strange to people who designate a few individuals to hunt for an extended family. Smith advocates letting the villages enact their own game regulations, provided they aren't wasteful.

In working with the native people, Smith must overcome their suspicion of environmentalists, who have fought subsistence hunting when they believed it threatened endangered species such as whales. Some environmental and animal rights groups are also opposed to trapping, which they consider inhumane. Other environmentalists simply don't trust the native peoples to conserve natural resources.

As Smith has learned more about native life, he has come to appreciate the importance of subsistence hunting to natives and has even changed his mind about motorized snow sleds and all-terrain vehicles after observing how useful they are for hauling water, wood, and one-thousand-pound moose.

Chapter 6

NADER AND HIS RAIDERS

I often wonder whether we do not rest our hopes too much upon constitutions, upon laws and upon courts. These are false hopes; believe me, these are false hopes. Liberty lies in the hearts of men and women; when it dies there, no constitution, no law, no court can save it.

—JUDGE LEARNED HAND

R alph Nader first suspected that he was being followed on a trip to Iowa on January 7, 1966. A stranger seemed to be shadowing his movements. Nader noticed the man twice in the hotel lobby and once near his room.

Nader, who was thirty-two years old at the time, had come to Des Moines to testify at auto safety hearings held by Iowa attorney general Lawrence Scalise. As the author of *Unsafe at Any Speed*, Nader blamed the auto industry for many of the fifty thousand deaths and five million injuries that occurred each year on the nation's highways. He claimed that 1960–63 Corvairs were especially dangerous because General Motors had ignored the advice of its engineers and built a car with a tendency to roll over on turns.

Nader wasn't afraid of confronting the powerful automobile industry. After publication of his book, he held a press conference in Detroit and challenged the auto companies to debate him. Nader's publisher was hoping to provoke a response, creating a controversy that would publicize the book. But the auto manufacturers didn't take the bait; instead they cordially invited Nader to visit their proving grounds.

Nader accepted the offer and on January 14, 1966, he proceeded to GM's Technical Center at Warren, Michigan, where he was met by a group of senior GM executives. His hosts went out of their way to be friendly and insisted that everyone address each other on a first-name basis.

The GM officials said they wanted to provide Nader with data about the design and handling characteristics of the Corvair, but first they needed to know if he was involved in the lawsuits brought by plaintiffs injured in Corvair accidents. After Nader assured the executives that he wasn't, they escorted him to a nearby conference room where he was shown a film and given an illustrated lecture by GM engineers who tried to convince him that the Corvair was safe.

Nader was also given a tour of GM's proving ground. A vice president with practiced bonhomie suggested, "Why don't you come over and join us and put your ideas to work here?" Nader ignored the remark, which was reiterated three times that day. He considered the offer a thinly disguised bribe to buy him off. But his beliefs weren't for sale, and none of the information presented to him that day raised his regard for the Corvair.

That same day, Senator Abraham Ribicoff announced another round of hearings on auto safety. Nader had been an unpaid behind-the-scenes adviser to the Senate Subcommittee on Executive Reorganization, sharing his voluminous research on automobile hazards with it and preparing questions for committee members that had embarrassed GM executives by forcing them to admit how little they spent on safety research. Now Nader was scheduled to testify before the committee as a witness.

Soon after Ribicoff's announcement, Nader began to receive late-night telephone calls at his Washington rooming house. At first the anonymous calls seemed innocuous: "Mr. Nader, this is Pan American . . . [click]." "Mr. Nader, please pick up a parcel at Railway Express . . . [click]." "Cut it out. Cut it out. You're going to cut me off . . . [click]." Some of the voices were male, others female.

"As the Senate hearings approached, the calls increased in frequency and became more personal: "You're supposed to know all about cars. Well, why don't you come and help me? I can't get mine started." "Why don't you change your field of interest?" "You are fighting a losing battle, friend. You can't win. You can only lose." At 3:30 A.M. the night before he was scheduled to testify, the phone rang and the caller threatened, "Why don't you go back to Connecticut, buddy-boy."

The calls disturbed Nader's sleep and made him so anxious that more forceful means of persuasion might be employed against him that he lost several pounds from his already lanky frame. After all, billions of dollars were at stake in the debate over auto safety.

Following a sleepless night, Nader appeared as the first witness before Ribicoff's subcommittee. The panel of senators included Robert Kennedy of New York and Carl Curtis of Nebraska. Ribicoff introduced Nader and described *Unsafe at Any Speed* as a provocative book that raised serious questions about the design and manufacture of automobiles.

During Nader's testimony Curtis pretended he couldn't understand what Nader was saying and repeatedly interrupted until Kennedy exploded, accusing Curtis of attempting to stifle Nader. Nader was allowed to continue and then answered questions, spending nearly three hours before the committee.

The next day Nader went to the Dirksen Senate Office Building for a television interview. After the taping, he entered an elevator to descend to the cafeteria in the basement. Inadvertently, he pushed the wrong button and the elevator ascended. Realizing his mistake, he redirected the elevator down. Unbeknownst to him, two private detectives had been following him that day and his circuitous route threw them off his trail.

The men approached a building security guard and identified themselves as detectives. After describing Nader, they asked the guard if he had seen him. Suspicious, the guard called his supervisor who told the detectives in no uncertain terms that they weren't allowed to tail people in the Senate Office Building. He ordered them to depart immediately and they did so. A short while later Nader strode past the guard, who informed him of the detectives. For the first time, Nader had confirmation that he was under surveillance, but he didn't know who was following him or why.

The next week additional clues were unearthed. Old friends, classmates, and former employers informed Nader that they had been called to check his qualifications for an important job. One professor wrote him a warm letter congratulating him on his new appointment. But Nader hadn't applied for employment, and the callers were delving deep into his personal life. They had asked whether he drank alcohol, used drugs, or was anti-Semitic, and about his sex life. Realizing that someone was out to smear him, Nader decided to apprise several investigative reporters of his plight in the hope that they might be able to expose his pursuers. Morton Mintz wrote the first account of Nader's surveillance in a short article in *The Washington Post* titled "Car Safety Critic Nader Reports Being Tailed."

Several days later while standing at a magazine rack in a local drugstore, Nader was approached by an attractive brunette he had never met. "Pardon me," the young woman said, "I know this sounds a little forward—I hope you don't mind, but can I talk to you?" Before Nader could reply she invited him to attend a gathering that night with some friends to discuss foreign affairs. Nader politely declined. The woman persisted. Nader said he wasn't interested and turned his back to her. The woman departed without approaching any other patrons.

The following day Nader flew to Philadelphia to appear on *The Mike Douglas Show.* Afterward, as he hurried to the airport gate just minutes before his flight's scheduled departure, he noticed two men sitting in the lounge who boarded the plane after him. Nader suspected they were tailing him. After landing in Washington, Nader ducked in and out of several doors and jumped into a cab.

That same day, Frederick Hughes Condon, a classmate of Nader's from Harvard Law School, received a call from a man identifying himself as "Mr. Warren." Nader had dedicated his book to Condon, who had fallen asleep at the wheel of his car and crashed. His car rolled over, the doors opened, and Condon fell partially out and had his spine crushed, leaving him a paraplegic. Warren said he wanted to see Condon and ask him some questions about his friend Nader, who he claimed was being considered for an important research and writing assignment. Condon agreed to see him that afternoon at Condon's office in Concord, New Hampshire.

When Warren arrived, Condon asked the man, who now called himself Mr. Gillen, for whom he was working. Gillen refused to disclose his client. He appeared nervous and insisted on holding an attaché case in his lap which Condon assumed hid a tape recorder.

Gillen wanted to know if Nader had a driver's license, if he had owned a car at Harvard, and if he had ever been in an automobile accident. Then he began to delve into more personal matters. Why wasn't Nader married? Did he have any left-wing affiliations? Was he anti-Semitic?

Condon said that Nader's personal life was normal, that he didn't belong to any political groups, and that he most certainly wasn't anti-Semitic. After Gillen departed, Condon wrote up a memo summarizing the conversation and called Nader that evening to tell him about the encounter.

Two days later while Nader was shopping in a Safeway supermarket, an attractive blond woman in her twenties approached. "Excuse me," she said, "but I need some help. I've got to move something heavy into my apartment. There's no one to help me. I wonder if I can get you to give me a hand. It won't take much time." Nader politely declined, saying that he was already late for a meeting. The woman pleaded, "Please, it won't take long." Nader said he was sorry but he couldn't help. The woman then promptly turned and strode out of the store, past a number of unaccompanied men more than capable of helping her.

While Nader was tall and had an intelligent face, he wasn't so attractive that strange women approached him on the street. He suspected the women were trying to lure him to an apartment and seduce him before a hidden camera.

Nader told investigative reporter James Ridgeway about the detectives probing his personal life and the women who had made advances. Ridgeway then discovered that Vincent Gillen, who operated a large detective agency based in Garden City, New York, was investigating Nader. When Ridgeway confronted him, Gillen became flustered and admitted that he had made inquiries about Nader but refused to divulge the identity of his client, insisting that Nader was being considered for an important job. He also said that, while his investigation wasn't complete, he had found Nader to be an intelligent fellow and his report so far was "good for Nader."

A week later Ridgeway's article, "The Dick," appeared in *The New Republic*. According to Ridgeway, the automakers, who at first had ignored Nader, had now turned on him. "This is precisely the sort of knockdown public fight Nader was hoping for," he wrote, "but instead of open battle, he finds himself suddenly distracted from the task at hand and locked in a subterranean struggle against an uncertain enemy."

Ridgeway chronicled the campaign of harassment and surveillance against Nader and disclosed that Vincent Gillen was one of the detectives investigating him. Ridgeway's piece was an impetus to other journalists. *The New York Times* and the *New York Herald Tribune* published stories reiterating Nader's allegations that the auto industry was attempting to harass and discredit him. Industry spokesmen were quoted as saying that Nader's charges were ridiculous.

Senator Ribicoff, however, took the allegations seriously. On the floor of the Senate he announced that the harassment of Nader was an extremely grave matter and that he was asking the Department of Justice to investigate whether someone had attempted to intimidate or impede a witness before a congressional committee, a criminal offense. Senator Gaylord Nelson joined in the request and described the campaign against Nader as "a filthy business."

Reporters now besieged the auto companies with requests for more information. No longer content with unattributed denials from "industry spokesmen," journalists pressed for details. After a Ford vice president broke ranks and flatly denied that his company had investigated or harassed Nader, Chrysler and American Motors followed suit with similar statements. Only General Motors continued to refuse comment.

Then late at night, when most of the nation's morning newspapers had gone to press, GM issued a statement admitting that the company had hired a private detective to investigate Nader. GM claimed that its general counsel had "initiated a routine investigation through a reputable law firm to determine whether Ralph Nader was acting on behalf of litigants or their attorneys in Corvair design cases pending against General Motors."

GM claimed their investigation was limited to Nader's qualifications, background, and expertise and denied any harassment. The press release noted that GM had invited Nader to their Technical Center where he was given information proving that the Corvair was safe. That Nader nevertheless continued to criticize the car led GM to believe that Nader must have a financial interest in Corvair litigation. Apparently the company never considered the possibility that one of its critics might be motivated merely by a desire to save lives.

The controversy became front-page news. Senator Ribicoff announced on the floor of the Senate that he was requesting Nader, the president of GM, and detective Gillen to appear before his subcommittee. He wanted a public explanation of what appeared to be harassment of a Senate witness. The outrage of Congress was perhaps best summarized by Senator Gaylord Nelson, who stated:

> "What are we coming to when a great and powerful corporation will engage in such unethical and scandalous activity in an effort to discredit a citizen who is a witness before a Congressional committee! If great corporations can engage in this kind of intimidation, it is an assault upon freedom in America. No average citizen can face up to a corporation the size of General Motors which sets out to destroy him."

On March 22, 1966, the Senate Caucus Room was packed with reporters, photographers, television cameras, congressional staffers, and curious onlookers as Senator Ribicoff called the hearing to order. When Nader, who was scheduled to be heard first, could not be found, Ribicoff called James M. Roche, the president of GM, to take the oath and testify.

Roche, a tall, white-haired man who wore rimless glasses, was accompanied by attorney Theodore C. Sorensen, who had been retained to counsel him. Sorensen, a former adviser to President John F. Kennedy, was a close friend of both Ribicoff and Robert F. Kennedy, two of the senators on the panel.

In accordance with Senate tradition, Roche was permitted to make an opening statement before being questioned. He said he learned of his company's investigation of Nader only two weeks ago and since then he had attempted to obtain all the facts about what had transpired. To the best of his knowledge, the detectives employed by GM didn't use false names, didn't record interviews, didn't follow Nader to Iowa or Pennsylvania, and didn't telephone him late at night. While claiming that GM had the legal right to ascertain facts preparatory to litigation, he apologized, on behalf of the company, "to the extent that General Motors bears [any] responsibility."

Roche claimed he bore Nader no ill will and that the company never intended to "annoy, harass, embarrass, threaten, injure or intimidate Mr. Nader, to invade his privacy, to defame his character, or to hinder, impugn, coerce, or prevent his testimony before this or any other legislative body. . . . I personally have no interest whatsoever in knowing Mr. Nader's political beliefs, his religious beliefs and attitudes, his credit rating or his personal habits regarding sex, alcohol, or any other subject. Nor for the record was any derogatory information of any kind along any of these lines turned up in this investigation."

According to Roche, GM's general counsel had merely asked their Washington attorney, Richard G. Danner, to ascertain whether Nader was involved in Corvair litigation. Roche said detective Gillen had been overzealous in his investigation and taken it far afield of what was intended, running up a bill of $6,700 in the process. To hear Roche tell it, GM was a victim, not a perpetrator. Ribicoff and Kennedy commended Roche for his candor.

After lunch Nader testified. He apologized for his tardiness that morning, explaining that he had great difficulty hailing a cab. "I usually take no more than twelve minutes to come down to the Capitol from my residence by cab," he said. "In this instance I gave myself twenty minutes. And as I waited and waited and waited to get a cab, and as my frustration mounted, I almost felt like going out and buying a Chevrolet."

Nader then turned more serious:

"I am responsible for my actions, but who is responsible for those of General Motors? An individual's capital is basically his integrity. He can lose only once. A corporation can lose many times and not be affected. This unequal contest between the individual and any complex organization . . . bears the closest scrutiny in order to try to protect the individual from such invasions. . . .

"The president of General Motors can say he did not know of the specific decision to launch such an investigation. But is he not responsible in some way for the general corporate policy which permits such investigations to be launched by lower-level management without proper guidelines?"

Nader took the opportunity to introduce into the Senate record several voluminous exhibits documenting Corvair defects. By submitting the material, he ensured that it would be widely disseminated and readily available to plaintiff's attorneys and Corvair owners. Among the documents was a patent that had been applied for by a GM engineer in 1956. The patent was proof that GM knew of the dangers of the Corvair's swing-axle suspension and had ways of correcting it at least three years before the car was marketed.

At one point Senator Kennedy asked Nader why he was waging a campaign for automobile safety. Nader replied:

"If I was engaged in activities for the prevention of cruelty to animals, nobody would ever ask me that question. Because I happen to have a scale of my priorities which lead me to engage in activities for the prevention of cruelty to humans, my motivations are constantly inquired into.

"Basically, the motivation is simply this: When I see, as I have seen, people decapitated, crushed, bloodied, and broken—and that is what we are really talking about in auto safety when we get down to it, it is the fatalities and the horrible carnage involved—when I see that on highways, as I have seen all over the country, going back many years, I ask myself, what can the genius of man do to avoid it? And, frankly, I think this country and the auto industry are abundantly endowed with the genius of man to provide an engineering environment of both highway and vehicle which will protect the occupants from the consequences of their errors, and which will avoid the very perpetuation of these errors in the first place by a humane automotive and highway design."

The final witness was detective Gillen, who had busied himself during the proceedings by taking photographs of the participants with a miniature spy camera. Gillen began his testimony by reciting his qualifications and professional accomplishments. He was a former FBI agent and his detective agency was a large and prosperous business that had done work for three quarters of the Fortune 500 companies.

Gillen denied making harassing phone calls and using women as lures. He claimed that the interviews with more than sixty of Nader's friends and associates were undertaken on the pretext of a preemployment investigation. Unwilling to be the scapegoat in the affair, he stated he had done a good job for his client and was being smeared.

Kennedy questioned Gillen about the use of false names and delving into personal matters during the interviews. Gillen replied, "When you conduct an investigation under a pretext, you have to carry it out completely, sir. You have to ask all questions normally pertinent to that pretext."

"But you were lying," Kennedy pressed. "What you mean was that you were conducting an investigation under a lie and that you had to carry the lie out completely."

"Did you ever have that happen while you were the Attorney General?" Gillen shot back. Kennedy said no and continued to press Gillen.

"Oh, Senator, come on, come on," Gillen said. "For goodness sake, where did I learn to do this? In the FBI [which operates under the authority of the Attorney General]."

Nader emerged from the hearing with his reputation enhanced. All the witnesses conceded that GM's probe had failed to turn up any damaging revelations. Senator Ribicoff publicly told Nader, "I have read these reports very carefully, and you and your family can be proud, because they put you through the mill and they haven't found a damn thing out against you."

Nader had become a certified American hero, a man who had withstood the assault of a corporation whose assets were greater than all but five nations on earth. GM was hoist with its own petard; the publicity that arose from the company's overzealous pursuit of Nader increased sales of Nader's book and created a demand for him as a lecturer and guest on radio and television shows.

While others might have been satisfied with this public vindication, the conflict with GM only whet Nader's appetite for battle. He used his newfound stature and celebrity to press Congress to pass auto safety legislation, and he asked attorney Stuart M. Speiser to research a possible invasion of privacy suit against GM and Gillen.

On September 6, 1966, Ribicoff and Nader were invited to the White House to witness President Lyndon Johnson sign into law the National Traffic and Motor Vehicle Safety Act. With its passage, the automobile industry lost its power to decide how safe cars should be. From then on, the government would set vehicle design standards. While Nader was pleased with the legislation, he was concerned that the auto industry would eventually weaken it and believed an organization was needed to monitor enforcement and work to strengthen it.

The money to fund such a group might be obtained by suing GM. While the highest award ever recovered in an invasion of privacy suit was a mere $12,500, Speiser recognized that GM might be willing to pay a premium to bury the embarrassing episode. He drafted a complaint asking for $2 million to compensate Nader for mental distress and another $5 million to punish GM and Gillen for their misbehavior.

The suit, commenced on November 16, 1966, made front-page news across the nation. Nader said he had decided to sue in order to vindicate the right of citizens to speak freely without being intimidated or harassed, and that any money awarded him would be devoted to the cause of consumer protection. Most of the media misread the complaint and erroneously reported that Nader was suing for $26 million.

In a carefully worded public statement, GM said Nader's complaint had been turned over to its attorneys, who had advised the company that it had no legal liability whatsoever in the matter. The loquacious Gillen ridiculed the suit, calling the allegations "silly." Perhaps without thinking, he mentioned to one reporter that he usually gets paid $600 for a preemployment check but that in Nader's case GM paid him $6,700—a statement that appeared to bolster Nader's assertion that Gillen wasn't conducting an ordinary inquiry. Gillen disputed Nader's belief that he had been tailed in Detroit and Philadelphia, adding, "I would refer him to a psychiatrist. He was followed, but not at the times he claims."

Nader considered Gillen's suggestion that he see a psychiatrist defamatory and he instructed Speiser to file a $100,000 suit for damage to his reputation. While Nader and Speiser hoped the suit would deter Gillen from further prejudicial comments, the second lawsuit turned out to be a brilliant tactical move for other reasons.

Speiser served Gillen with the complaint, but he didn't file a copy with the court. Under New York law, suits are initiated by serving the other party—papers need be filed in court only when a party requests court action. Therefore, General Motors was unaware of Nader's second lawsuit.

Speiser quickly arranged to depose Gillen in the defamation suit and was pleasantly surprised to find Gillen willing to talk about GM's misconduct. Gillen was angered that GM had refused to pay his attorney fees, wouldn't reimburse him for his time spent in litigation, and wouldn't indemnify him against damages. If GM wasn't going to stand by him, he wasn't going to protect the company. With no GM attorneys present to object, Speiser had a field day.

Gillen provided letters he had received from GM's attorney that indicated that Gillen wasn't the overzealous detective GM had portrayed. On the contrary, GM had repeatedly complained that Gillen wasn't digging up enough dirt on Nader. The company encouraged him to look into Nader's personal life in order to find something embarrassing that could be used to silence him. GM officers specifically requested Gillen to investigate the possibility that Nader might be anti-Semitic, homosexual, or a drug user.

Moreover, Gillen told Speiser that he had secretly tape-recorded his conversations with GM. Especially illuminating was the recording of Gillen's initial meeting with Washington attorney Richard Danner, whom GM had retained to investigate Nader:

"This is a new client," said Danner. "They came to me and I'm anxious to do a good job because they have had trouble getting investigators. . . . It concerns this fellow who wrote this book. . . . They have not found out much about him. His stuff there is pretty damaging to the auto industry. . . . What are his motives? Is he really interested in safety? Who are his backers, supporters? . . . Some left-wing groups try to down all industry. . . . How does he support himself? Who is paying him, if anyone, for this stuff? How did he get all this confidential information from government reports or committees?"

"Is he an engineer?" asked Gillen.

"No evidence of it; he went to Harvard Law. . . . [There was] some half-baked investigation in Connecticut."

Danner handed Gillen a copy of Nader's book.

"This is dynamite," exclaimed Gillen. "I remember reading a review . . . in *The New York Times* recently. . . . This book got the biggest play."

"Yes," replied Danner, "that's why they are interested . . . apparently he's in his early thirties and unmarried . . . interesting angle there. . . . They said 'Who is he laying? If it's girls, who are they? If not girls, maybe boys, who?' . . . They want to know."

"Wow," said Gillen, "this is dynamite that might blow, Dick, you know that."

"Yes, he seems to be a bit of a nut or some kind of screwball. . . . Well they want to know, no matter what. . . . They want to get something, somewhere, on this guy to get him out of their hair, and to shut him up. I know it is a tricky one . . . that's why I called you. . . . You're a lawyer, as I recall."

Danner asked Gillen how he would handle the investigation. When Gillen suggested that he use a preemployment interview as a pretext for obtaining information, Danner thought the idea wonderful and suggested that Gillen and he act as co-counsel. That way Gillen could claim attorney-client privilege and refuse to identify his client. Gillen agreed.

Finally, Danner said, "I'll tell you in the strictest confidence, to be revealed to no one, even in your own organization. . . . If we handle this right, both of us will get a lot of business from them [GM]."

Two months later by telephone Gillen bragged to Danner that he anonymously called a reporter from *Newsweek* and "put a little bug in his ear," suggesting that the reporter go to Nader's hometown of Winsted, Connecticut, where he would discover that the Nader family was anti-Semitic. "Now, let him defend his mother and his brother and his father," Gillen laughed.

"Yes, that would be good for Ribicoff to know," Danner said.

Gillen pointed out that such an allegation might alienate several Jewish journalists who had been writing about the GM-Nader controversy.

After deposing Gillen and reviewing his documents, Speiser concluded that GM had engaged in a massive coverup. Roche's assertion that GM was only interested in learning if Nader was involved in Corvair litigation was patently false. GM officials had given Gillen a laundry list of potentially embarrassing areas to explore and had never even asked Gillen to investigate if Nader was involved in Corvair litigation. If that was GM's motive, the company didn't need a private investigator. GM could have phoned the Corvair defense lawyers and easily obtained a list of all plaintiff witnesses and consultants.

Perhaps the most devastating revelation was Gillen's admission that GM's legal department had asked him to destroy incriminating documents. Gillen had nevertheless retained copies, foreseeing their value if GM tried to make him a scapegoat.

Speiser now had enough ammunition to devastate the defense erected by GM. But evidence obtained in one suit isn't necessarily admissible in another. Speiser would have to schedule another deposition of Gillen for the *Nader* v. *General Motors Corp.* suit if he wanted to use Gillen's evidence. This time, however, GM's lawyers would be there to object, and they could delay proceedings for years with lengthy appeals.

Nader was eager to expose GM's wrongdoing and to harpoon the GM public relations machine, which had managed to convince the Senate and a large segment of the public that GM was the victim of an overzealous detective.

Because Nader and Speiser were concerned that the media and the public might tire of the story during a long delay, Speiser decided to serve a request for admissions on GM. The device asks an opposing party to admit or deny the truth of matters of fact. Parties who refuse to admit facts that are later proven can be assessed the cost of proving those facts. Using Gillen's deposition as a guide, Speiser drafted a list of questions for GM. The questions and Gillen's deposition were filed in court and became public records open to the news media. On February 5, 1967, Morton Mintz wrote a front-page story for *The Washington Post* based on the court papers. The story was titled "Detective Admits GM Instructions to Muzzle Nader—Auto Executives Lied at Hearing, Gillen Swears."

GM's attorneys immediately filed a motion to strike Nader's request for admissions and asked that Nader's suits be consolidated into one action—thereby preventing Gillen from disclosing additional information in the absence of GM's attorneys. In an affidavit, GM claimed Nader's action against Gillen was a sweetheart suit, "a vehicle for obtaining pretrial discovery against defendant GM . . . without affording GM its fundamental right to participate in any such discovery proceedings and protect its rights."

Speiser responded that there was no collusion between Nader and Gillen, that GM was merely objecting to Gillen's telling the truth: "At no time has General Motors ever charged that any of the statements made by Mr. Gillen . . . were in any way false. Apparently, they think it is most unsporting of Mr. Gillen to tell the truth after he had been hired as an agent for General Motors."

The motion was argued before Justice Saul S. Streit on March 23, 1967. On April 3, Streit said he was unable to determine from the affidavits whether Nader's defamation suit was brought in good faith and referred the question to a referee.

The referee found that GM's allegations were based purely on "suspicion, surmise and conjecture." Granting that Gillen volunteered information and was often unduly loquacious, the referee determined that that wasn't proof of collusion or bad faith. Gillen's motive, according to the referee, might well have been his anger at GM for refusing to indemnify him.

After Justice Streit confirmed the referee's report, GM promptly appealed; and the Appellate Division unanimously affirmed the decision. GM then sought permission to appeal to New York's highest court, the Court of Appeals, but its request was denied. After twenty-two months of wrangling, the issue of Gillen's admissions was settled.

Meanwhile, GM's lawyers had opened a second front by filing a motion to dismiss parts of Nader's complaint. After arguments were heard, Justice Joseph A. Brust upheld the complaint. GM appealed and lost in a three-to-two decision. GM requested leave to appeal again and its request was granted.

The Court of Appeals ultimately declined to dismiss any of Nader's complaint. They did rule, however, that the allegations concerning Gillen's interviews of Nader's friends, the harassing telephone calls, and the advances by strange women couldn't support an action for invasion of privacy. These charges could only substantiate Nader's action for intentional infliction of emotional distress.

After more than three years of wrangling, GM had little to show for its effort other than establishing that it was willing to spend unlimited amounts of money to defend itself. However, Nader and his attorneys had demonstrated equal determination. With the prospect of years of motions, appeals, and delays before them, the parties began to discuss an out-of-court settlement of their dispute.

GM realized that it couldn't prevent Nader from ultimately proving his case—the Gillen disclosures alone were sufficient to do that. The company was also chagrined to be losing the public relations battle. Every time a motion was filed or a decision made, the public was reminded of GM's misconduct.

While Nader relished the idea of a trial that would expose GM's nefarious activities, he recognized that his opponent would assert the attorney-client privilege in an attempt to suppress evidence and that appeals could delay proceedings for years. Meantime, his small staff struggled to survive, living hand to mouth.

After extended negotiations, Nader agreed to settle for $425,000, an amount thirty times the largest previous award for an invasion of privacy action. While GM issued a statement denying any wrongdoing, the denial wasn't convincing. The *New Rochelle Standard-Star* published a cartoon showing a GM official taking cash out of a company vault and handing it to Nader with the caption: "Of course, we don't admit we invaded your privacy. But anyway, here's $425,000 to offset your embarrassment at becoming internationally famous."

After Speiser deducted his fee, Nader was left with

$300,000. With that sum and the lecture fees he has earned over the years, he has funded numerous public interest organizations including the Public Interest Research Group, the Aviation Consumer Action Project, the Center for Auto Safety, the Clearinghouse for Professional Responsibility, the Corporate Accountability Research Group, Congress Watch, the Health Research Group, and the Tax Reform Research Group.

Nader and his task forces of energetic staffers followed *Unsafe at Any Speed* with a number of hard-hitting investigative reports, exposing the shortcomings of government agencies such as the Food and Drug Administration, the Federal Trade Commission, and the Interstate Commerce Commission, as well as Congress itself.

By revealing mismanaged government agencies that were captives of the very industries they were supposed to regulate, the exposés led to reforms. After the report on the FDA, for instance, top officials resigned; and the agency banned cyclamates and stopped manufacturers from adding MSG to baby food—two of the report's principal recommendations.

Nader and his associates have also been responsible for passage of such major pieces of consumer legislation as the Wholesome Meat Act of 1967, the Natural Gas Pipeline Safety Act of 1968, the Federal Coal Mine Health and Safety Act of 1968, the Radiation Control for Health and Safety Act of 1968, the Wholesome Poultry Product Act, the Occupational Safety and Health Act (OSHA), the Safe Water Drinking Act, and the Consumer Product Safety Act. Largely as a result of his work, Congress passed more than twenty-five pieces of consumer, environmental, and safety reforms between 1966 and 1973.

In the wake of the National Traffic and Motor Vehicle Safety Act, the National Traffic Safety Agency (later renamed the National Highway Traffic Safety Administration) was established and given the authority to recall defective cars. Since then, more than 100 million defective automobiles have been recalled for repairs. GM stopped manufacturing Corvairs in 1969 after sales had plummeted 93 percent.

Nader's influence is obvious in the design of today's cars. Dashboards and steering wheels are padded; headrests prevent whiplash, instrument knobs are rounded and sharp edges don't protrude; rearview mirrors break away on impact; doors and locks are reinforced; passenger restraints are mandatory; and air bags will soon be standard equipment. These safety measures have saved at least 170,000 lives, and eliminated millions of injuries.

Ralph Nader was raised in Winsted, a New England town nestled in thickly wooded forests of northwestern Connecticut. In this compact community of ten thousand, the town hall, post office, library, grade school, and firehouse were within a fifteen-minute walk of the Nader home.

Models of participatory democracy, Winsted residents addressed their elected officials by first name and had the right to override their decisions by convening a town meeting. Among the most vocal and vibrant citizens were the Naders, one or another of whom would often attend town council meetings to question how tax monies were being spent.

The Naders never hesitated to challenge authority. When the phone company tried to cut back a large tree in front of the Nader home, Ralph's older brother Shaf climbed the tree and refused to let the workmen proceed. The tree escaped unscathed.

Ralph's father, Nathra, also tangled with the phone company. He objected when the company tried to remove the pay telephone in his restaurant because it wasn't earning enough revenue. In Nathra's view, if it made ten cents a month that was more than the phone company would earn without it.

The company's real motivation became apparent when officials revealed their plans to install phones along the sidewalks and to charge six dollars a month rent to businesses that wanted to retain indoor phones. Nathra considered the policy foolish since patrons would be inconvenienced and he believed it unfair to ask businesses to pay rent to house a device that earned money for the phone company. So he refused to let the phone be removed and refused to pay rent.

The local and then regional managers of the phone company trekked to Nathra's restaurant to plead for his cooperation. When that failed, a succession of executives from company headquarters in Hartford visited him. Nathra remained obstinate. Although intensely patriotic, he told one executive to go back to company headquarters and tell his colleagues, "It is people like them who will make communists out of people like me." The phone company eventually relented and Nathra earned the distinction of having the only rent-free pay phone in Connecticut.

In Winsted the highly opinionated Nathra was considered a colorful character, although some found him insufferable. Residents said of his restaurant that for ten cents you could get a cup of coffee and a dollar's worth of talk. He enjoyed conversing with his customers and wasn't reluctant to express his views and rail against injustice wherever he saw it.

Ralph was also contentious although he never rebelled against his parents. While Nathra and Rose encouraged their children to be freethinkers, they set firm moral and ethical boundaries for them. Misbehavior simply wasn't tolerated and an errant child would be sent to stand in the corner of the dining room facing the wall. Ralph was generally well-behaved; conflict arose only when his voracious appetite for books interfered with the completion of his chores.

Nathra had immigrated to America when he was nineteen because he yearned for the freedom of a democracy. As a young man in Lebanon, he had chafed under the oppressive rule of the Ottoman Turks. Like other immigrants, he had an idealized vision of his new homeland.

He arrived in America in 1912 with twenty dollars in his pocket and settled in Newark, New Jersey, where he worked in a succession of factories. After several years he had saved enough to go back to Lebanon to find a wife, and in the village of Zahle he married nineteen-year-old Rose Bouziane.

They returned to the United States and settled in Danbury, Connecticut, where he operated a small bakery-diner-health food store. Five years later he bought a larger building in Winsted and opened the Highland Arms restaurant. It had counter service, a bakery, a delicatessen, and a dining room. Nathra worked long hours, seven days a week.

Years later, after achieving a modicum of prosperity, Nathra, with his own funds and those he raised, financed the construction of a sewer for the village of Zahle in Lebanon and later persuaded Winsted to build a new one for itself.

There were four children in the Nader family: Shaf, Claire, Laura, and Ralph, who was the youngest. They were taught to work hard, be frugal, stretch their imaginations, and enjoy life. And whatever they chose to do, they had an obligation to make society better for succeeding generations.

Nathra liked to play Socrates, asking his children difficult questions to stimulate their thinking. He had a proverb for every occasion and would find it amusing when one contradicted another. He might cite "Look before you leap," and "He who hesitates is lost" and ask his children to reconcile the two.

Rose Nader stayed home to care for her children, a role she took seriously. She carefully monitored their activities and read historical novels to them over lunch. If they wanted to see a movie, she would call her neighbors to find out if the film was worthwhile.

She taught her children to think for themselves and resist peer pressure. One day Ralph came home upset after his classmates teased him for wearing short pants. His mother told him his clothes weren't the problem—the problem was that his classmates were unable to tolerate nonconformity. Then she showed her son pictures of tough Scottish soldiers in kilts and asked him if they looked like sissies.

Both parents took an avid interest in their children's education, and dinnertime was an opportunity to nourish one's mind as well as one's body. The family discussed current events, various injustices, and the distribution of power in society. The animated conversations sometimes lasted until 11:00 P.M. The children were spoken to without condescension, and they were never asked to go to bed early.

When Ralph was five years old, his father took him to visit the courthouse. Although he was too young to understand much of what transpired, he understood that the judge was mediating a dispute and that his decision would please some people and disappoint others. He was impressed that here was a place where a person could bring an injustice; and if one made a good argument, it would be remedied. Seeing how the lawyers helped people, he decided to become one himself. Soon he began to visit the courthouse on his own. When he came home late his mother would ask him where he had been, and he would matter-of-factly reply, "In court."

Nathra taught his children that they had a duty to speak out and act on their convictions. One day when Ralph's teacher had a different opinion from his, he was ashamed that he hadn't had the courage to speak out and challenge her. He confessed his failure to his father who gently reminded him that America was founded so that everyone would have the freedom to speak freely, and that freedom needed to be exercised or they might as well live under a tyrant. The incident made a lasting impression on all the Nader children.

Like his father, Ralph was industrious and thrifty. He

had the largest paper route in Winsted, delivering 129 papers a day and earning ten dollars a week, a considerable sum in those days for a young boy.

As a teenager, he was expected to work without pay in the family restaurant. After school and during summers, he would wash dishes, cook food, bake bread, and wait on tables. Like his father, he enjoyed talking to customers and learning about their lives. He was deeply affected listening to local factory workers complain about their exposure to toxic chemicals and hearing about their dreary lives, which left them perpetually exhausted.

Ralph's views were also shaped by the books he read. The librarian once remarked that she had never seen such an active library card as his. Ralph replied that the card would be even more active if she would let him take out more than two books at a time. He enjoyed reading about the adventures of the early pioneers and liked historical novels, especially *Ivanhoe.* He was also fascinated with the work of the muckrakers, having particular regard for Ida Tarbell's exposé "History of the Standard Oil Company."

At age thirteen he began reading the encyclopedia, the dictionary, and French and Greek philosophers. He found it challenging to try to understand difficult material. His older brother introduced him to the *Congressional Record*— which induces sleep in most readers. Ralph, however, found the debates of senators and congressmen fascinating.

After graduating high school, Ralph attended Princeton University, majoring in Far Eastern politics and languages. Although he could have applied for a scholarship, the proud Nathra forbade his children to seek any financial aid, feeling that such programs should be reserved for the truly needy. Because money was tight, Ralph lived in the least expensive room on campus, and used his thumb for transportation. Instead of feeling deprived, he liked his thirty-five-dollar-a-month room and enjoyed meeting interesting people on his hitchhiking forays.

Ralph thrived at Princeton. Perpetually browsing the

library stacks, he voraciously read whatever caught his eye regardless of whether it was relevant to his coursework. He loved to engage his classmates in lengthy intellectual discussions and learned to speak Russian and Chinese. Many years later, after he became a famous consumer advocate, the government of China invited him to visit their country. He surprised his hosts by speaking their language—and probably shocked them by criticizing their countrymen's unsanitary habit of spitting in the streets.

In the summer of 1955, Ralph worked in Yosemite National Park. While he was in California, a hurricane drenched Connecticut in a torrential rainstorm that caused the Mad River to overflow its banks and sweep away half of Winsted's main street. The flood roared through his father's restaurant, breaking windows, destroying tables, and depositing several feet of silt on the floor.

Ralph learned of the disaster from a California newspaper. On the front page was a picture of Winsted's devastated main street and his family's restaurant in ruins. He frantically tried to phone home to learn the fate of his family, but the telephone lines were down. He hitchhiked East and reached Chicago before being able to get through to his mother. He was relieved to hear that his family was safe and their home undamaged. The restaurant, however, was completely destroyed. The restoration depleted the family's savings, and Ralph would have to take out student loans and work part-time managing a bowling alley in order to continue his education.

After graduating from Princeton magna cum laude, he entered Harvard Law School. He didn't like Harvard's urban campus nearly as much as Princeton's pastoral setting. Moreover, he felt that the law students were narrow-minded and only interested in obtaining high-paying jobs upon graduation and that the faculty was blind to social injustices and had a very limited view of what lawyers could do. Disillusioned, he often cut classes, remaining absent for days at a time while he devoted himself to outside interests.

He joined the staff of the law student newspaper and in

his second year became its managing editor. After hitch-hiking to several reservations, he wrote a long piece about the plight of the Native American, asserting that Native Americans had been portrayed as savages in order to justify the appropriation of their land. The article delighted Native American activists and several hundred reprints were sold, earning the paper a handsome profit.

Nader next wrote a long article about Puerto Rico's commonwealth status. Expecting another best-seller, the newspaper printed many extra copies; but this piece didn't please partisans on either side of the issue and sales were slow.

Nader's interest in auto safety arose from the accidents he witnessed on his hitchhiking travels. Once he came upon a wreck in which a young child had been decapitated. Her body had been thrown forward against the glove compartment which had popped open and sliced her neck like a cleaver.

Perplexed as to why auto manufacturers and the public weren't more concerned about automobile safety, Nader took a medical-legal seminar at Harvard and began to research the topic. He was shocked to learn that automobiles had killed three times as many Americans as all the wars in United States history. Nevertheless, little effort had been made to prevent injuries.

Nader received an A for his third-year paper on the subject. After graduation, he wrote a piece for *The Nation* about automobile design and accidents. But he had to put aside his newfound interest when he joined the Army Reserves. At Fort Dix, New Jersey, he received basic infantry training and then became a cook. He was fascinated by the methods and machinery used to prepare large quantities of food, and the highlight of his military career was the day he filled in for the baker and successfully prepared banana bread for two thousand soldiers.

After leaving the Army, Nader established a desultory law practice in Hartford, Connecticut. He taught a course on government at the University of Hartford, traveled to

Latin America, Europe, and the Soviet Union, and wrote articles for *The Christian Science Monitor* and *The Atlantic Monthly.* He also worked on auto safety and consumer legislation pending before the Connecticut legislature before becoming a consultant to the U.S. Department of Labor, where he drew up a report on auto safety for Assistant Secretary Daniel P. Moynihan, a leading advocate of auto safety.

When Richard Grossman, a fledgling publisher from New York, asked Nader to write a book about auto safety, he jumped at the invitation. Grossman and Nader discussed the project over a three-hour lunch and agreed that the book would not contain gory pictures of accident victims and that Nader would receive a two-thousand-dollar advance.

The book was supposed to be published on Memorial Day, 1965, but Nader wasn't able to complete it on time. Grossman spent the summer of 1965 in a Washington hotel room working with Nader on the manuscript; and it was Grossman who suggested the title *Unsafe at Any Speed,* a phrase borrowed from John Keats's book *The Insolent Chariots.*

Detroit didn't tremble upon the publication of Nader's scathing indictment. Although Nader called the design of the Corvair "one of the greatest acts of industrial irresponsibility in the present century," General Motors and the auto companies didn't even bother to refute the charges. Many reviewers also ignored the book, their magazines fearing that reviewing the work might jeopardize their automobile advertising. A reviewer for *Life* candidly admitted, "I wouldn't touch this book with a ten-foot pole."

Ralph Nader has become an American institution. Although he is best known as a consumer advocate and crusader against unsafe cars, his interests are much broader. He has tackled issues in the areas of insurance reform, energy policy, environmental protection, government integrity, and union democracy.

His Spartan office in Washington, D.C., is cluttered with publications and cartons containing the thousand-plus letters he receives each week from people requesting help. Their complaints range from broken toasters to defective nuclear reactors. Some are addressed, "Ralph Nader, Washington, D.C."; others read, "Ralph Nader, The White House." Like mail sent to Santa Claus, each piece gets delivered regardless of the address.

Nader makes a point of reading his mail although he doesn't have the time to reply to much of it. Noteworthy complaints are sent to an appropriate public interest organization, often one Nader himself has founded. Complaints about cars, for instance, are sent to the Center for Auto Safety.

Nader's days are packed with speeches, press conferences, interviews, and meetings. His stamina legendary, he rushes from one event to the next from early morning until late at night. On one trip he brought along a nineteen-year-old staffer as his assistant. Although the young man was a tremendous athlete and a marathon runner, after three days of accompanying Ralph he was exhausted.

While Nader earns several hundred thousand dollars a year from speaking fees and from the sale of publications, he puts most of his money into his work. In 1988 he spent only ten thousand dollars on personal expenses, which he doesn't find remarkable since he doesn't have a family to support or own a house or a car.

He has little interest in being fashionable. While in the Army in 1959 he bought twelve pairs of basic black Army shoes because they were on sale for six dollars apiece, as well as four dozen pairs of calf-length socks for thirty-five cents apiece. Nearly thirty years later he continues to wear both and only regrets that he didn't buy more.

Deriving tremendous satisfaction from his work, he is rarely depressed—even in defeat. While not hesitating to criticize those he disagrees with, he is also quick to laud those who deserve commendation. Although his condemnation is considered newsworthy, his praise is usually not.

Trying to persuade others that civic activity can be personally rewarding, he explains, "Engaging in civic activism is really a form of human happiness that too few people have discovered. Striving for justice, helping other people, decreasing hostilities, preserving the environment . . . is a form of human happiness. And we've got to redefine hedonism to include that because people who think it's . . . fun are most likely to become civic activists."

If Nader can be described as an ideologue, his ideology is based on empowering citizens and breaking up undue concentrations of power in government and industry. Believing that government will only respect the rights and interests of citizens who actively participate in government, he says, "What we don't need is to transfer one concentration of power into another. . . . That's been the Achilles' heel of idealistic ideologists who think by just taking power from corporate capitalists and putting it in socialistic enterprises . . . that the abuses are not going to be transferred. They will always be transferred unless the victims change their psychology, their use of time, their knowledge level, and their expectations.

"My daddy told me a long time ago, 'Whenever you read about a revolution, don't ask the revoluntaries [what is the meaning of the revolution], ask the presumed beneficiaries [how their lives have improved].' That's the key . . . so many revolutions go sour because they don't want to go through the hard work of improving the character of the people. They think they have found the formula for justice and all they have to do is deliver it to the people. Do you think communism has changed the character of egalitarianism of the Russian people? If you removed communism from Russia and put in capitalism, U.S. style, you'd have the fastest growth of bourgeois mentality in modern history. . . .

". . . Reform is a cottage industry. It's got to come from the top and the bottom at the same time . . . people have got to change. We've had a lot of good laws which people don't even use. One of them is the right to vote. Another is the right to be a candidate. We're not taking advantage of a fraction of the rights to change society that we already have.

"We don't spend enough public-citizen time, we spend too much private-citizen time. We spend too much of our twenty-four hours a day on our private lives, which is important, but we are shortchanging a necessary increase in public-citizen time . . . [needed in] a complex society. We have got to spend ten, fifteen, twenty percent of our time on civic duties. The real movements in history are marked by shifts in use of time. Nomad farmers, industrial revolution, the shift from manufacturing to a service [economy]."

Nader isn't the advocate of ever-more government regulation that his conservative critics charge. Opposing regulations that are anticompetitive or designed to insulate an industry from marketplace forces, he pushed for the deregulation of the trucking and airline industries (with the proviso that tough antitrust and safety enforcement measures remain).

He doesn't have much faith in government regulations, having come to the realization that citizens cannot rely upon the government to protect them. Therefore, he urges consumers to organize themselves into buyers' groups and co-ops where they can use their leverage in the marketplace to obtain lower prices and better-quality goods. Such devices as class-action suits are desirable because they enable victims to hold corporations accountable. And ratepayers should establish Citizen Utility Boards to resist price increases.

Despite his criticism of American government, Nader doesn't believe Marxism or socialism provides a solution. "The theory of socialism is that the government would own the means of production and since the government represents working people, the working people would basically run society. The big flaw in that theory is one word—it's called bureaucracy—and there never was sufficient recognition of the fact that if the government becomes a bureaucracy with its own momentum and ability to be secretive, heady, corrupt, introverted, then the society is basically trading one master for another." To him, communism breeds a particularly invidious and unresponsive form of government because of its triple concentration of economic, military, and political power in the hands of a small ruling group.

According to Nader: "Whichever way you opt for in reorganizing the society, you have to follow one principle of responsive power: Power has to be insecure to be responsive. It's got to have something to lose. And the definition of perfect tyranny is an institution that really has nothing to lose. And that's the problem with government bureaucracy—it has nothing to lose."

He believes the problem confronting Marxist regimes today is how to increase production without unleashing unbridled greed in the marketplace that could destabilize their regimes. "They're in a real dilemma. They don't see a way out except in recent years a kind of liberalization so that people can sell some vegetables at road stands or engage in minor repairs or small businesses. And when they do that, productivity goes up quite rapidly. So while the capitalist regimes confront the problem of excessively unleashed greed leading to abuses of power in the marketplace, communist regimes confront the problems of excessively little production which undermines their whole pretense for being which is to give the masses a bigger slice of the pie."

In Nader's view the Western democracies don't really function as capitalist economies but rather are "corporate socialist" economies dominated by large corporations, noting that when big companies are mismanaged and in danger of bankruptcy, the government will bail them out as it did with Penn Central Railroad, Lockheed Aircraft, and

Chrysler Motors. He says that much of our country's fiscal and monetary policy isn't designed to help workers or consumers but to help corporations.

Nor should America's economy be judged solely in terms of production, Nader reasons, explaining that the concept of productivity must be redefined so that it includes cars that kill fewer people, don't pollute the environment, and conserve energy. "We need a consumer-sovereign economy, not a seller-sovereign economy. We need consumer standards to judge seller performance. If someone says to you that the drug industry has increased its sales and profits by forty percent from last year, is that progress? The seller's standard of performance would say yes. What would the consumer standard of performance say?

"[It] would say, 'Wait a minute. We don't have enough information. Have these increased sales of pharmaceuticals gouged patients because there's no competitive pricing? Have they harmed patients because of their adverse effects? Have patients been sold drugs that don't work?' Unless we have answers to these questions, unless we can conclude that the increased sales of the drug industry have advanced health in America, rather than retarded it, we cannot say the drug industry has progressed from a consumer standpoint.

"So, here we are, free as a bird to rush over to some poor fellow who's just been hit by a car, blind, bleeding, and dying on the highway, and we can say to that fellow, 'Cheer up, you're at least contributing to the gross national product. You're generating an economic demand for repairs, for funeral service, for hospital service, for lawyer service, for insurance service. You're creating jobs, sales, profits. Why are you so glum?'"

According to Nader, America could compete successfully with Japan and other countries if our industries were better managed because the United States devotes more money for research and development, has a bigger national market, and has dominated the modern world marketplace longer than any other country.

"Why did we slip?" he asks. "Product quality. Service quality. That's the main reason. German autoworkers now make twenty percent more than U.S. autoworkers. Japanese autoworkers make eighty percent [of what United States workers make] and they have a lot of fringe benefits that U.S. autoworkers don't have. . . . The Japanese companies that are opening auto plants in this country, like Honda, use American workers and produce a product that they say is slightly superior to the Honda coming out of Japan. So what's the excuse?

"It's bad management. Inflated, complacent, overpaid, overpampered, overinsulated corporate management. It's the biggest cause of our industrial decline. Not only that, these bad managers . . . have lost their allegiance to the U.S.A. They will ship capital and their plants to any country if that will reduce their costs. . . . [They will] use serf labor and operate in highly polluted areas as long as they can sell back into this market. That's what they are doing. [They're] exporting jobs. . . . That's what the trade deficit means."

Nader isn't interested in running for office himself. "I view democracy like a tree," he tells audiences. "The people are like the roots and the trunk and the elected representatives in politics are the branches and the twigs. I've always liked to work at the roots and the trunk. I've always been impressed by how many good people who go into politics end up unable to do anything because they're surrounded by special interest groups. When they look for the support of organized citizens, the organized citizens are not there. Good politics come from active, involved citizenry behind the politicians."

Nader has earned the enmity of many powerful people with his penchant for unsparing criticism combined with a willingness to name names. He accused Ronald Reagan "of building a government of the Exxons, by the General Motors, for the Du Ponts." It is time, he said, "to forget about law and order for the powerful and put the wood to the weak and the disadvantaged."

Calling former Budget Director David Stockman and Ronald Reagan "consummate bullies," Nader said, "They cut the infant nutrition program, cut housing for low-income people, but don't cut corporate subsidies. Don't cut the corporate welfare system. Don't cut the defense contracting budget, those massive budgets where hundreds of millions of dollars fall through the cracks." In Nader's opinion the Strategic Defense Initiative ("Star Wars") missile defense system is a fictional program that is "insupportable empirically."

"You see, we're living in a period when the experts take away our common sense and when the politicians take away our indignation. The experts take away our common sense by telling us, Who are you to challenge? Who are you to ask? Who are you to decide? You're not a biochemist, you're not a nuclear engineer. And the political leaders tell us how wonderful we are. They flatter us into subservience. Have you ever met a politician who doesn't flatter the people? Show me one. Show me a politician, left, right, or moderate, who doesn't flatter the people all the time, and I'll show you a visiting Martian."

Nader doesn't flatter his listeners; he enjoys challenging them. He opened a March 1987 speech at Harvard by asking how many students were determined to become leaders in the advancement of justice. Several listeners raised their hands while others shifted uncomfortably in their seats. "Now, how many have decided that there's no future in that," he said to the audience's nervous laughter, "and you are going to go to work for the Fortune Five Hundred or some law firm?" A few students raised their hands. "That still leaves a slight majority of you who, shall we say, who still have this pressing question under contemplation."

He told the students that their schooling has put blinders on them. How many of them could write a thousand-word essay on how their university was governed? How many could name the members of their university board of directors? "Don't you even know who your rulers are?" he taunted. "Maybe you're like members of the AAA, all you care about is towing service. . . . [All you care about is that] they give you a degree and a scholarship. How about this for a debate topic: 'Is the governance of Harvard University closer to that of the Kremlin or that of the United States?' "

In the early 1970s, a majority of Harvard students signed a petition to raise their student fees several dollars to establish a Public Interest Research Group (PIRG) on campus, like those at many other universities across the nation. Never had so many Harvard students petitioned for a program. The proposal was sent to the dean of students, who referred it to Harvard's Boston law firm, from which it never emerged. Nader was greatly disappointed when the administrators defeated the students by wearing them down and waiting them out, realizing that student activism would wane by exam time and eventually the troublemakers would graduate.

"As students of Harvard University," Nader said, "you have less rights than students at many community colleges, you have less rights than students in European universities, you have far fewer rights than students at Canadian universities. . . . [But] that doesn't seem to bother Harvard students. 'Who needs these rights, when we got this status, man? We got the Harvard insignia, the trademark, the emblem.'

"Don't ever excuse yourself on the grounds that you're too busy and you're trying to make it through your courses and that you'll open your eyes and thoughts to these issues of governance when you get out and go to work for IBM or the Department of Defense, or a law firm or a hospital. It doesn't work that way.

". . . You will never again be as free to experiment, pioneer, challenge, question, and innovate as you are now as a student. . . . You are reaching your peak of that kind of freedom. Later you will ask yourself, 'Shall I break away from the law firm that's paying me eighty thousand dollars a year?' " He warned the students that as they entered the work force, they would censor themselves and the sharp edge of their dreams would dull. They would begin to rationalize that they have to toe the line because they have families to support and debts to pay.

Cautioning them that they shouldn't immerse themselves in their studies and lose touch with the outside world, he recalled that during his first year of Harvard Law School while walking across campus with some of his classmates, he heard Ravel's *Boléro* being played in a nearby lounge. When he suggested that they stop and listen, his classmates looked at him as if he were crazy. One turned and said, "Do you realize there are only eight weeks left until exams?"

Lamenting that universities don't teach students how to be smart consumers, Nader said that an insurance salesman without a high school diploma can take a Harvard Ph.D. in economics to the cleaners on life insurance. "This is because universities teach lawyers how to sell legal services and doctors how to sell medical services but they don't teach anybody how to buy anything."

Nader told his audience that they weren't even aware of the chains imprisoning them. "Control mechanisms are in place in this country that are extremely efficient. They are so efficient, they are self-integrated. They are so efficient, they don't need police in jackboots walking down the street, knocking on your door at three in the morning . . . [because] the most efficient control systems are the ones where the people who are the victims are also the enforcers of the control systems."

He cited multiple-choice standardized tests as an example. "Multiple choice tracks you from kindergarten all the way to the licenses you get in the professional and occupational arena. Now most students say to themselves, 'I will accept that standard of measurement. I will take cram courses . . . I'm not interested in what this measures . . . I'm just interested in scoring, because that's the way up.' As a result, educational curriculum in high school is tailored to these multiple-choice tests. Experiences that don't get you a reward on these tests get you a low status, a low priority. . . . These tests do not measure the most important aspects of your personality, your chances for success in life.

"It's a system of control. If you're a high school student who wants to get a good score on the SAT, are you going to spend your time learning about social organizing techniques? Are you going to spend your time learning about philosophies of life? You're going to spend your time learning about the topics that are tested . . . a whole range of educational maturity [is screened out] because it doesn't score points for you."

Another example of a control mechanism is the cosmetics and beauty industries, he said. "Who sets the standard of personal beauty in our country? The cosmetic companies and the fashion magazines. They set it. So that they can generate proper anxieties in your mind, proper deteriorations of self-esteem, so you can then crave for the products that will diminish the gap between you and Revlon and you and *Vogue* and you and *Playboy*'s ads. Millions of people accept it. It's a cosmetic uniform. If they don't wear the stuff, something happens at the workplace, they get the raised eyebrow. Maybe they are not considered properly dressed.

"Millions of people put this stuff on their hair, on their eyes, on their skin, on their nails without asking: 'What are these toxic chemicals? How many are carcinogens? How many are mutagens?' There are plenty. How many are getting into the bloodstream, through the perms and the hair dyes? What about the millions of people who work in the beauty salons and are exposed to this stuff eight hours a day? Higher respiratory ailments, cancer experiences— the studies are showing. For what? In order to meet an externally imposed standard of increasing centralization, commercialization, and exploitation. . . .

"Now you may think that's trivial. Try reading some of the letters of teenagers on the verge of nervous breakdowns because they don't think they appear the right way. How about all these middle-aged women who are on the brink of serious anxiety spasms because they've discovered brown spots on their hands? How about all the elderly people desperately putting on lipsticks and mascara in order to cater to the demands of a youth-oriented culture? How about this personal narcissism, this personal concern, this personal anxiety? What is left for the civic culture? What is left for more important issues which need self-confidence? We need an individual definition of beauty that involves characteristics of achievement and personality and compassion and wit instead of whether you are a reasonable facsimile of a picture in *Seventeen* magazine."

Nader concluded his speech by noting that his book, *Unsafe at Any Speed,* arose from research he had done as a student at Harvard. "How many of you can transform what you think is important . . . into a movement that will make a difference? You know what the answer is? Plenty of you. Plenty. So, let me tell you something that no one's ever told you before as a Harvard student. Stop selling yourself short. You're overrated and underactive."

The next day Nader addressed the students and faculty of Suffolk University Law School, and television was the object of his wrath. He criticized it for stigmatizing intellectuals, portraying them "as nerdy and somewhat on the lunatic fringe. Never fitting in with mainstream society and being somewhat aberrant. . . .

". . . It's just generally more socially acceptable for people to be conformists and not to question the system. To just go along and let your values be dictated by television. . . . Thinkers are dangerous people to the establishment. They might think of alternative ways to have power used in a society for the benefit of the many instead of the few.

"One day when I was ten years old, I came home from grade school and my dad said, 'Well, what did you do today, Ralph? Did you learn how to think or believe?' I said, 'Well, gee.' And I went to my room to try to figure it out. Suddenly it occurred to me. Day after day we went to school and we were told believe, memorize, regurgitate. Don't question, don't think, don't challenge. Even these students I spoke to at Harvard yesterday, they got to Harvard by being hard-working and obedient. Toeing the line.

"And that's what television is exuding again, and again and again. To the extent that they put on dissenters, they paint them out to be freaks, mavericks, bizarros. Behavioral mavericks, like [those who wear] punk dress will be put on, but not thinking mavericks. You see, they are potentially dangerous. You know somebody could come up with a plan on how workers could take control of hundreds of billions of dollars in pension monies. They are owners of huge blocks of stock on the Fortune Five Hundred. You don't have an hour show devoted to that. They say, 'That's dull, nobody would be interested in that.' Male strippers [though are okay].

"Television is ninety percent entertainment, ten percent news and zero percent mobilization. . . . The overall message, is [the same as] the Roman circus. Titillation, diversion. It's . . . an electronic narcotic."

He accused corporations of using television subversively. "Corporations are trying to bust up some of the most important value systems in our society, even economic value systems like competition, replacing it with oligopoly or monopoly. Look what they've done to the family. They have undermined and subverted the American family by going directly to their kids on the tube. In Western Europe, advertising aimed at children is unlawful. You do not advertise to four-, five-, six-, seven-, eight-year olds. In this country, they're open game. The tube is raising the kids. Training them to nag parents.

"In fact, Madison Avenue has a way of describing whether a children's ad is really effective: They say it has a high nag factor, that is, a high percentage of the children watching are going to go nag their parents to buy the product. Go out and get those Hostess Twinkies. . . . And you get somebody like Tony the Tiger becoming an authority figure. And Tony the Tiger says eat this. Millions of kids are going to eat this. I mean, who elected Tony the Tiger? Who appointed Tony the Tiger? Who monitors Tony the Tiger? . . .

"And look at the violence on TV. How many programs have peace themes compared to violent themes? They are killing so many people on TV that they can't even wait for them to fall. They're zapped, they're evaporated by electronic weapons.

". . . A lot of times parents use the TV set as an electronic baby-sitter. There was a survey taken recently that the average time parents spend with their children (once they're no longer infants) was seventeen minutes a day. Working parents. I mean they hardly see, they hardly talk to them anymore. It's rush, rush, rush back and forth. The kids have their own rooms, their own TVs, video games, whatever. We're paying a penalty for this. You're seeing it right now, all over."

In 1971 Nader established Public Citizen, a nonprofit organization to supervise and fund his public interest endeavors. Under its banner, he established a Litigation Group to wage his courtroom battles.

A student who had worked for Nader suggested Alan Morrison to head the group. Morrison, aged thirty-three, was assistant chief of the Civil Division in the United States Attorney's Office for the Southern District of New York. He had been a prosecutor for three and a half years and was thinking about setting up his own public interest law firm— something akin to the National Resources Defense Council but with a focus on economic issues.

Morrison told Nader he was interested in running the Litigation Group but the $5,000-a-year salary Nader was offering couldn't support his wife, child, and himself. Nader suggested $15,000; and although Morrison was already making $23,500, he agreed to come to Washington to discuss the position.

Upon Morrison's arrival, Ted Jacobs, Nader's chief assistant, asked to see his resume. Morrison hadn't brought one so he wrote his credentials on a yellow legal pad. He had served four years as a Navy officer and had worked for a Wall Street law firm for two years. He had an undergraduate degree from Yale and a law degree from Harvard where he wrote for the law review, was president of the university's legal aid society, and graduated magna cum laude.

Nader emerged from his office an hour later, only to tell Morrison that he was late for a speech at George Washington Law School and suggested that Morrison come along.

Morrison found the energy and vision of Nader's speech electrifying, and it hadn't escaped his notice that day that Nader had been mentioned in three separate articles in *The New York Times*. As they walked back to the office, Nader asked Morrison if he had any ideas about the kind of lawsuits he wanted to bring. Morrison rattled off several possibilities. Impressed, Nader offered him the position.

Morrison returned to New York to ponder the offer, and he spent the night tossing and turning in bed. The next morning he realized he hadn't been able to sleep soundly because he kept thinking of all the exciting suits he could bring with Nader. And so in February 1972, he moved to Washington to become the director of the Litigation Group.

While the pay was modest, there were some benefits. Working for Nader meant instant credibility, which opened doors and attracted news coverage. Since Nader provided all operating funds, Morrison was relieved of any fundraising burden. Moreover, Nader allowed his protégé to take full credit for his accomplishments. One of Nader's most admirable qualities is that he isn't a glory seeker.

From Nader's point of view, Morrison was an ideal staffer because he was self-motivated and needed little supervision. Nader is happy to provide an office, a modest salary, and some direction to his staff, but he doesn't have a lot of time to give them and expects staffers to take the initiative. Some people find this freedom invigorating; others are uncomfortable in such an unstructured environment.

In the beginning, Nader reviewed all of Morrison's briefs and asked to be kept regularly informed about the progress of each case. But in time he came to trust Morrison's judgment and turned his attention to other pressing matters. While Nader would occasionally suggest a lawsuit, he allowed Morrison to set his own agenda. There were so many things that needed to be done that it was a waste of time to quibble about what to do first. As long as Morrison was doing good work, Nader didn't interfere.

When conflict arose, it was over such extraneous matters as Morrison's refusal to give Nader his home phone number because of Nader's penchant for telephoning his associates late at night. Only after Nader promised not to call after 11:00 P.M. did Morrison relent.

Another dispute revolved around Morrison's desire for a photocopy machine. Nader felt carbon paper and periodic trips to a local copy center would be more economical and would discourage unnecessary copying. Morrison believed a photocopier was an essential tool for a litigator who might have to prepare voluminous briefs quickly. He considered Nader penny-wise and pound-foolish. The argument escalated; and when Morrison threatened to resign, Nader gave in.

But there has been no dissension over the suits brought by the Litigation Group. Morrison has successfully sued government agencies for violating the Freedom of Information Act and challenged President Nixon for impounding funds and firing prosecutor Archibald Cox. The group has also tangled with organized labor over the rights of rank and file members to democratically elect their union officials.

Morrison confronted the legal profession in *Goldfarb* v. *Virginia State Bar* (1975). He persuaded the Supreme Court that lawyers were subject to antitrust laws and that minimum-fee schedules constituted price fixing. In *Virginia*

State Board of Pharmacy v. *Virginia Citizens Consumer Council* (1976), he won a landmark Supreme Court ruling that increased First Amendment protection for commercial advertising. Subsequent cases ended the prohibition on lawyer advertising.

The Litigation Group's record before the United States Supreme Court is impressive, with eleven victories in eighteen suits, the most notable of which occurred in 1983 when Morrison persuaded the Court in *INS* v. *Chadha* to strike down all laws permitting Congress to veto executive branch actions. In one stroke more than two hundred laws, including the War Powers Act, were invalidated.

The decision infuriated some of Morrison's public interest colleagues but he is a purist on separation-of-power issues. To him, the legislative veto was unconstitutional because it violated the separation-of-power clause. Moreover, the veto was bad public policy, he reasoned, because it allowed officials to block action with less public scrutiny than if they voted directly on an issue.

Morrison also succeeded in contesting the Gramm-Rudman-Hollings automatic-spending-cut bill to balance the federal budget. Four hours after Ronald Reagan signed the bill into law, Morrison filed suit, finding the law a gimmick that allowed Congress to take a shortcut to avoid making tough political decisions. He believes that if congressmen don't want to stand up and be counted, they should stand aside and let others be elected.

By 1988 the Litigation Group's annual budget had grown to $450,000. Ten attorneys work out of a Spartan office overlooking Du Pont Circle with none of the trappings of a successful law firm. The attorneys share one full-time and one part-time secretary; most do their own typing. The office doesn't subscribe to computerized research.

Morrison, who either runs or bikes to work, often appears in jogging shorts. His bicycle rests against a dilapidated chair next to an old metal file cabinet. A wooden cable spool serves as a coffee table.

Beginning lawyers receive salaries of $17,000 to $18,000 a year, about one third of what they could earn elsewhere. Veteran attorneys earn up to $40,000. With income from part-time teaching jobs at Harvard and New York University, Morrison earns about $50,000. Despite the low salaries and humble surroundings, there is no shortage of applicants.

After sixteen years with the Litigation Group, Morrison remains as energetic and enthusiastic about his work as the day he started. Friends and foes alike describe him as bright, competent, aggressive, and shrewd. He can be impatient and abrupt with others—nobody has ever accused him of being humble, and his critics call him brash and arrogant.

He works long hours and is considered a good motivator and teacher. His staff has an average tenure of more than seven years, considerably longer than that of attorneys for other public interest groups where the arduous hours, low pay, and poor working conditions make employment a short-term proposition for many.

Morrison says his staff remains loyal because they enjoy their work, believe it is important, exercise a great deal of responsibility, and like each other. He considers his job the most wonderful in the world. Where else, he asks, could he wake up each morning, read the newspaper, and then file suit over anything that outrages him?

Since the Litigation Group doesn't accept money from clients, Morrison selects cases without regard to the plaintiff's ability to pay. He is fiercely independent, and his views don't fit neatly into liberal or conservative categories. On many consumer, health and safety, and open access issues, he is aligned with liberals; but on constitutional issues he is often with the conservatives.

The cases he favors have broad ramifications for social policy or are based on novel theories. Representing the underdog and bringing cases that everyone else is afraid to pursue are particularly satisfying.

The Litigation Group's limited resources, however,

compel Morrison to avoid cases that require lengthy trials in favor of those where the facts aren't in dispute and a decision can be rendered on the basis of a judge's interpretation of the law. Morrison uses the discovery process to uncover facts and then moves for a summary judgment. On the appellate level, he keeps his briefs concise and to the point and he doesn't spend enormous amounts of time researching esoteric theories.

Lawsuits brought by Morrison and other public interest lawyers have induced regulatory agencies to become much more careful in promulgating regulations. The agencies always were cautious in making decisions that affect industry because they knew businessmen had the resources and incentive to contest them. Now the agencies take care to dot their *i*'s and cross their *t*'s when they enact rules affecting consumer and citizen interests as well.

Although Nader resigned in 1980 as president of Public Citizen, he still maintains informal contacts with many staffers. Uninterested in building a personal empire, he spun off the organization so that it could establish an identity of its own.

He continues to travel and lecture incessantly, urging his listeners to become active citizens. After a speech, he is often besieged by worshipful admirers asking him to help resolve some local dispute or personal problem. He sighs, realizing that they've missed the point; after offering some suggestions, he reiterates that they have to lead the fight themselves.

Chapter 7

BUSTING THE MAFIA

*If there were no bad people there
would be no good lawyers.*
—CHARLES DICKENS

On September 7, 1986, the Mafia was prosecuted as
an ongoing criminal conspiracy for the first time. If
its leaders were convicted, their lengthy jail terms
would deal the secret society a devastating blow.

The prosecutors were three relatively inexperienced
attorneys—the oldest only thirty-two. The wholesome appearance and fresh faces of these young men were hardly
likely to frighten hardened criminals, except perhaps those
who fear yuppies. Many doubted that these legal tender-
foots could succeed against a foe that had withstood the
assaults of Thomas E. Dewey, Robert F. Kennedy, and
J. Edgar Hoover. The mob's bookmakers would have called
it a long shot, especially since the three were up against
eight veteran defense attorneys—five of whom were
former prosecutors.

The trial was unusual. The boss of the Colombo family
defended himself. His cousin was the prosecution's star
witness—a witness whose testimony was impeached by his
wife and stepchildren.

The case against the Mafia's ruling Commission was based on an extortion scheme and a murder. Paradoxically, the first required a remarkable degree of harmony among mobsters from different families, while the second showed just how ruthlessly these men could deal with each other.

The "hit" was unexpected, but then most are. On July 12, 1979, at about two o'clock in the afternoon, Carmine Galante, boss of the Bonanno crime family, arrived for a late lunch at Joe and Mary's, a modest Italian restaurant on Knickerbocker Avenue in the Bushwick section of Brooklyn. Accompanied by Moe Presenzano, seventy-one, a family captain, Galante was driven to the restaurant by his nephew, Jimmy Galante, forty-three, who then left to run some errands.

To the average passerby, Galante, balding, pudgy, and a mere five feet four inches in height, looked like just another sixty-nine-year-old grandfather. But those who knew his reputation for viciousness and cruelty weren't fooled. Galante, who had worked his way up in the mob as a feared executioner, was said to have committed eighty hits and had been arrested numerous times for assault, bootlegging, extortion, and gambling.

The son of Italian immigrants who came to America in 1907, he had his first brush with the law when he was eleven. By the time he was twenty he had been arrested for robbery and killing a policeman in the ensuing gun battle. Four months later he was involved in another armed robbery and a second policeman was shot. Galante was sentenced to twelve years in jail, and after he was paroled, he worked as an enforcer for the Genovese, Bonanno, and Profaci (later renamed Colombo) crime families, three of the five families that operate in New York City.

In the 1950s, as the underboss, or number two man, in the Bonanno family, he went to Italy to meet with Lucky Luciano, who was living in exile, and arranged to smuggle opium from Marseille to Canada to the United States, forg-

ing the so-called French Connection. When he was convicted of narcotics trafficking in 1960, he was the largest
single heroin importer in North America.

This time Galante served fourteen years of a twenty-
year sentence, receiving parole in 1974. Upon release, he
tried to reassert his control over the narcotics trade, which
was now dominated by brothers Frank and Carmine Consalvo of the Gambino family. After Carmine Consalvo was
found splattered on the ground beneath an upper-story
window, a bloody underworld feud began, and in its after-
math Frank Consalvo was dead. Galante had indeed re-
gained his influence over the narcotics trade. He then
moved to eliminate black and Hispanic competitors and to
establish new drug links with Southeast Asia.

Galante's aggressive tactics aroused alarm even within
the Mafia. Santo Trafficante, the Florida boss, complained,
unavailingly, to the Mafia's ruling commission that Galante
was infringing on his narcotics trade from South America
and Sicily.

Galante was also disliked by his criminal peers because
he was greedy. Where rackets were joint ventures run by
several families, he would take a larger share than he deserved. To aggravate matters, he actively sought to become
the *capo di tutti capi*—the "godfather of all godfathers."

The honorary title, on the few occasions it was bestowed,
traditionally went to the most senior and respected boss—
the man who could resolve internal conflicts because of his
stature. Galante, who apparently thought he could gain the
position through force, considered the role more akin to
dictator than conciliator. If mobsters received report cards,
Galante's would have read, "Does not play well with others."

But the few stragglers finishing lunch in Joe and Mary's
restaurant didn't know who Galante was, so they didn't take
much notice when he entered and walked to a rear courtyard behind the restaurant, which was reserved for the use
of the owner and his family. The small patio was bordered
by grapevines and tomato plants and enclosed with a chain
link fence. Here Galante and Presenzano sat at a picnic table

covered with a plastic tablecloth while Galante's cousin Joe Turano, forty-eight, the proprietor, cooked a piece of fish on a charcoal grill for him. As they talked, they partook of the salad, prosciutto, bread, fruit, and a gallon jug of red wine on the table.

Joe and Mary's was a neighborhood restaurant favored by members of the Bonanno clan because Joe and Mary were Sicilians from the town of Castellammare del Golfo, the ancestral home of the Bonannos. Before a large influx of Puerto Ricans, this part of Brooklyn had been a tight-knit Italian community, but the restaurant now shared the block with a bodega and Miguel's TV service.

Shortly after Galante arrived, Nino Coppolla, forty, a suspected narcotics dealer and Galante confidant, entered the restaurant accompanied by two twenty-eight-year-old Bonanno family soldiers, Caesar Bonventre and Baldo Amato, who were wearing leather jackets despite the oppressive summer heat and humidity. The three sat in the front section of the restaurant and ordered coffee.

When Galante learned of their arrival, he sent a waiter, John Turano, seventeen, the owner's son, to invite them to the courtyard. The men approached warily because Coppolla and Turano harbored ill feelings toward each other. Two months earlier, when Coppolla accused Turano's wife Mary of stealing money he had given her to deliver to an insurance broker, an infuriated Turano had kicked Coppolla out of the restaurant and told him never to return.

Galante urged the old friends to forgive each other and celebrate Joe's imminent departure to Sardinia for a vacation. After a grudging rapprochement, Coppolla took a seat at the table, while the younger men positioned themselves on opposite sides of the patio, keeping an eye on the entrance. Several minutes later Presenzano excused himself, went to the front to make a phone call, and then left the restaurant.

At about a quarter to three, the restaurant's phone rang. John Turano answered. "Is my uncle still there?" Jimmy

Galante asked. "Yes, he's here," said John. "I'll be right over," replied Jimmy.

Within seconds a blue, four-door Mercury Montego screeched to a halt in front of the restaurant. Four men wearing blue jeans, T-shirts, and woolen ski masks jumped out of the car. Three rushed toward the restaurant. One carried a sawed-off double-barreled shotgun, another a pump shotgun, and the third two pistols. The driver, armed with a carbine, remained by the double-parked car.

The men burst into the restaurant and headed toward the rear. As they passed John Turano, one gunman pointed his shotgun at him and warned him to remain still and keep his mouth shut. Another gunman told three workingmen eating lunch in the front of the restaurant to get their heads down. They quickly obeyed, bending over into their plates.

As the gunmen approached the rear doorway, John Turano shouted, "Watch out, watch out!" But the warning was too late, the gunmen opened fire. Galante was hit with two blasts from a double-barreled shotgun, two blasts from a pump-action shotgun, and bullets that pierced his left eye, leg, and back. Half of Coppolla's head was blown off. Joe Turano was shot repeatedly.

When young John Turano rushed to the storeroom to retrieve a gun hidden there, the assassin with the two handguns chased him, broke down the storeroom door, and shot him four times.

Meanwhile, Edward Brunck, a deliveryman for Berkey Photo, was driving down Knickerbocker Avenue heading to the A&P supermarket on the corner. He slowly maneuvered his way along the narrow street toward the assassin's double-parked car. As he passed he saw a man wearing a ski mask and holding a carbine hanging over the car door and heard gunshots emanating from the restaurant. The masked man pointed his gun at Brunck and told him, "Get the fuck out of here or I'll kill you." Brunck drove to the corner, got out of the truck, and walked to the A&P. Near the entrance were two armed security guards standing by an armored truck. Brunck told the guards what he had witnessed; but when they made no move to intervene, Brunck proceeded with his delivery.

Across the street from Joe and Mary's, Migdalia Figueroa, thirty, was cooking in her third-floor apartment when she heard what she thought were firecrackers. She went to her front window to investigate and saw a blue car double-parked across the street and a man standing by it waving a gun and screaming at people to hit the floor. Then she saw several men, wearing ski masks and carrying guns, run from the restaurant, jump into the car, and speed off.

A few moments later she saw two other men, Bonventre and Amato, flee the scene. One of them carried a handgun. Next, a bleeding John Turano limped into the street screaming for help, while the restaurant patrons scurried away. She momentarily left the window to attend to her child, and then wrote the license plate number of the get-away car on a scrap of paper.

From the moment the blue Mercury pulled up in front of the restaurant to the instant the hit men returned to their car and fled, not more than sixty seconds had elapsed. A dozen residents immediately called the police to report gunfire. Police units responded quickly. Officers Robert Dixson and John Bobot, who were three blocks away when the radio call came in, were first on the scene.

As Dixson swung his patrol car in front of a hydrant near the restaurant, Bobot jumped out, drew his gun, and entered the restaurant. Bobot quickly returned and shouted, "We got two down and two going." Dixson called central command and requested an ambulance.

Bobot reentered, while Dixson remained outside questioning passerbys and preventing the growing crowd of onlookers from trampling on any evidence. A Hispanic man handed Dixson a scrap of paper that Ms. Figueroa had given him. On it was the license plate number of the get-away car. After questioning her, Dixson called in the plate number and make of the car, which she had described as a Chevy Nova.

In the courtyard, Bobot observed Galante's bloody body lying on the ground amid overturned chairs and a floor littered with shotgun shells. He was slumped on his back, knees drawn together, with a limp hand resting near his chin and a smoldering cigar still firmly clenched in his mouth. Blood from his left eye had dripped down his face onto his shirt. The hole in his chest was large enough to put a fish through. Coppolla was also obviously dead, his brains splattered across the floor. Joe Turano remained alive despite many wounds.

An ambulance appeared and Joe and John Turano were taken away. Joe died on the way to the hospital. John survived. Miraculously, none of the bullets proved fatal—two grazed him and two lodged in his buttocks.

As soon as the homicide detectives arrived, they immediately began gathering evidence and photographing the scene. A sergeant chalked the location of spent rounds. Galante's pockets were emptied and his keys, driver's license, Social Security and Medicaid cards, and $860 in cash were removed. No guns were found on the victims or in the vicinity. Autopsies later revealed more than one hundred pieces of lead in Galante, forty in Coppolla, and twenty in Turano.

The detectives questioned everyone in the restaurant. Unharmed were a male cook, Joe Turano's elderly mother, and his sixteen-year-old daughter, Constanza. Only Constanza had observed what had transpired in the courtyard when the shooting began. From her hiding place behind a refrigerator in the kitchen, she had looked out a window and seen Amato crouching behind a table, his gun drawn. She was unsure if Amato fired his gun but she was certain he had one. The police deduced that Amato must have been in collusion with the killers; otherwise they would have shot him too.

Outside, the street was soon filled with policemen, patrol cars, camera crews, and a large crowd of spectators. Galante's sobbing twenty-three-year-old daughter was seen standing outside her Manhattan apartment waiting for a black limousine to take her to Joe and Mary's. "They've killed him," she cried. When a *Daily News* photographer tried to take her picture, she lashed out, kicking him in the shins and throwing his electronic pager in the street.

News of the Godfather's death quickly spread across the city. New York newspapers proclaimed: GODFATHER GALANTE SLAIN, and GALANTE GUNNED DOWN. The *New York Post* blared: GREED! with the subtitle MOB CHIEFS KILLED THE GODFATHER FOR GRABBING TOO MUCH.

The getaway car was found an hour after the shooting, abandoned six blocks away on a street bordered by small factories with no overlooking windows—an ideal place to switch cars. The license plate was checked and no one was surprised to learn that the car was stolen. Detectives who combed the car remarked that it was one of the cleanest they had ever searched. Nonetheless, they were able to lift four prints, two of which were adequate for identification. One was from a window, the second from the inside surface of an interior door handle. The police would later misfile the window print; the door print was checked against prints of two hundred possible suspects without a match.

While the police understood little about the inner workings of the Mafia, they knew that the nation's twenty-four Mafia families were controlled by a Commission, which prohibits the killing of a boss without its permission, a rule that lets ambitious underlings know that they're signing their own death warrant if they knock off their superior.

The police also were aware that Galante had antagonized other mobsters. Indeed, the FBI had warned him that a contract had been put out on his life, but Galante had shrugged off the warnings.

The police later learned through informers that Amato and Bonventre were promoted soon after the killings. It thus became apparent that members of the Bonanno family had conspired to kill their own boss, probably at the behest, or at least with the consent, of the Commission. A second theory was that Joe Bonanno, the retired patriarch of the family, ordered the killing because Galante wasn't sending him his full share of profits.

The police put out an APB (all-points bulletin) for Bonventre and Amato. Although they were only wanted for questioning, the bulletin warned they might be armed and dangerous. For eighteen days a nationwide manhunt was conducted, and airports and bus terminals were checked. Then their lawyer called the Brooklyn District Attorney's Office and offered to bring the men in if the DA would promise not to arrest them. When they arrived for questioning, they claimed they had nothing to do with the killings and professed to be lucky to be alive.

When they took lie detector tests, Amato failed. With Bonventre, however, the lie detector couldn't get an accurate reading because the subject didn't react emotionally to any questions. "You could have brought his mother into the room and tortured her and I don't think you'd get a reaction out of him," said one observer. The polygraph just showed a flat line—as if he were dead.

The ballistics evidence contradicted Amato and Bonventre's story. After determining everyone's placement, the detectives compared the trajectory of bullets and the location of spent shells on the ground, and deduced that Amato and Bonventre fired at the victims with Amato failing to hit anybody and Bonventre wounding Coppolla three times. But the case against Bonventre was based entirely on the placement of the spent shells since no guns had been recovered. The evidence was considered too tenuous for prosecution and the investigation continued.

Eight months after the Galante slaying the Brooklyn District Attorney's Office learned that the Manhattan District Attorney's Office had been withholding evidence relevant to the murder. On the day of the murder, detectives working with the Manhattan DA had the Ravenite Social Club in Little Italy in lower Manhattan under videotape surveillance. Thirty minutes after the murder, Bonanno soldier Anthony Indelicato arrived outside the club and was congratulated by high-ranking mobsters of several different families.

The Brooklyn DA initiated a search for Indelicato, who was in hiding from members of his own family, which had split into two warring factions after the Galante murder. Almost two years later, on May 5, 1981, Indelicato's father, "Sonny Red," and two of his associates were murdered; and Phillip Rastelli, the new boss of the Bonanno family, put out a contract on Indelicato's life through Joseph Pistone, an undercover FBI agent who had infiltrated the mob.

When Pistone's identity was discovered, the contract to kill Indelicato was lifted, and the family was soon so immersed in legal difficulties that it lost interest in pursuing Indelicato. After remaining underground for four years, he surfaced in 1985 when he was arrested on a gun possession charge. A full set of prints was taken and his palm print was found to match the one taken from the rear door handle of the getaway car, proving only that he had been in the car, not that he had committed the murders.

Two years after the murder, the police discovered that the misplaced fingerprint taken from the window of the getaway car had been filed with a batch of prints from glassware and utensils found in the courtyard. These prints had been put aside when it was learned that the gunmen hadn't entered the courtyard. After the window print was checked against police files, it was found to belong to Santo Giordano, a Bonanno family associate who had prior convictions for car theft and gun possession. The police believed they now knew the identity of two of the assassins.

Giordano later was shot in the back and permanently paralyzed during a gunfight between members of the Bonanno family. Despite his disability, he continued to pilot his own plane, which mysteriously blew up in midair a day after he talked to law enforcement officials.

In the spring of 1984, Bonventre was discovered dead, his body deposited in two oil drums in a New Jersey dump. He had been cut in half through the waist with a butcher's saw—while alive, according to the medical examiner. Police intelligence suggested he was murdered because he was so cold-blooded he frightened his colleagues.

Five years after the killings, the case file sat in the Brooklyn DA's office collecting dust. No prosecution was planned.

Sitting in his office in lower Manhattan, Rudolph Giuliani, the United States attorney for the Southern District of New York, considered how best to attack the Mafia. His intense dislike of the Mafia was inherited from his father, who blamed it for smearing the reputations of all Italian-Americans.

That was not the only trait he inherited. His sixty-nine-year-old father liked to take late-night strolls on the dangerous streets of New York despite his wife's pleas that he stay home or go out during the day. But his father insisted that it was his right to walk whenever and wherever he chose, and that he would rather be dead than live in fear. One night, when two men jumped him, he smashed one with his fist and hit him with a garbage pail, breaking his jaw. The second fled.

Giuliani shared his father's smash-in-the-face attitude toward crime. Since his appointment in 1983, he had gone after white-collar crime and insider trading, and recovered almost $200 million in one tax-fraud case alone. He had fought terrorism, convicting the head of the Cuban group Omega 7, which was responsible for thirty bombings and two deaths. He had indicted 38 mafiosi for narcotics trafficking in the so-called Pizza Connection case. He even prosecuted a sixty-seven-year-old peddler of umbrellas at Grand Central Station—convicting her of tax fraud after she reported an income of $20,000 dollars while netting $100,000 a year on umbrellas and another $400,000 on stock investments.

Giuliani grew up in Brooklyn and Long Island, attended Catholic schools, and for a while considered becoming a priest. But he went to New York University Law School instead, made the school's law review, clerked for a federal judge, and then became an assistant United States attorney in the office he would later head.

As a young prosecutor he established a reputation as a hard-driving attorney who relished trials and would volunteer to work on the most interesting cases even if it meant increasing his already heavy workload. The long hours contributed to the breakup of his first marriage, but by age thirty he was the number three prosecutor in the office.

During the Knapp Commission investigation of police corruption in the early 1970s, he was assigned to work with Robert Leuci, a cop caught pocketing eighteen thousand dollars and granted amnesty in return for his cooperation. After federal officials promised that his partners wouldn't be indicted, Leuci agreed to wear a bug for eighteen months to record illegal activities by fellow narcotics officers.

Giuliani befriended Leuci but suspected he was withholding evidence. Leuci didn't want to betray his buddies but in turn was worried that he might subject himself to additional charges if he didn't. Finally, Giuliani gave him an ultimatum, demanding that he choose one side or the other. Leuci confessed all and implicated close friends who were later indicted. One partner went insane and two others committed suicide. The story was dramatized in the 1981 movie *Prince of the City*.

In another celebrated case, Giuliani went after Brooklyn congressman Bertram Podell, who was accused of accepting bribes of more than forty thousand dollars in return for pressing the Civil Aeronautics Board to grant a route to a Florida airline. Podell's defense was that there was no conflict of interest because he had two law firms, and the one in which he was a partner didn't receive the money.

Giuliani grilled Podell mercilessly, sarcastically asking if any stationery had been printed for the alleged second law firm, and who were some of its clients. When he casually got Podell to admit that all law firms are listed in the Martindale-Hubbell legal directory, he promptly pulled out a copy hidden at the prosecution table, plopped it in front of Podell, and asked him to find his firm's listing.

Podell was so shaken that he fumbled with his eyeglasses, knocking out a lens. As he leafed through the directory, Giuliani said, "Well, Congressman, you're reading it very quietly, none of us can hear you, why don't you read it louder?" Podell finally conceded there was no listing, asked for a recess, and then pled guilty. It was the kind of courtroom scene that rarely occurs except in lawyers' dreams and television shows.

In 1975 Giuliani moved to Washington. After eight years there with the Justice Department and a law firm, he returned to New York in 1983, at age thirty-nine, to head the Southern District office. Giuliani's decision to accept the post surprised many of his associates who viewed the move as a step down.

As the newly appointed federal prosecutor with jurisdiction over most of New York City, the capital of organized crime in America, Giuliani could hardly ignore the fact that the five most powerful Mafia families in the nation were operating under his nose. But if the Mafia didn't tremble at Giuliani's appointment, it was understandable, for there had been many previous attempts to crush the mob, none of which had succeeded.

In 1907, for instance, Lieutenant Joseph Petrosino, commander of the New York Police Department's Italian Branch, decided to fight the Mafia by traveling to Italy to obtain the criminal records of immigrant mobsters. He barely got off the boat before he was assassinated.

In the 1930s Thomas E. Dewey, the Manhattan district attorney, had more success. He convicted Lucky Luciano on prostitution charges and sent Tammany Hall politicians in cahoots with the mob to prison. Political ambition, however, induced him to abandon his prosecutorial career to become governor.

In 1950 Senator Estes Kefauver held hearings that revealed the existence of the Mafia, but nothing much was done to dismantle it.

In 1963 Attorney General Robert F. Kennedy unveiled mob informer Joe Valachi and announced that the mob had been struck "a blow from which it will never recover." In 1973 Denis Dillon, then head of the Eastern District Organized Crime Strike Force, proclaimed that a series of indictments had "decimated" the Colombo family and predicted that within two years the Bonanno and Gambino families would be on the ropes. In each instance, the glare of publicity was merely a temporary inconvenience for the Mafia and, in the long run, only served to emphasize its apparent invincibility.

Giuliani understood how resilient the Mafia was, and he realized the special problems he would face prosecuting its leadership, which lets underlings do most of the dirty work. The bosses are exceedingly careful when speaking on the phone and don't put anything in writing that can be used against them. On the rare occasion when a mob boss had been convicted, it was usually for a white-collar crime such as tax evasion, not for the rackets and murders he directed.

Giuliani shaped his plan of attack after reading Joseph Bonanno, Sr.'s, autobiography, *A Man of Honor*. Although Bonanno was careful not to incriminate any living persons, he did describe in some detail the inner workings of the ruling Commission, which in recent times has been comprised of the heads of the five New York crime families (although Phillip Rastelli, Galante's successor as head of the Bonanno family, wasn't invited to sit on it). While Bonanno's book couldn't be used as evidence—it's hearsay—it got Giuliani thinking. He met with Ronald Goldstock, in charge of the Organized Crime Task Force for the state, and learned that during recent wiretaps Anthony Corallo, the boss of the Lucchese family, had made repeated references to the Commission, unaware that the FBI had bugged his Jaguar. Up to this point, mafiosi assumed it was safe to talk in cars, and conducted much of their business there.

Giuliani's idea was to go after the Commission itself instead of prosecuting one racket or family. No one had had the audacity or vision to bring such a case before. Dazzling in scope, the plan, if successful, would cut off the head of the Mafia with one blow, the kind of dramatic gesture Giuliani liked.

Giuliani planned to prosecute the Mafia under the Racketeer Influenced and Corrupt Organizations (RICO) statute, a 1970 law designed to target criminal enterprises. Before RICO, prosecutors could convict individual mobsters but lacked the means to attack the infrastructure of organized crime. Like the mythical Hydra slain by Hercules, no sooner had one of the monster's limbs been cut off than it grew others.

The Genovese crime family, for instance, survived numerous losses, beginning with Lucky Luciano's conviction in the 1930s. In the 1950s his successor, Frank Costello, was found guilty of federal tax evasion. The next boss, Vito Genovese, was convicted in 1962 for participating in a drug conspiracy, and his successor, Frank "Funzi" Tieri, was convicted of racketeering in 1980. Yet the family had continued to thrive, with Anthony Salerno as its current boss.

Under RICO, prosecutors only needed to prove two acts of racketeering for conviction. Unlike ordinary criminal trials, where the jury is instructed to ignore a defendant's prior criminal record, RICO allowed prosecutors to introduce evidence of past crimes; and convictions under the law could lead to $25,000 fines, twenty-year jail sentences, and forfeiture of the proceeds and profits of the enterprise as well as civil penalties that would permit victims to recover triple damages and attorney fees.

Initially prosecutors didn't really understand the full implications of RICO; then it was used successfully against Philadelphia mobsters. After that, the floodgates opened.

Nonetheless, the law had come under severe attack. Business representatives claimed RICO was never intended to be applied against "legitimate business." So-called legitimate business, nevertheless, is engaged in a surprisingly large amount of illegal activity. A 1979 study sponsored by the United States Department of Justice found that the nation's 582 largest publicly owned corporations committed 1,554 violations of the law in a two-year period. A 1985 study found that about two thirds of America's five hundred largest corporations were involved in some illegal behavior over the past decade. So far business lobbyists haven't succeeded in narrowing RICO.

To obtain convictions under RICO, Giuliani would have to prove that a criminal enterprise existed and that each of the defendants committed two criminal acts in furtherance of that enterprise. That was difficult because Mafia activities are typically confined to a single family. Essentially a loose confederation of crime lords who met to resolve disputes and avoid costly wars, the ruling Commission had no soldiers of its own.

Giuliani knew of at least one instance, however, where crime families jointly ran an enterprise. As a result of an ongoing investigation, the FBI had collected evidence that the four New York families that then formed the Commission operated a scheme to extort money from the concrete industry. Giuliani also knew of the Brooklyn DA's investigation that suggested that Carmine Galante's murder was the work of the Commission, but it was uncertain whether there was sufficient evidence to obtain a conviction for either crime.

Giuliani had his assistants wade through hundreds of hours of surveillance transcripts that had been collected over the past thirty years. With a chart listing their best evidence, he flew to Washington, D.C., and urged William French Smith, the attorney general, and William Webster, the director of the FBI, to give him the manpower he needed to gather additional proof. His request was granted, and agents in fourteen cities were assigned to him. Sixteen months later he brought charges against ten members of the Mafia, all of whom had previous convictions for one or another offense, including:

Anthony "Fat Tony" Salerno, seventy-five, the head of the Genovese family, the largest of the Mafia families with some two hundred members

Carmine "Junior" Persico, Jr., fifty-three, the head of the Colombo family

Gennaro "Gerry Lang" Langella, forty-seven, underboss of the Colombo family

Anthony "Tony Ducks" Corallo, seventy-three, boss of the Lucchese family

Christopher "Christie Tick" Furnari, sixty-two, *consigliere* (counselor) of the Lucchese family

Salvatore "Tom Mix" Santoro, seventy, an underboss of the Lucchese family

Ralph Scopo, fifty-seven, a soldier in the Colombo family and the president of the Concrete Workers District Council, which controlled the workers who did high-rise construction

Anthony "Bruno" Indelicato, thirty, a soldier in the Bonanno crime family

Paul Castellano, the head of the Gambino family, was indicted, but by the time of the trial, he had been assasinated in front of Spark's steak house in Manhattan. Giuliani also brought charges against Phillip Rastelli, sixty-eight, who had succeeded Galante as head of the Bonanno family, but he was later severed from the case pending the outcome of his trial for racketeering in the Eastern District of New York.

After the indictments were handed down, Giuliani subpoenaed Joe Bonanno to testify under oath. The author who had written so eloquently about the mob refused to talk and was jailed fourteen months for contempt of court.

To assist him, Giuliani chose Michael Chertoff, a hardworking young attorney, whose balding head and mustache made him appear older than his thirty-two years. Although Chertoff was new to the office and had prosecuted only a few minor cases, his inexperience didn't bother Giuliani, who intended to personally try the case.

A former history student, Chertoff was thrilled to be working on what looked like a precedent-setting case. The walls of his Upper-East Side apartment were decorated with sketches of famous lawyers and his bookshelves filled with books about the law. He saw the defendants as some of the most powerful, notorious, and vicious predators in America, and he relished the opportunity to go after them.

And so the Super Bowl of Mafia prosecutions was set to begin. But before the kickoff, a surprise substitution was announced: Giuliani was dropping off the team. Stanley Friedman, the Bronx Democratic leader, had been charged with racketeering and bribery in a scandal involving the Parking Violations Bureau. If there was a target Giuliani found even more appealing than mobsters, it was corrupt politicians. He held a press conference and dashed off in pursuit of his new quarry, leaving the Mafia Commission trial in Chertoff's hands.

For Chertoff, a challenge of this magnitude was a once-in-a-lifetime opportunity. "It's like a movie about an understudy who gets the starring role," he said. Ordinarily, the assignment would have been given to a veteran prosecutor, probably the head of the Criminal Division; but with the trial date rapidly approaching and Chertoff already familiar with the intricacies of the complex case, Giuliani decided to let him try it, confident that the young prosecutor would succeed.

Having grown up in New Jersey, Chertoff wasn't exactly unfamiliar with organized crime. The son of a rabbi, he was raised in Elizabeth where he read lurid newspaper accounts of the exploits of "Sam the Plumber" and other mobsters. While Chertoff was a high school student, a bound and gagged body was dumped gangland-style in a driveway several blocks from his house.

But he had only a passing interest in crime then. A private-high-school student who went to Harvard, he took the law boards in his senior year to keep his career options open. When he was accepted at Harvard Law School, he decided to become a lawyer.

He excelled in law school, making the law review, and after graduation obtained a clerking position with Supreme Court justice William Brennan, where he reveled in the majesty and tradition of the Supreme Court. His only concern was that he might never again have such a heady experience.

After his year clerking, he joined a large and prestigious law firm where, still very much the idealist, he was shocked to discover the mercenary nature of big-time practice. While he revered the tradition of lawyers who courageously followed the dictates of their consciences, the attorneys he encountered were preoccupied with the number of hours they billed and their ability to attract new clients. Even more distressing, he found that clients didn't consider lawyers trusted advisers but hired technicians.

His first appearance in court was equally disillusioning. Assisting a senior partner, he found the trial process mysterious, difficult to grasp, and boring. But a year later, when he was allowed to try a case on his own, his reaction was dramatically different. This time he was intimately familiar with all aspects of the case and could follow what was going on. After that first day in court, he walked out of the courthouse thinking, "This is terrific, what a kick," and decided then and there to become a trial lawyer. A short while later he applied to the United States Attorney's Office, where he believed he could try more and bigger cases than anywhere else.

As his number two man, Chertoff was assigned Assistant United States Attorney John Savarese, thirty-one, a winningly handsome fellow with prematurely gray hair, an Ivy League wardrobe, and a Boston accent that disguised his upbringing in Westchester and Schenectady, New York.

His background was remarkably similar to Chertoff's. Both attended Harvard undergraduate and law schools, made the law review, and clerked for William Brennan. They met when Chertoff returned to the Supreme Court to visit Brennan while Savarese was clerking there. Chertoff's enthusiasm for the U.S. Attorney's Office encouraged Savarese to apply.

Savarese had serious reservations about becoming a prosecutor, however. He has described his thinking at the time as that of the "fuzzy-headed" liberal variety, which didn't lead him to like prosecutors. He was nevertheless impressed upon meeting Giuliani, finding him thoughtful, smart, funny, and interesting. Then, at a reunion of Brennan clerks, he was encouraged by a federal district court judge who told him that the U.S. Attorney's Office was the best training in the world for a lawyer and that he would have "a ton of fun" there.

Notwithstanding the long hours, modest salary, and austere working conditions, Savarese was immensely happy in his new work. His small office had unadorned concrete walls and was furnished with gray government-issue desks and file cabinets; the hallways overflowed with cardboard file boxes; and the secretaries were slow-moving civil servants. But he felt intense satisfaction in accomplishing something worthwhile.

Savarese was delighted to play such a prominent role in the Commission case. As an Italian-American, he objected to the stereotype of Italians as gangsters.

The third member of the prosecution team was brought in from outside the office. Because Giuliani wanted to use the Galante murder as one of the predicate acts for a RICO conviction, he felt it would be politic to involve the Brooklyn District Attorney's Office. They assigned Gil Childers, thirty-one, to the case.

Childers had the clean-shaven all-American look of Clark Kent sans eyeglasses. Although his credentials weren't nearly as sterling as Chertoff's or Savarese's—he had attended Trinity College and Boston College Law School—he had more street smarts and practical experience than either, having prosecuted the dregs of humanity for five years for shoplifting, burglary, assault, and child abuse. Many of the misdemeanors he handled would be considered felonies elsewhere, but in Brooklyn they used the "fifty-stitch rule": If a victim gets less than fifty stitches, it's a misdemeanor.

Childers joined the Brooklyn District Attorney's Office right out of law school. In his first year, he was assigned to the Investigation Bureau, where he rode with the police to crime scenes to ensure that evidence was properly collected. Other attorneys hated the twenty-four-hour shifts; he loved them.

Chertoff, Savarese, and Childers complemented each other and soon became fast friends. They shared ambition, idealism, and a determination to win. They immersed themselves in the evidence collected against the Mafia over many years and read about its history and lore. Pretty soon their conversations were peppered with such expressions as "sits," "getting whacked out," and "made men."

Savarese listened to so many surveillance tapes that he found mob lingo creeping into his everyday speech. He was especially intrigued by the defendants' values, the foremost being greed. "They want to make as much money as they can," he explained, "as easily as they can. They're intensely lazy and don't want to work to make an honest buck. They think that anyone who does is a chump. The wise-guy way to lead your life is to always have a scam, always a freebie. Better to go to the Poconos for free than go to Paris and pay for it. They're constantly running little schemes, some of which are kind of cockamamie. They will go to enormous lengths to accomplish very little as long as they can get something for free."

The prosecutors also learned that in the Mafia of the 1980s the men who rose most quickly were the big "earners" who put together lucrative insurance and credit card scams, a large percentage of whose spoils were passed to the bosses.

In order for the prosecutors to obtain convictions they had to persuade a jury that: (1) the Mafia existed (a fact apparently never before established in court), (2) the ruling Commission controlled the Mafia, (3) the crimes alleged were committed, and (4) the defendants were responsible for those crimes.

The wiretaps produced many incriminating conversations. On one tape Anthony Corallo said, "We should kill them. . . . We should have some examples. . . . Say we kill the first cocksucker . . . that gets to their fucking ears." On another tape Ralph Scopo told a small contractor that he couldn't obtain a job because it was worth more than two million dollars. "Who do I gotta see?" asked the contractor. "You gotta see every Family," said Scopo. "And they're gonna tell you 'no.' So don't even bother."

While the conversations showed the defendants to be tough and vulgar men, the prosecutors were uncertain whether the evidence was sufficiently incriminating to obtain convictions, since a sharp defense attorney can offer innocuous interpretations of the most damning conversations. And the defense only needed to raise a reasonable doubt in order to prevail.

The prosecutors expected the defense attorneys to portray their clients as a bunch of over-the-hill men who sat around drinking coffee, cursing, telling war stories, and talking big, without ever doing anything. The argument was believable only because Mafia bosses are such masters of deception. They often reside in modest homes, drive Chevys, and congregate at unpretentious social clubs and bars. Their mansions on Long Island and other expensive assets are kept hidden or held in the names of others.

The prosecutors faced additional problems. The concrete industry extortion racket was so subtle that a jury might not believe it even existed. Dealings between the mob's bagmen and the contractors were invariably polite and gentlemanly. No threats or beatings occurred. The Mafia's reputation for violence was so well established that they didn't need to break anyone's legs.

As the prosecutors organized their presentation, they tried to envision how a juror might react to each piece of evidence. Savarese would try to think what it would be like to hear each fact for the first time. Like a film director, he wanted to set the scene and let the evidence unfold naturally as in a good story. But he also had to be thorough, because if the jury was confused or missed a crucial piece of information, the entire case could collapse.

Each of the prosecution's witnesses was interviewed and prepared for trial. They were asked to stick to the facts and not speculate, which could open them to ridicule on cross-examination when the defense would try to impeach their credibility by challenging any inconsistent statements. The defense would also attempt to discredit them by raising any prior convictions. Consequently, the prosecutors planned to expose the warts of their own witnesses, a tactic that they also hoped would impress the jury by its candor.

Preparing for trial became an all-consuming task, filling their evenings and weekends. Childers left home at 6:30 A.M. before his wife Anne awoke and returned at 1:00 A.M. after she was asleep; he telephoned to speak to her. On the rare occasion when the prosecutors weren't working, they were usually too exhausted to socialize. Chertoff's sole relaxation was an infrequent movie—the only activity that could take his mind off the case.

As the trial approached, Chertoff became increasingly anxious. He bought two new suits and after an investigator jokingly pointed to the hole on the bottom of his shoe, he quickly ran out and had it repaired. When his best typist was called for jury duty, he worried whether he and his colleagues would have enough time to correct all the transcripts and label the evidence before the trial began.

In order to see more of Savarese, his fiancée, Lynn Ashby, suggested that the men and their significant others dine together Saturday evenings. The restaurants they went to were near the office, either in Little Italy or Chinatown, and the conversation was inevitably about the case. The women were nevertheless happy just to be with their men and socialize a bit. Chertoff's girlfriend, Meryl Justin, and Ashby were lawyers; Anne Childers was an actress. The women were lonely, but they didn't complain.

Jury selection began on September 8, 1986. In federal courts, attorneys aren't allowed to question prospective jurors—the judge conducts the voir dire while the attorneys and defendants observe. If prejudice is disclosed, either side can move to eliminate a candidate. Because some citizens don't want to serve, impaneling a jury can be difficult, especially when a trial is expected to be lengthy and involves organized crime.

One candidate confessed that he couldn't be impartial because a relative of his had been indebted to a loan shark and was badly beaten as a result. Fat Tony quipped to his codefendants, "You should have come to me, I would have straightened it out." The man was excused.

In the proceedings, Chertoff was surprised by how few prospective jurors tried to shirk their duty. To allay fears of retaliation and to protect them from being badgered by the press, the jurors were granted anonymity, standard practice in organized-crime trials. Moreover, they were informed that every day during the trial marshalls would escort them to a secret dispersal point and precautions would be taken to ensure they weren't followed. The defense complained that these procedures were inherently prejudicial because they signaled to the jurors that the defendants were dangerous men. The objection was overruled.

After two weeks of voir dire, twelve jurors and six alternates had been chosen. The jury was comprised of seven women and five men, more than half black or Hispanic. Ages varied from late twenties to retirees. One man was a musician, another a weather forecaster. One woman was in cooking school, another worked in social services.

Chertoff liked the serious and attentive demeanor of the jury. He was worried about the fifth alternate, however, a young man who looked like androgynous rock star Boy

George and always seemed lost in thought. Chertoff didn't want an oddball of any sort on the jury because he believed oddballs were inclined to disagree with the majority on principle, thereby producing hung juries. The defense, on the other hand, often reasons that a hung jury is the next best thing to an acquittal since the government frequently won't go to the expense of another trial and will either accept a lesser plea or drop the case.

The presiding judge was Richard Owen, a 1950 graduate of Harvard Law School and a former assistant U.S. attorney and antitrust prosecutor. An experienced judge who had been on the bench since 1974, he had a reputation as a no-nonsense man who ran his courtroom in a brisk, businesslike manner. He liked to begin on time and work a full day; he didn't engage in levity in the courtroom; and he pushed attorneys to move forward quickly. In his free time he enjoyed sailing and was a musician and composer who had written four operas.

On Wednesday, September 18, 1986, the trial was set to begin. That morning, however, a woman juror, apparently seeing the trial as an opportunity for some free-lance journalism, informed the judge that she had written an article about the case that she planned to submit to the Long Island newspaper *Newsday*. The judge and the attorneys read her piece.

Chertoff, who found her subjective impressions of the defendants bizarre and the tenor of the piece frivolous, worried that the much feared oddball had slipped onto the jury. The defense was equally unhappy, however, since her article referred to the defendants as mobsters before any evidence had been presented. Consequently, the judge and all the attorneys agreed to her dismissal, and the first alternate took her place.

At 10:00 A.M. the trial began with Judge Owen admonishing the jury to keep an open mind until all the evidence was in and not to discuss the case before then. Dressed in his new navy blue suit with a faint windowpane pattern, a white shirt, and red tie—traditional colors for a prosecutor's opening—Chertoff rose and walked to the lectern to begin his statement as his parents and girlfriend watched from the gallery.

Chertoff told the jury that the evidence would show the real-life workings of the Mafia. "It's not romantic or glamorous," he said. "It's not like TV or movies or books.

"What you will see is these men, these defendants, these organized crime leaders, fighting with each other, backstabbing each other, each one trying to get a larger share of the illegal proceeds which their organization rakes in. You are going to learn that this Commission is dominated by a single principle—greed. They want more money and they will do what they have to do to get it."

Chertoff said La Cosa Nostra was a nationwide criminal network composed of families, five of which were located in New York City. "It's not a fraternal organization. It's not the Boy Scouts or the Rotary. It's an organization which has a specific purpose in mind, and that purpose is to make money by committing crime. . . . And to that end this criminal group is rigidly organized and it's governed by fear and violence."

As Chertoff spoke he became more relaxed. He left the podium and walked about the front of the courtroom. At one point he strode up to the defendants and introduced each of them, giving their nicknames and their positions in the Mafia hierarchy. Salerno glared at him; the other defendants reacted with studied indifference.

As Chertoff spoke, Savarese looked at the defendants sitting just a few feet away and thought, "How bizarre that I'm here. I'm just a kid who has gone to law school, and here I am in a suit and a tie and hanging out, in a sense, with these guys who are the bosses of the mob and used to a world of incredible violence, and ordering that people get killed . . . yet I have to be civil with them and treat them as sort of normal human beings."

Despite the defendants' bravado, Savarese didn't feel personally threatened. There was simply no profit for the Mafia in killing him. He would be quickly replaced and the case prosecuted with even greater vigor. The fungibility of prosecutors is their greatest protection.

Childers had nothing but contempt for the defendants. When he first began work on the case, he found a certain glamour connected to the Mafia: the secret society, the pricking of the fingers and the oath of blood brothers, the code of honor. But as he listened to the tapes, his perceptions changed. Now he saw the members of the Mafia as sick human beings, sleazy cold-blooded killers, men without honor, who would do whatever was expedient.

Childers believed Mafia bosses weren't all that different from politicians: Both were driven to accumulate power. He knew that police would often search a boss's house and find shoeboxes full of cash, enough to quietly retire and live in luxury for a lifetime. Yet the bosses refused to forsake their criminal empires because of their love of power.

Childers's wife, Anne, had a different impression. Sitting in the gallery, she found it difficult to believe that these ordinary-looking people committed the horrific crimes they were charged with. Tony Salerno looked like a cute little old man. Anthony Indelicato was quite attractive. Without realizing it her eyes were drawn to him; she found him fascinating to watch. When he began to return her gaze, she became frightened as she realized what this man was capable of.

Savarese's mother was also in the gallery. Happening to sit near Persico's daughter and his wife Joyce, an attractive blonde in her forties, she was upset to overhear the Persico woman making rude remarks about the prosecutors and later told her son what they had said.

Meanwhile, Chertoff described how the Commission operated. Although the members occasionally met as a group, usually they would get together in pairs or communicate through intermediaries. "These men are very aware of keeping their activities secret and inconspicuous," he said. "Because this is a criminal organization, they don't meet in an office. They don't have a telephone directory that says La Costa Nostra Enterprises at such and such an address. . . . They hold meetings in basements or in houses in out-of-the-way residential neighborhoods. . . .

"Again and again you will hear these men talking on tape about how concerned they are about being watched and being surveilled and being listened to, and how much trouble they take to conceal their activities and to keep their activities secret and hidden from prying eyes.

"And, again, because most of the men here are the senior men, the older men, the men who make the decisions, they don't go out on the street. They don't expose themselves."

Chertoff finished his opening statement by urging the jury to rely on common sense in reaching a verdict: "Because that's why we have jurors, that's why we don't have professional decision-makers."

The defense then argued its case. Each of the defendants had an attorney, although Persico spoke for himself, relying on his lawyer for advice only. Attorney Samuel Dawson, representing Salvatore Santoro, underboss of the Lucchese family, was the first to speak.

"Despite everything you've heard by counsel for the government who gave a very nice opening statement," he said, "this case is not whether or not there's an organization in existence known as the Mafia or La Cosa Nostra.

"I tell you now, plainly and simply and directly, that there is [a Mafia] right here in New York City. And if the government is going to spend the next two and a half months playing tapes, recorded conversations, over and over again or bringing in witnesses from various places to try and convince you there's a Mafia, I'm prepared to save them all the time and trouble.

"Assume it. Accept it. It is."

The prosecutors were shocked by the admission. In previous mob trials the defense always ridiculed the notion that something known as the Mafia existed. Obviously, the defense felt the prosecution's evidence would be too overwhelming to deny. To maintain credibility they were staking out a back-up position. Chertoff thought they had made a shrewd decision.

Dawson told the jury that being a member of the Mafia wasn't a crime. He reminded them that they had taken an oath pledging that they would be fair, impartial, and open-minded. "We selected you because we needed a sophisticated jury," which he defined as one that would understand the dramatic and exciting history of the Mafia without letting it prejudice them.

According to Dawson, the "club" of construction firms that controlled the construction industry wasn't run by the ruling Commission but was simply a bid-rigging scheme by the contractors. As far as he was concerned, the government had the case upside down. It was the contractors who should be on trial.

After admitting the existence of the Commission, Dawson claimed that it had only two functions: first, to approve or disapprove new members coming into the Mafia, and second, to resolve disputes. "Because what does conflict do?" he said. "It gives you notoriety. The last thing you want is notoriety so you try to avoid conflict." He never explained the kind of disputes the Commission resolved or why it was so important for them to avoid notoriety.

Over lunch the prosecutors discussed the proceedings. They were relieved their opening went smoothly and were surprised at how quickly the case was progressing. The judge allowed only an hour-and-ten-minute break, so the prosecutors got into the habit of sending out their lunch orders in the morning and eating in their office. On Mondays and Wednesdays, Chertoff ordered a turkey sandwich; Tuesday and Thursday he got tuna fish. It was a boring diet but he didn't want to risk an upset stomach during the trial.

After lunch, Carmine Persico, Jr., the first mob boss ever to represent himself, made his statement. Persico might have felt he had little to lose since he and Langella had recently been convicted of racketeering in a trial in which he had professional representation.

Judge Owen had been concerned that Persico might try to turn the courtroom into a circus. But anyone expecting a show trial was disappointed. Persico presented himself in a dignified manner, maintaining decorum and being respectful of the judge while making a good faith effort to abide by the rules of evidence.

Many lawyers believe that a layman representing himself is as foolish as a patient attempting to be his own surgeon. While that overstates the case, a layman acting as his own attorney is at a serious disadvantage because of his ignorance of the law and courtroom procedure.

Nonetheless, lawyers dislike lay opponents because the judge often ends up trying their case for them, and the jury is inclined to empathize with the layman. Moreover, the nonlawyer can use ignorance as a weapon, wreaking havoc with the rules of evidence by asking improper questions. The judge may ask the jury to disregard testimony, but will they? Indeed, when they retire to deliberate, can they even be expected to remember which bits of evidence they're supposed to have forgotten?

Persico had decided to address the jury, even though he, like the other defendants, wasn't willing to take the stand and risk cross-examination. Perhaps he was hoping that the jurors would get to know him and come to believe that such a charming, courteous, and articulate man couldn't possibly be guilty of the crimes he was charged with. Besides, the dangers of self-representation were minimized for Persico because of the seven experienced defense attorneys sitting beside him who could be counted to raise technical objections and ask questions that he might miss.

Persico had worked hard preparing his opening argument, tape-recording and reviewing his speech and then rehearsing it at the Metropolitan Correction Center where he was incarcerated. His codefendants and their lawyers critiqued his performance. The verdict: too much like a lawyer. Attorney John Jacobs told him to try to be himself.

When it was his turn to give an opening statement, Judge Owen simply looked over and said, "Mr. Persico."

Persico stood and faced the jury. A short, ordinary-looking man with an overbite, he wore a dark gray pin-striped suit, white shirt, red tie, and gold-rimmed glasses, the very model of a well-dressed attorney.

"Judge, gentlemen of the defense, ladies and gentlemen of the jury," he said. "By now I guess you all know my name is Carmine Persico and I'm not a lawyer. I'm a defendant. Sitting at this table."

Persico told the jury that the witnesses the prosecution was going to present were "people that committed murder, committed extortion, bribery, every crime you could think of. Dope dealers, polluted the city with dope, drugs. . . . These witnesses are going to get up on the stand and they're going to tell you they reformed, they are here to tell you the truth."

Persico urged the jury to observe how bold and brave these witnesses would be. That's because they have agreements with the government which grants them immunity, he said, explaining that some witnesses were promised freedom in exchange for their testimony, while others were paid $5,000 dollars a month by the government.

"I don't have the power to do that," he said. "I can't pay a witness five thousand dollars a month, that's illegal for me to do it . . . I can't tell a witness that's in jail come and testify for me, I'll give you freedom."

Persico argued that the government was very powerful and that witnesses were afraid of it. He asked the jury to use its common sense when they listened to the prosecution's witnesses. He said that when Mr. Chertoff will ask them a question they will answer every question directly and without evasion. But on cross-examination, he predicted, these same witnesses would say, "I don't remember, I don't recall."

"Count the I-don't-remember's and the I-don't-recalls," he said. "When Mr. Chertoff asks them questions they'll remember everything. They'll go back twenty years and remember. We'll ask them what they had for lunch and they may not recall."

After several minutes Persico lost his train of thought. "Bear with me please," he said, "because I have so many notes here I don't know, I'm getting a little confused. I'm a little nervous, too."

All in all, it was a bravura performance, sure to evoke sympathy.

The first major witness for the prosecution was former Cleveland underboss, Angelo Lonardo. As the highest-ranking Mafia member ever to turn informer, he had earned the FBI code name Top Notch.

The seventy-five-year-old mobster had been convicted in 1983 on a narcotics charge and sentenced to life without parole plus 103 years. He wanted some hope that he wouldn't spend the rest of his life behind bars, and so after two years of negotiations, Giuliani was able to win his co-operation. In return, his life sentence without parole was dropped, making him eligible for parole in ten years. If he testified in future trials, the Justice Department was likely to move to reduce the sentence further, believing it was better to let one elderly mobster out early if his testimony could convict dozens of others.

The government went to extraordinary lengths to pro-tect him. In jail he was segregated from other prisoners. As he toured the country testifying at Mafia trials, he was guarded twenty-four hours a day by FBI agents. If and when he gained his freedom, he would be given a new identity and resettled in some out-of-the way community where the Mafia was unlikely to find him.

So the jury would be under no illusions as to his char-acter, Chertoff had Lonardo describe his background. His father ran the Cleveland mob in the 1920s and was killed by Sam Todaro when Lonardo was eighteen. Using his un-witting mother as bait, Lonardo drove to Todaro's hideout to seek revenge. When Todaro came out to speak to the widow, Lonardo shot and killed him.

In the 1930s the Cleveland family was headed by a

physician, a Dr. Romano. When one of Lonardo's cousins died after an appendectomy performed by Romano, Lonardo killed the doctor, thereby crossing the ruling Commission, which even then had a rule against killing a boss. But the new head of the Cleveland family, a longtime friend of the Lonardos, pleaded with the Commission for leniency. Lonardo was spared on the grounds that since he wasn't a member of the Mafia, he didn't know of its prohibitions.

Defense attorney Dawson objected to Lonardo's testimony on the ground that the Cleveland killings were irrelevant to the present case. The judge overruled his objection and allowed the evidence admitted for the purpose of assessing the credibility of the witness. He explained that the government has a right to "bring out all the warts on a witness," even one of its own.

Lonardo explained that he became a member of the Mafia in the 1940s and rose to become the underboss of the Cleveland family, which communicated with the ruling Commission through defendant Anthony Salerno, the head of the Genovese family.

Lonardo said that he and Salerno often met at the Palma Boy Social Club in East Harlem, Salerno's headquarters. One meeting was convened to gain the Commission's backing of Roy Williams for president of the Teamsters. The mob approved of Williams, who was elected but later convicted of bribery. Lonardo then proposed Jackie Presser to replace him. Presser, backed by the mob, was also elected.

By telling the jury about the history and operations of the Mafia and by identifying some of its members, Lonardo's testimony was damaging even though the witness had no firsthand knowledge of any of the crimes charged in this case. Such evidence is admissible under RICO because it explains the nature of the criminal conspiracy; ordinarily, it would be considered irrelevant and highly prejudicial.

Carmine Persico was the first to cross-examine Lonardo. He asked if Lonardo had ever met him before. Lonardo replied, "Never." Persico then asked about Lonardo's 1982 federal narcotics conspiracy conviction. Lonardo claimed he was innocent of the charges.

"You were tried in the federal court with a federal judge and a federal jury?" asked Persico.

"That's right."

"Are you saying they brought witnesses against you?"

"There were three witnesses. . . ."

". . . And you were sentenced to life?"

"Life."

"Plus one hundred twenty-three years?"

"One hundred three years."

Persico cleverly showed that if Lonardo's claim of innocence was to be believed, the government had unfairly convicted him. On the other hand, if Lonardo was lying, why should the jury believe anything he said. Either way the defense won.

Langella's attorney, Frank Lopez, got Lonardo to declare that he was never personally involved in narcotics and didn't know of his underlings' involvement. He thus used the government's witness to establish that Mafia bosses didn't necessarily know what their men do.

After further questioning of Lonardo by both sides, Chertoff turned the floor over to Childers, who called several policemen as witnesses. They testified about an infamous mob meeting in 1957 at a farm in Apalachin, New York, where more than sixty underworld leaders had gathered three weeks after Albert Anastasia's death to confirm Carlo Gambino as his successor. (Anastasia, the chief executioner of Murder, Incorporated, was gunned down while sitting in a barber's chair.) The meeting would have passed without notice if an alert policeman hadn't become suspicious of so many out-of-town license plates. When he drove up to the farmhouse to investigate, the mobsters panicked and ran into the woods. Most were apprehended, looking fairly comical in their mud-splattered clothes with burrs clinging to them.

At the time, the American public had been shocked to learn the extent and power of organized crime. Now the incident was used as evidence that the ruling Commission had existed for more than thirty years.

On cross-examination, Persico pointed out that no arrests were made and no crimes were committed. The meeting was just a bunch of men with notorious reputations having a barbecue.

However, Persico was soon confronted with more incriminating testimony when John Savarese put Joey Cantalupo on the stand. Cantalupo was an unsavory character who worked closely with the Colombo family, although not a member of it. In organized-crime parlance he was an "associate." Cantalupo testified that Persico was the boss of the Colombo family and that Persico continued to run the family while incarcerated from 1972 to 1977.

On cross, Persico first got Cantalupo to concede that they barely knew each other. "So everything that you spoke here in this courtroom about me was knowledge you picked up from other people?" Cantalupo agreed.

Persico then suggested that Cantalupo was testifying against him because Persico's brother had beaten him up over a ten-thousand-dollar loan shark debt. Cantalupo denied his motive was revenge.

"You was angry because you was beat up," Persico shouted. "And you was beat up because you didn't pay back the money."

Chertoff felt Persico had hurt himself in the exchange by revealing his belief that Cantalupo deserved the beating for not paying his loan shark debts on time—a perception not likely to be shared by the jury. Moreover, it showed Persico to be a man familiar with the world of loan-sharking and violence.

Persico's real nemesis turned out to be the next witness, his cousin by marriage, Fred DeChristopher. DeChristopher, fifty-nine, explained that he didn't grow up in the mob; his father had been a Pinkerton detective.

In the late 1960s, DeChristopher met and became friendly with Andrew Russo, a member of the Colombo family. He accompanied Russo to Nestor's, a social club in the Carroll Gardens section of Brooklyn that served as Persico's headquarters. There DeChristopher observed a brazen marketplace for loan-sharking, gambling, and other illegal activities. Truckloads of television sets and other hot merchandise were nonchalantly unloaded in full view.

DeChristopher prospered from his relationship with the mob. Russo arranged for him to sell insurance to a company he had his hooks into. He earned a commission of $60,000, although he had to give Russo $38,000 of it. Unsure how to claim the money on his income tax returns, he stopped filing returns.

In 1973 DeChristopher married Russo's sister, Catherine. Four months later, he contacted the FBI and began secretly informing on Russo and the Colombo family without compensation.

In 1983 Russo arranged for DeChristopher, now semiretired from his life insurance job, to work on a cruise ship. DeChristopher supervised the casino, keeping a false set of books and skimming money for the family. Asked to hold onto $200,000 of diverted cash, he hid it in the bathroom ceiling of his house.

In 1984 JoJo Russo, Andrew's son, asked DeChristopher and his wife if they would hide Persico for two weeks at their home in Wantagh, Long Island. A *New York Post* reporter had tipped off Persico that an indictment was pending against him. After DeChristopher and his wife agreed to take Persico in, JoJo requested that someone be with him at all times because Persico didn't like to be left alone.

Persico stayed with the DeChristophers for the next three months. Every day he would awake at around 3:00 P.M. and come downstairs for breakfast and to read the papers, paying particular attention to any articles about the Mafia. He often listened to audiotapes of evidence obtained against him in another case and liked to watch the news on television. In the evenings either he or Fred DeChristopher would cook dinner, and then Persico would play cards or watch television game shows. At around two or three in the morning he would retire.

As Persico sat in the courtroom and listened to DeChristopher's testimony, he appeared to become increasingly aggravated. He was particularly incensed to hear DeChristopher say that Persico bragged that not a yard of concrete was poured in New York City without his getting a piece of the action. DeChristopher also said that Persico claimed he had voted against Galante's murder.

DeChristopher explained that on February 12, 1985, he met with FBI agents Jim Nelson and Damon Taylor in Manhattan and told them Persico was hiding at his home. He informed them of the $200,000 hidden in the bathroom ceiling. It was agreed that the FBI would arrest DeChristopher along with Persico, so as not to arouse suspicion.

After DeChristopher was released from jail he went to his mother-in-law's house where relatives and friends had gathered in a festive atmosphere. Then a stranger in a suit arrived and the men, in ones and twos, went downstairs to confer with him. DeChristopher was the only man not invited downstairs. He thought he detected a subtle shift in attitude toward him and he began to worry that he had been exposed and might soon be blown away.

DeChristopher told his wife it was time to leave and they departed for home. He hid his anxiety from her. She was unaware that he had been informing on her brother and Persico. The next day he dropped her at their daughter's home and called agent Taylor and told him what had happened. Taylor advised DeChristopher not to return to his house. Instead he drove to the train station, and with no more than the clothes on his back and six dollars in his pocket, he fled. He didn't even return home to retrieve his false teeth.

DeChristopher received a $50,000 reward for turning in Persico, who was one of the FBI's ten most wanted fugitives. The FBI relocated him and paid him $5,500 a month while he testified against the mob. He had had no contact with his wife or stepchildren until he saw them in court the day he testified against Persico and Andrew Russo in the Colombo family racketeering trial.

Frank Lopez was the first to cross-examine him. He had DeChristopher confirm that he had always been legitimately employed and had never been a member of a crime family. Lopez then elicited the fact that DeChristopher knew of Russo's background when he married into the family. He asked him why he called the FBI.

"They are the most despicable people on the face of the earth," DeChristopher replied.

"And knowing that Andrew Russo was one of these despicable people, you nevertheless married into that family, is that right?"

DeChristopher said he married Catherine, not the family, although he conceded that he made money from his relationship with Russo. DeChristopher also admitted that he had asked Russo to intervene on behalf of a friend of his, Adam Liotti, the owner of a restaurant who was being blackmailed by a waiter aware that Liotti had been cheating on his taxes. Russo brought the matter to Persico, who said he would send a man named Shorty to speak to the waiter. Shorty must have been a persuasive fellow because the matter was quickly resolved. Liotti was so pleased that he gave DeChristopher two thousand dollars for Persico. But Persico refused to accept it, saying he had taken care of the matter as a favor.

Lopez attempted to introduce into evidence a photograph of DeChristopher dressed as a gangster, holding a machine gun. Chertoff objected. The judge called the attorneys to the side bar to discuss the issue out of hearing of the jury.

"As Mr. Lopez knows," said Chertoff, "this is part of a series of Coney Island pictures . . . where people dress up. . . . This is being put in only to be argumentative or ridiculous . . . it's an attempt to embarrass the witness."

"He was never embarrassed," said Lopez. "It shows his

state of mind. He could have picked several things and this is the way he saw himself. . . ."

". . . He also dressed up as a sheriff," said an exasperated Chertoff.

"Objection sustained," said the judge.

Defense attorney Anthony Cardinale was DeChristopher's next sparring partner. He elicited an admission that the witness had accompanied Russo as he went about his illegitimate activities.

"And you were impressed, weren't you?"

"Yes, sir."

"You weren't disgusted, were you?"

"Yes, I was."

"You were impressed and disgusted at the same time?"

"I never liked them. . . ."

". . . Nevertheless, night after night, you would travel along the highways and byways with Mr. Russo to the various places that he would go to?"

"That's true."

Cardinale concluded by bringing out the fact that De-Christopher hadn't filed income tax returns for twelve years.

The day Persico was set to cross-examine DeChristopher the gallery was packed. The left side was dominated by family and friends of the defendants including several expensively coiffed women in high heels and elegant dresses. Also in the crowd was actor Robert Duvall, who had played the *consigliere* to the Corleone family in the movie *The Godfather*.

Persico's strategy was to persuade the jury that DeChristopher became an informer because he was in dire financial straits and wanted the reward money and the $200,000 hidden in his bathroom. Persico began with a review of DeChristopher's debts and got the witness to admit that he owed restaurant owner Adam Liotti and his wife $8,000, and that he hadn't mentioned this debt when he had been questioned earlier by Lopez.

Persico accused DeChristopher of shaking down the Liottis, a charge DeChristopher denied, although he did admit that he rarely paid for meals at their restaurant.

"Adam didn't make you pay for your food because you were good friends?"

"That's right . . ."

"Anybody that was his friend came in there didn't pay?"

Persico then attacked DeChristopher's credibility. He got him to admit that he lied when he said Adam Liotti was his cousin. Despite the pointed questions, DeChristopher kept his poise.

"Did you tell your children . . . you got wounded fighting the war?" asked Persico.

"I got hurt."

"Did you tell your children you were hurt fighting the war when in fact you fell down a ladder? . . ."

". . . I fell down a ladder while they were shooting the guns."

"Were you running to hide?"

"No, I don't hide, Junior, that's the problem."

Persico also questioned DeChristopher about their conversations while Persico was staying at the DeChristopher home.

"Did Mr. Persico ever use the word 'crime family'?"

"Well, the actual word crime family you never used. . . ."

". . . Did you ever hear me describe anybody as a made member?"

"You used to say 'my very close friends.' You always used the words [*sic*] friends."

"Did you know me to have a lot of friends? . . ."

"You hated Paul Castellano, you called him your close friend."

Finally, Persico set DeChristopher up to administer what he hoped would be the coup de grace.

"Okay. When you left on . . . February seventeenth, you left your whole world behind?"

"Right. . . ."

". . . Tell us what you left behind. . . ."

288

"I left my family. I left my job. I left everything. . . ."

"Was there any other reason [besides that] for you leaving?"

"No other reason."

Persico then confronted DeChristopher with evidence of an affair he was having with a woman named Patricia Northover. DeChristopher conceded that she was his girlfriend, that he paid eight hundred dollars a month rent for her house and that when he left his home in the morning for work, he often went to visit her instead.

"So when you left your whole world behind . . . ," said Persico.

"I thought I left that part too," replied DeChristopher.

"Or maybe you took it with you?"

"No."

Then DeChristopher burst out, "Wouldn't you like to see me down the sewer altogether?"

"You want to ask me? . . . I don't think the judge would permit me to answer that question," replied Persico.

"I know. I know what your answer would be. We both know."

"I wish I could tell you."

Persico concluded by saying, "Mr. DeChristopher, isn't it true that you stole the two hundred thousand dollars that was in your ceiling, that you turned me in for the fifty thousand dollars, and that you came here to lie about me so that you could be with Pat, is that true?"

"That's not true, Junior."

Persico turned to the judge: "I have no more questions."

Chertoff felt that Persico's hatred of DeChristopher was so palpable that the jury was able for the first time to see his dark and vicious side. It was obvious that Persico would love to kill DeChristopher, and to do so in as slow and cruel a fashion as possible. He had shown the jury menace—something the prosecution hadn't been able to demonstrate.

DeChristopher's travail was hardly over. Under interrogation by John Jacobs, Scopo's attorney, he conceded that his government grant of immunity included protection from prosecution for having failed to pay back taxes and admitted that he was skilled at deception—having fooled Persico, Russo, and his own family about his intentions.

Fred DeChristopher's credibility was further assaulted when Persico called his wife Catherine to the stand. Persico noted that she hadn't received thirty-five hundred dollars a month to testify, nor did she receive immunity. He asked her if she had ever heard him, Persico, utter the words "Commission," or "Mafia." "No, you don't talk like that," she said.

Although she professed that she still loved her husband, she contradicted virtually everything he had said, even stating that she never saw him listening to tapes with Persico and that Persico used headphones anyway. She claimed that Persico and her husband never excused themselves to talk privately, and that Persico couldn't have whispered because Fred was hard of hearing and deaf in one ear.

According to Catherine, Persico planned to surrender to the FBI the very day he was captured, but Fred had urged him not to do so. Finally, she complained that her husband hadn't called her or the kids, or sent any money, since he had fled.

As Chertoff listened, he contemplated how to impeach her testimony. The usual method would be to contradict her with prior inconsistent statements. But few statements existed. He decided instead that he would encourage her to make increasingly outrageous statements, hoping the jury would recognize her bias.

He asked her about her husband's deafness, and whether she learned sign language in order to communicate with him. No, she replied, but you had to scream for him to hear you. So Chertoff had her raise her voice and demonstrate just how loudly she had to speak to him. What she must not have realized was that for several days the jury had been observing DeChristopher readily answer questions asked in a normal voice.

Chertoff then took the jury on a tour of Catherine's world.

"You are not aware that your brother Andrew is connected with anything called the Colombo family, correct?" he asked her.

"Read it in the papers but my brother never told me."

"Never mentioned it?"

"Never confirmed it."

"Did you ever ask him about it?"

"No, I would not."

"You understand what in general discussion the Mafia is, right?"

"Yes, I do. . . ."

"In fact, when you were asked about it yesterday you said that Carmine Persico wouldn't talk like that, right?"

"He doesn't talk like that. . . . I read that in the papers, about Mafia. . . . He doesn't [talk like that] . . . in front of ladies."

"And that's because the Mafia is not something you speak about in front of ladies, right?"

"No. My cousin or my brother wouldn't speak like that."

"And you've understood from the way you've grown up all your life that there are certain matters and certain things that your brother does that you are not to speak about?"

"Objection," shouted Persico.

"Overruled," said the judge.

"Isn't that correct?" asked Chertoff.

"I don't know what my brother does. . . ."

". . . Certain things are none of your business, isn't that correct?"

"Of course."

"And one of those things is whether your brother is a made guy [member of the Mafia], correct?"

"I don't know the use of the word 'made.' Explain."

"You've never heard the word—"

"I heard it but I do not know what it means."

Chertoff asked her if she had ever wanted to ask her

brother about the newspaper stories that alleged he was a member of the Mafia.

"I asked him once. He said: 'You believe everything you read?' "

"And that was all he said about it?"

"That was it."

"What was your response?"

"I just never elaborated on it."

"You didn't say to him: 'But Andy, this is a terrible thing they are saying about you?' "

"No."

"Did you suggest that Andrew Russo sue the newspapers for defamation?"

"No. . . ."

". . . You know Gerry Langella, right?"

"All my life. . . ."

". . . And you've also read that Gerry Lang is a member of the Mafia, right?"

"I read it in the papers all the time."

"Of course you asked Gerry, 'Are you a member of the Mafia?' "

"No, I don't speak to Gerry that way. . . ."

"Do you know what Gerry Lang does for a living?"

"I have no idea."

"Did you ever know what he did for a living?"

"No."

Under further questioning by Chertoff, she admitted that she knew an indictment was outstanding against Persico and that, during the three months he lived with her, two people were always kept at home with him so that if one had to leave, another would be there to answer the door. Although this practice severely restricted her social life, she claimed Persico's presence was no imposition at all. Nor did it bother her that he never contributed to household expenses. Her loyalty was all the more remarkable considering that she wasn't particularly close to her cousin—before he moved in, she had seen him only twice in the previous five years.

Finally, Chertoff asked her if she was bitter that her brother Andrew was convicted in an earlier trial in which her husband testified against him. She claimed she wasn't bitter or angry. "I happen to love him very much. I am just hurt and disappointed with what he did," she said. "My husband lied and robbed from his family in order to go away with his girlfriend, and that's it in a nutshell."

"And you still love him?" asked Chertoff.

"I sure do."

"Do you love Junior Persico, ma'am?"

"I sure do. He is my cousin."

"And you love Andy Russo?"

"Yes, he is my brother. . . . I love all my family. All my cousins, all my aunts."

Persico then called Catherine's son Richard Santaniello, twenty-three, as the next witness. Santaniello, who claimed he had spent more time with Persico than any of the other members of the family, stated he never heard Persico discussing the contents of his audiotapes with his stepfather or anyone else. He also said that Persico never uttered the word "Mafia" and didn't talk about construction. His testimony added little beyond what Catherine had stated but allowed the prosecution an opportunity to cross-examine him.

Chertoff first brought out that during Persico's stay Richard was neither attending school nor working. He would wake up at noon, and spend his days watching television, shopping, and visiting his girlfriend. The jury, comprised of working people, weren't likely to be sympathetic.

Richard claimed he spent a lot of time talking about old times. "Your old times?" Chertoff asked.

"No. His old times," the witness replied.

"Well, tell us some of the old times he told you about."

"Well, like the prices of things. Going to the movies, what they cost then and what they cost now. You know, I thought that was—it amazed me."

"You had a lot of conversations about this? . . ."

"Yes."

"Would you say you talked about the prices in the old days every day you were with Carmine Persico?"

"Not every day, no."

"That wasn't really too interesting a subject, was it?"

"To me it was."

"Did Mr. Persico talk to you about his activities in the old days?"

"No. Never."

"You weren't interested in those?"

"No."

"Did Mr. Persico ever talk about what he did for a living?"

"No."

"Did you ever ask him what he did for a living?"

"No. I would never ask. . . ."

"Weren't you curious as to what he did for a living?"

"No. Not at all."

"He was living in your house for three and a half months and you never once wondered what he did for a living?"

"It wasn't really my business. I would never ask somebody that question. . . ."

"You knew, didn't you, that your cousin, Mr. Persico, had had an interesting past life, right?"

"I didn't know him."

"You had heard about him, right?"

"I have read about him."

"In the newspapers, right?"

"Yes."

"So here was your opportunity to sit down with Carmine Persico, your relative, in the flesh, and you never asked him about any of those stories you read in the newspaper about him?"

"No."

"Never?"

"No."

"There wasn't one time over coffee that you didn't turn to him and say, 'Tell me, what was it like in the Gallo wars'?"

"No."

"Objection," shouted Cardinale.

"I will sustain that," said the judge.

Persico next called Kim Roggeman, Catherine's daughter, Fred's stepdaughter, as a witness. She complained that when Fred borrowed her car and left it at the train station, she found its interior torn, cigarette burns on the seats, and a traffic ticket on the windshield.

Chertoff undercut her credibility by bringing out that the ticket was dated two days after she had recovered the car. She also didn't know what Persico did for a living.

To win their case, the prosecutors had to prove that Anthony Indelicato murdered Galante, Coppolla, and Joe Turano at the ruling Commission's behest. Constanza Turano, deliveryman Edward Brunck, and Migdalia Figueroa all described what they had witnessed at the time of the shooting. But John Turano, twenty-five, who had bravely intervened in an attempt to save his father and been shot four times for his efforts, was extremely reluctant to testify. On the stand he stared at his fingers and muttered, "I don't remember," to Chertoff's questions.

A day earlier Turano had confided to Childers that he was afraid to testify, saying, "Hey, you do this for a living. But you don't know these people the way I know them. I have to live with them."

His testimony was important because he was the only eyewitness who could establish the seating arrangement in the courtyard. Calculating bullet trajectories and making deductions based on the location of spent shells wasn't possible if you couldn't fix the position of gunmen and victims. The prosecution was especially anxious to establish where Bonventre sat, so it could prove that members of Galante's own family were involved in the murders. Since Amato and Bonventre were subsequently promoted, the killings must have been done with the Commission's approval.

Turano said he didn't remember where everyone was

sitting. By confronting him with his prior grand jury testimony, Chertoff was eventually able to get him to recall where Bonventre sat.

To help establish that Indelicato was one of the assassins, the prosecution called Detective Zachary Levin, who testified that the prints taken from the getaway car belonged to Santo Giordano and Indelicato.

On cross-examination, Indelicato's attorney, Robert Blossner, elicited the fact that no matches were made when the prints were first taken from the car in 1979 although more than two hundred comparisons had been tried. Levin explained that Giordano's match wasn't made until 1981 because the print of his lifted from the car was misfiled. Indelicato's match wasn't made until 1985 because only then did police obtain a copy of his palm prints for comparison.

Blossner pointed out that Levin had received a promotion after he had made the match, insinuating that the promotion and pay raise were a bribe.

On redirect, Chertoff asked, "When you were promoted did anyone tell you you had to reach a particular result in order to get your promotion?"

"No," said the detective.

Blossner called Indelicato's aunt, Frances Diliberto, as an alibi witness. A tough old gal who looked as if she had been chiseled out of granite, she testified that at the time of Galante's murder her nephew was involved in a neighborhood fistfight, testimony that neatly explained why Indelicato had a bruise on his face and a limp in his stride when he was congratulated outside the Ravenite Social Club in Little Italy half an hour after the murders—a scene secretly videotaped by the Manhattan District Attorney's Office.

Her testimony completely surprised the prosecutors. Although the defense was required to give notice before calling an alibi witness, the rule wasn't enforced against them. But the prosecutors had a surprise of their own. David Brodsky, an assistant district attorney who happened to be sitting in the gallery that day, recognized the witness as the subject of another investigation. As soon as there was a break in the proceedings, Brodsky hurried to the counsel table to tell the prosecutors before rushing off to gather evidence for them.

Chertoff began his cross-examination by asking the witness if she knew what her nephew did for a living. She, like the other defense witnesses, was stymied by this simple question. Nor did she know the occupations of the mafiosi friends she had grown up with. And she couldn't explain why she had not called an ambulance or a doctor for her nephew after the alleged beating.

"Ma'am, did you ever receive or possess stolen airline tickets?" Chertoff asked out of the blue.

"No."

"Did you ever have a discussion with Vinny DiPenta in which you told him about a scam in which you can get stolen airline tickets and use them to fly free . . . ?"

"No. Not to my knowledge."

"Well, you would remember if you had a conversation with someone concerning a fraud, wouldn't you?"

"Possibly. . . ."

". . . And isn't it a fact, ma'am, that you told Mr. DiPenta that you were involved in a fraud involving Delta Airlines?"

"No. . . ."

"I am going to object at this point," said Blossner. "This is a collateral issue."

The judge directed the attorneys to come to the side bar where he asked Chertoff to explain the basis for his questions.

"Your Honor, she is on tape . . . fully outlining a scheme in which she obtained blank airline tickets and filled in fictitious names. . . ."

"Do you expect to play that tape for us?" asked the judge.

"If necessary, yes."

"It's a collateral issue," asserted Blossner.

"No. It isn't," said the judge, "because it goes to credibility."

Chertoff resumed his cross-examination. "Do you remember telling Mr. DiPenta that you had tickets for Fort Lauderdale in December of 1981?"

"I don't remember."

"Do you remember telling him that you were going to go under the name Harris?"

"No. I don't remember. . . ."

". . . Did you tell Mr. DiPenta in the presence of your brother that, 'They can't stop me. I've got my money order. Harris. I'm going under Harris.' Did you say that?"

"I don't remember."

"Is it the kind of thing you would remember, ma'am?"

"Probably."

"So when you say you don't remember, you are telling us you didn't say it? Is that your testimony?"

"I don't remember."

"Did you tell Mr. DiPenta, 'What do I care? First-class, second-class . . . I'm going for nothing.' . . ."

"I don't remember. . . ."

". . . Ma'am, do you know at the time whether Vinny DiPenta was wired with a tape recorder?"

"I don't know."

"Do you think you would recognize your voice on tape?"

"I might."

"Would it refresh your memory if we played a tape for you?"

"Possibly."

"Objection," said Blossner. "If we can be heard at side bar."

"I will come to the tapes in a minute, Your Honor," said Chertoff. "I will proceed first with something else." Turning to the witness he asked, "In addition to the airline ticket scam, isn't it also a fact, ma'am, you have also been involved with a checked luggage scheme."

"No. . . ."

". . . Did you say to Mr. DiPenta, 'Never mind that. And when I get home Vinny, I lose my suitcase'?"

"I don't remember."

"... Is it the kind of thing you think you would remember, ma'am?"

"Possibly. ..."

"... Do you consider lying to get money a serious matter, ma'am?"

"... It depends on the situation. I could lie to my mother to get money. I wouldn't consider that serious."

"... What about to lie to an airline to get money?"

"I guess that is a crime. ..."

"... And what about to lie to help a member of your family, ma'am, would you consider that serious?"

"It depends on the lie. ..."

"... Isn't it a fact that the only thing that would stop you from lying is if you thought you would get caught at it?"

"Yes. I would be afraid. It stops me from lying if I am afraid that I would get caught."

"That's what stops you?"

"That's right."

"But if you thought you could get away with it, you would do it, isn't that correct, ma'am, depending on the circumstances? Take all the time you need to think about that."

"Could you repeat that question?"

The judge had the reporter read back the question.

"Depending," said the witness.

Chertoff's cross-examination was so devastating that the defense attorneys looked as if they wanted to crawl underneath their seats. At the side bar, Gaudelli moved for a mistrial arguing that his client had been prejudiced by the spillover effect of the testimony. LaRossa claimed he didn't know the witness was going to be called and asked the court to sever his client from the trial. Dawson joined in the request. The witness had fractured the defense.

The judge refused to declare a mistrial or sever any defendants. He did offer to instruct the jurors that the witness's testimony should only be considered in regard to Indelicato. Blossner objected on the grounds that such an instruction drew more attention to her testimony and asked that the instruction be given after all the witnesses for the defense had been called. The other defense attorneys disagreed. They wanted the instruction now. Chertoff offered an acceptable compromise: The instruction was given at the end of Blossner's case, and a similar one would be given after each of the defense attorneys rested, thereby reminding the jury who called each witness and for whose defense the testimony should be considered.

Chertoff then handed the witness a pair of earphones and played a tape for her. First, she said she couldn't hear the recording. Then she claimed she didn't recognize any of the voices: not DiPenta's, not her brother's, not even her own.

The Mafia derives its revenues from a wide variety of illegal rackets including extortion, corruption of labor unions, gambling, bribery of public officials, fraud, and loan-sharking. According to the President's Commission on Organized Crime the nation's crime families generate income of $47 billion a year, which is 1.13 percent of the nation's gross national product. Their illicit activities reduce the disposable income of every man, woman and child in the United States by $77 a year.

The ruling-Commission trial provided a rare glimpse into the inner workings of a mob racket—in this case a very successful scheme to extort money from construction companies in New York. It was based on the Mafia's control over half a dozen labor unions, including the Teamsters, who drive the mixing trucks that deliver concrete; Laborers, who pour the concrete; Carpenters, who build the plywood forms into which the concrete is poured; and Masons, who finish the concrete. The crime families' domination of some unions is so complete that the President's crime commission concluded that they own labor unions the way ordinary citizens own property, and can pass that interest from one crime family to another.

"Mayor Koch may think that he's running the streets of New York," an informer told a committee of the New York State Assembly in 1984, "but let me tell you something— he's in for a rude surprise. Any time that the mob wants to teach him a lesson, they control one of the most powerful weapons in the world: the stink of the garbage that is picked up from thousands and thousands of commercial establishments in New York."

Through their control of labor unions, the Mafia persuaded the major concrete contractors in New York to join a bid-rigging club. Members agreed not to compete against one another and each paid a tribute of 2 percent of the price of their contracts to the four families that controlled the club. A *Newsday* survey found that the price of concrete in Manhattan was nearly twice as high as in other major cities. The assurance of labor peace gave contractors an additional incentive not to expose the scheme.

To prove the existence of the racket, Savarese called to the stand contractor Stanley Sternchos, whom the FBI had caught making payoffs to defendant Ralph Scopo, a Colombo family soldier and president of the Concrete Workers District Council. Sternchos cut a deal with the prosecution that allowed him to plead guilty to a misdemeanor in return for his cooperation and willingness to testify.

Sternchos was a forty-one-year-old college graduate who had taught junior high school before going into construction. In 1980 he and two partners established Technical Concrete Construction Corporation. Soon thereafter, Scopo told them they had to pay 1 percent of their contract price plus $2 for every cubic yard of concrete poured. Periodically, the partners would give Scopo a few hundred dollars to keep him at bay. At that time, they were handling small jobs in the $10,000 to $250,000 range.

In the fall of 1980, Technical participated in several joint ventures with a New Jersey demolition company run by Philip Palmieri—a man with reputed underworld connections. When Technical later acquired a job on its own,

Palmieri, upset that he wasn't brought in on it, threatened Technical, telling them that he expected to be their partner on everything. The partners, afraid he would resort to sabotage or violence to enforce this unwanted marriage, countered Palmieri's moves by taking in a fourth partner, Anthony Mancuso, whose father-in-law had underworld connections of his own. Mancuso was unable to solve the problem, however, and the partners were forced to ask Scopo for help. Scopo met with Palmieri and told him to back off, that Technical was his.

The original three partners later tried to rid themselves of Mancuso, and representatives of Mancuso's family met with Scopo and the Technical partners and demanded half a million dollars' compensation. Upon Scopo's advice, they accepted.

Technical prospered and was soon bidding $5.8 million for a job, when Scopo, telling them that the job had been allocated to another contractor who had bid $6.8 million, advised them to raise their bid or withdraw it. Realizing they couldn't do the work without Scopo's cooperation, they withdrew.

Scopo explained to the partners that they couldn't bid on jobs above $2 million because those jobs went to contractors in "the Club." However, they were invited to join the Club. At the time the largest contractor in the city was in a dispute with the Mafia over its payments, and the families decided it wasn't worth the bother to kill the owner since he was going out of business anyway. Technical could have their allocation if they were willing to give half of their company to the mob. The partners declined.

In August of 1981, Technical's concrete supply was abruptly halted. They called Scopo, who was in Florida attending a conference. He told them he didn't know why the deliveries were stopped, but he would find out and have them resumed. No deliveries were made for the next nine days. The company lost $10,000 a day and its reputation suffered. Scopo blamed the Teamsters, saying he had spoken to their family and threatened that if Technical's concrete was ever withheld again without his permission, he would stop all deliveries throughout the city.

Scopo subsequently arranged for Technical to receive permission to do a $3-million job, pointing out that if his family was a partner in the company he would have greater strength in interfamily councils and would be able to get them more big jobs. The partners didn't want to be in business with the mob, but they reluctantly agreed to give the Colombo family 2 percent of their contract price as well as giving Scopo $10,000 per job.

On cross-examination the defense attorneys tried to pin the blame for the scheme on the contractors, asserting that there was no extortion and that the Mafia was acting at the behest of the contractors. Sternchos admitted that Scopo was generally courteous and soft-spoken in their dealings, that he never threatened them with physical violence, and that the company had turned down some of Scopo's requests for rigged bids. Moreover, Technical had haggled over the amount of its payments and delayed remitting them. Although the partners had paid about $800,000, they owed another $600,000 at the time Scopo was indicted.

Persico asked Sternchos if he had cheated Scopo. Sternchos responded that Scopo was a criminal and why should he give him a fair count.

"He was just as much of a criminal as you were," said Persico. "You went to him."

"We went to him to sign a union document because we needed laborers on the job. He came to us with his proposal that we couldn't work unless we paid him. . . ."

". . . Did you decide to go to the police department, or the FBI, or any law enforcement agency?"

"No, we didn't."

When Persico asked about Scopo's help in ridding them of Mancuso, Sternchos replied that they ended up paying Mancuso twice as much as his shares were worth. Persico said, well, what about his help getting your concrete shipments resumed? Sternchos claimed Scopo was probably responsible for stopping them in the first place.

On redirect, John Savarese had Sternchos explain that he feared Scopo because of stories of mob beatings. According to one story, Scopo's son had beaten someone senseless.

After eight weeks of trial, in which 85 witnesses were called, 150 audiotapes were played, and hundreds of surveillance photos were introduced, the attorneys began their closing arguments. John Savarese summarized the case for the prosecution:

"When Ralph Scopo tells a contractor that he has to pay two points on his job, it's not just Scopo talking. It's the four families as regulated by the Commission that stands behind him. And it's the fear, the fear of what the mob might do that gives the Mafia its greatest power.

"Every victim sits there and has to decide: What will they do to me? What will happen to my business? Every victim asks himself those questions and then decides it just isn't worth fighting these guys, I'm going to try to make the best of this bad situation. . . .

". . . [The defendants] live in a world of power, fear and violence. They have decided . . . to ignore the rules of decent legitimate society. They ignore laws and take money from people any way they want. When these people use the word family, they don't mean a group of relatives seated around Thanksgiving dinner table. A family is not like the Elks Club or the Rotary, it's a group of men, dedicated, as you heard them say, to this thing, this life of ours. Dedicated to making money strictly through crime. . . .

". . . You, ladies and gentlemen, have learned an enormous amount in the last couple of months about a small but dark segment of our society that is unfortunately with us. It is a world filled with selfish men and is a special, chosen way of living. . . . The responsibility for the crimes they committed is theirs.

"The government asks you to lay that responsibility at

the feet of these defendants. The government asks you to find these defendants guilty as to each and every charge."

The court adjourned for the weekend. The following Monday, the defense gave its view of the case:

"At the beginning of the case," said Persico, "I told you I wasn't a lawyer. I guess you found out that was true. I don't think I could speak as well as all these people did, but I am going to try to make you understand what the facts are in the case.

· "What I am going to try to do is to tell you what I think of the whole case. To me it is like a bus ride in a sightseeing bus tour. . . .

". . . Mr. Savarese . . . put us all on the bus, the whole bunch of us, and he was going to take us through the tour and show us what the evidence was, as he has seen it. We got on the bus. And where did he take us? He took us to tinseltown, Hollywood town, cardboard town. Big maps, big signs, marquees.

"In a movie, in a Hollywood production, you always try to use top names, stars, to attract attention; Genovese family, Gambino family, names that have been around for a lot of years and everybody is familiar with it. So that is part of the tour. . . .

". . . And who do they bring in? Who . . . did they bring in to prove Carmine Persico was a boss? Cantalupo . . . Cantalupo is one of them witnesses I told you about in my opening. Immunity. Paid substantially. Called him back whenever they needed him. Threw him out of the program whenever they didn't want him. Brought him back again. I hope they don't try to say he is my friend because I never received a Christmas gift off of him. I never went out to dinner with him. I never partied with him. . . .

". . . I guess you'll be the judge of whether he lied or not. Full immunity. Bold and brazen and he was bold and brazen. You seen it. I told you to look for it. And I think I proved that. . . . All the stickups, all the robberies, narcotics he sold. They didn't put him in jail. They kept putting him on the stand, kept putting him on the stand to testify against everybody. And every time he got on he had more to tell."

Persico ridiculed Sternchos as a victim who became a millionaire. As for DeChristopher: "He did pretty good for a man that ran away from home with six dollars and no teeth. The government gave him a new life . . . to start with his girlfriend.

"Dedicated family man, worried about his children, left his whole life behind. Never even called them. Never even bothered to find out how they were doing. Never bothered to send them the money. Didn't care whether they had money or not.

"Despicable? How much more despicable could you be than Fred DeChristopher? . . ."

". . . Ladies and gentlemen, I can't say I never did anything wrong because you know I have been in jail . . . the only thing in this country that makes anybody have faith in this justice system is the jury. Ask someone that knows. We have no faith in the prosecutor. We have no faith in the courts. We have faith in the juries because the juries are people and they have no ax to grind . . . thank God for the jury system in this country. That is what makes us separate and apart from any other country. . . .

". . . You gave us your promise that you won't be prejudiced, that you will look for the evidence, and I say if you look for the evidence, you will find no evidence against Carmine Persico."

Defense attorney James LaRossa reminded the jury that they had sworn to give the defendants a fair trial regardless of whether they were members of the Mafia; and that promise was more important than any crime that may have occurred. It requires a great deal of heroism and fortitude for a jury to act on principle, he said, "the same kind of heroism that is required when this country is in war."

When the defense attorneys finished, the prosecution was given an opportunity for rebuttal. Chertoff rose and turned to the jury. First, he expressed his sympathy for the

jurors, saying that after eight weeks of hearing about killings, extortion, and loan-sharking they must be numb.

Chertoff refuted Persico's complaint that he was being
tried on his reputation. "The reputations these men have
are reputations they wanted. . . . And when they were sitting in the Palma Boy Social Club and going over the list of
money that the contractors were paying, had paid, and were
going to pay, what were they thinking? What did they think
the money was coming to them for? Did they think they
were a charity? . . . Or did they know why they got the
money? Did they know they got the money because their
underlings went out and used the reputation of the Mafia
. . . to collect that money for these men?"

The fact that the Mafia didn't use guns and threats
against the contractors, Chertoff argued, was because they
didn't want to frighten the contractors out of business.
They preferred to slowly bleed their victims, letting them
remain alive so that they could continue to feed off them.

"As for the claim that DeChristopher turned in Persico
for the money, even if you assume that was true, it didn't
explain why DeChristopher was willing to testify. He could
have taken the money and fled to Brazil. He could have sat
on a beach there instead of being attacked and humiliated
in the courtroom. And when he took the stand, he was fair.
He could have said Persico voted for the hit against Galante.
But he said just the opposite.

"Now you heard Mr. DeChristopher's family testify. I
won't go over that. They blamed him for everything. Catherine DeChristopher. If the question had been, 'Who
started World War Two?' you would have heard Fred De-
Christopher started it. . . ."

". . . What Junior Persico finds despicable about Fred
DeChristopher is that he testified, he broke the code of the
Mafia. . . . And Junior Persico wants you to . . . accept his
values, accept his view that you are a rat when you testify;
that it is okay to hide behind people; that when the victim
doesn't want to pay the full amount to the extorter, it's the

victim's fault; that when Allie Boy Persico, his brother, beats up Joey Cantalupo over a loan shark debt, that is the loan shark victim's fault. That is the code of the Mafia that Carmine Persico wants you to buy."

Chertoff urged the jury to use their common sense: "Step by step. . . . Go systematically, building up. Not every brick in the building has to support the entire structure. A building is a lot of bricks meshed together. You have to look at the whole pattern."

After four hours of refuting the defense, Chertoff concluded by saying: "[The defense] sometimes makes it sound as if the jury is here only because the defense wants it, that the government doesn't want a jury. That's very wrong. The government wants a jury. The government wants to present evidence to a jury because you jurors are picked and selected to represent the community. And that's really what this is about. The community makes the laws and the laws are made to protect the community so that people are free to go about their pursuits to work as they please to live unmolested and it is very fitting that when someone breaks the law it should be representatives of the community who judge them.

". . . These men placed themselves above the law and they made their own law. They didn't have courts, they had sitdowns; they didn't have police, they had soldiers. . . . What's remarkable, what's fitting about this case more than anything else, is that these bosses of the Mafia, these mobsters are brought here finally to answer to you, the jury, sitting in a court applying the law. That is very fitting. And it's a responsibility and a privilege that you have to serve on this jury. . . ."

". . . And now it's time for justice and, ladies and gentlemen, you are going into the jury room and that is what you must do. You must reach a verdict and you must do justice. And that's what we ask of you. Thank you again and good luck."

The judge instructed the jury and then sequestered them. According to an *Us* magazine article later written by a juror, all the jurors except one were inclined to find the defendants guilty. The lone holdout, an elderly woman, didn't believe the government had proven its case or even the existence of the ruling Commission.

The other jurors, aghast because they found the evidence overwhelming, tried not to pressure her. They began to carefully review the evidence, returning to the courtroom periodically to listen to the tapes. On one, Salerno bragged, "If it wasn't for me, there wouldn't be no mob left. I made all the guys." At another point, Corallo coldheartedly commented, "You pick 'em and ya kill 'em. All right. He survived. He's in . . . bad shape. He's crippled. But we do it."

While the jurors deliberated, Persico and Langella were sentenced in another courtroom to thirty-nine and sixty-five years, respectively, on their prior racketeering conviction for running the Colombo family. The news was kept from the jurors who spent their nights at a hotel in Clifton, New Jersey. They were watched around the clock by marshals who accompanied them to the bathroom and listened in on their telephone conversations.

After several days of waiting for a verdict, the prosecutors were becoming tense and antsy. Savarese felt as if he were on a roller coaster. Sometimes he believed they would win, at other times he became despondent. The first two days they spent by the courtroom expecting a decision any moment. Then they returned to their office and tried to do other work. But they found it difficult to concentrate, their thoughts always returning to the case. They mentally reviewed what they had said and done, second-guessed their actions, and tried to reassure themselves that they hadn't committed any serious errors.

Whenever the jurors returned to the courtroom to review evidence, the prosecutors scrutinized their expression looking for a hint of which way they were leaning. They believed the pattern of notes from the jury—the trial lawyer's equivalent of reading tea leaves—was favorable. At the very least, the notes demonstrated that the jury was proceeding in a careful and meticulous manner.

At 11:30 A.M. on Wednesday, November 19, after five days of deliberations, the jury asked for a clean verdict form. The request had the impact of a bolt of lightning. The courtroom quickly filled with spectators and lawyers. Chertoff became surprisingly calm as he realized the long trial was about to end.

In the jury room the jurors hugged each other and then resolutely walked into the courtroom and took their seats, all dressed in their Sunday best. At 12:20 P.M. the forewoman, a thin black lady in a red blouse, stood and began to read the verdict in a firm resonant voice: On count 1, Anthony Salerno, guilty; Carmine Persico, guilty; Gennaro Langella, guilty. As she read each defendant's name the same word was heard: "Guilty." Tears rolled down her cheek.

Reading the verdict took a long time. Her throat became sore and she had to pause for some water. The judge suggested she sit. She did and continued reading. She spoke for twenty-eight minutes and repeated, "Guilty," 151 times. Not once did she say, "Not guilty."

As the verdict was being read, none of the defendants showed any emotion. Across the aisle, Chertoff, Savarese, and Childers beamed with joy. Chertoff felt an enormous sense of relief once he knew that each defendant had been convicted on at least one count. Savarese was tremendously impressed with the courage of the jury.

After the judge praised the jurors for a job well done and excused them, they returned to the jury room where several women broke down and cried. They made plans for a reunion the following year and were then led into a van that was escorted by two carloads of federal agents. With sirens blaring, the convoy rushed out of the courthouse garage and took the jurors to their drop-off points for the last time, their anonymity still intact.

The defendants were remanded to jail, including Corallo, Santoro, Furnari, and Scopo, who had been out on bail. At the prosecution table the three prosecutors shook hands and congratulated each other. Not wanting to hang around and gloat, they quickly left the courtroom. Chertoff was so relieved he felt numb. "Thank God, we were able to convict them," he thought.

As the prosecutors walked down the courthouse steps, they were surrounded by a large crowd of reporters thrusting microphones and cameras in their faces and shouting questions. To Chertoff, the scene was something out of a movie. He patiently answered their questions, offering the usual homilies about justice being done, after which the prosecutors returned to their office for an impromptu celebration. They popped open cans of beer as they accepted the congratulations of their peers and watched television news reports of the verdict.

Rudolph Giuliani heard about the verdict in New Haven where he was in the midst of prosecuting Bronx Democratic boss Stanley Friedman (Friedman would be convicted). Ecstatic, he telephoned his congratulations.

On January 13 the defendants returned to court for sentencing. The attorneys for Corallo and Scopo moved for a postponement, pleading clients' ill health. The judge denied their requests. Cardinale asked for leniency for his client Salerno, asserting that he was seventy-six years old, in ill health, and that many people could testify to his numerous charitable activities and good deeds. The judge, who had a reputation as a tough sentencer, replied that Salerno had spent his life feeding off the community, engaging in killings and beatings and threats. His sentence, said the judge, would be a statement to those out there who are thinking of taking over the reins of power. He gave Salerno one hundred years in prison and fined him $240,000.

"This case was prejudiced from the very first day," said Persico. He claimed the attitude of the prosecutors and the court was "in conformance with this mass hysteria, this Mafia mania that was flying around . . . deprived every one of us in this courtroom to our rights to a fair and impartial trial by all the spectaculars that youse made of this case." The judge replied that in his opinion the jury found him guilty on overwhelming evidence. Persico was given one hundred years and a $240,000 fine.

Santoro complained that the convictions were unjust because they were based on testimony from government-paid witnesses. The judge replied that the defendants incriminated themselves on the tapes. "Aw, give me the hundred years and get it over with," Santoro said, rising from his chair. "I am about to do that," said the judge, who promptly sentenced him to one hundred years and fined him the same amount as the others.

Scopo pleaded for a lesser sentence on the grounds that he wasn't a member of the ruling Commission and didn't even know of its existence. Then what about this picture of you with Commission members outside a house in Staten Island? asked the judge. Scopo claimed he was just walking down the street when he encountered the men. Savarese began to refute the claim, but the judge told him not to bother. The sad thing about you, said the judge, was that you were a union leader with a duty of faithfulness to the people you were representing, which you absolutely threw down the gutter to enrich yourself. The judge added that it was perfectly clear that Scopo was a member of the Colombo family, and he was also given one hundred years and the same fine.

The judge asked Indelicato if he had anything to say. "No," replied Indelicato.
"No?" asked the judge.
"No," repeated Indelicato.
The judge noted that the evidence that Indelicato killed Galante for the Commission was more than sufficient for conviction. "We have the incredible happenstance of your fingerprint on the stolen getaway car in the backseat," said the judge, "and the even more incredible circumstance of the fact that the agents just happened to be videotaping the Ravenite Social Club that day when thirty minutes later you

heave into view, if I can use an old nautical term, to receive your congratulations."

Indelicato, who wasn't involved in the concrete extortion scheme and wasn't charged with murder, a state offense, was given the maximum punishment possible under RICO, forty years and a $50,000 fine.

Although the defendants were eligible for parole in ten years, the judge recommended that none of them be released early and also ordered them to reimburse the government the cost of the prosecution. On appeal all the convictions were affirmed except one of the RICO counts against Indelicato, which was overturned because of the statute of limitations. Indelicato's sentence was reduced from forty years to twenty. Ironically, the Commission defendant who had committed murder received the shortest sentence.

And so, fifty-five years after the bosses of the New York crime families established the Mafia's ruling Commission in a Brooklyn restaurant, the law finally caught up with it. Nobody believed that this prosecution had destroyed the Mafia. Indeed, nine months after the convictions, a rash of mob killings broke out across New York as captains and soldiers struggled for control of the criminal empires.

But the convictions did send a chilling message to the underworld: that the code of *omerta* (silence) was broken and even top mobsters could become informers; that the FBI could bug their cars and social clubs, making it increasingly difficult for them to communicate with each other; and that even the most powerful Mafia bosses were not immune from prosecution and conviction for their crimes.

Perhaps as important was the message given the public: that you could go to the authorities for help and something would be done. The Mafia's success has been largely based on its ability to exploit a climate of fear and hopelessness among its victims. Its reputation enabled it to extort money quickly and easily from people who believed they had no alternative. But when citizens fight back, organized crime becomes a less profitable and riskier endeavor.

For the prosecutors, winning convictions enhanced their reputations and brought them much praise and even some fan mail. Chertoff received a congratulatory call from a woman in Alabama who read about him in *Time* magazine and wanted to know if he was single. Several months later he accepted an appointment as first assistant United States attorney for the District of New Jersey and became engaged to his girlfriend, Meryl Justin. Savarese was appointed deputy chief appellate attorney and later joined a large law firm. He and Lynn Ashby have married.

For Childers, who thinks big-city cops are the greatest people on earth, the most gratifying aspect of the victory was the kudos he received from policemen. Veteran officers, who for years had been frustrated watching the Mafia operate with impunity, told him it was great finally to see justice done. One cynical cop gushed, "My God, we never thought this could happen."

THE AUTHOR

The author is always interested in learning about lawyers of vision and daring involved in provocative cases. He can be reached by writing:

Mark Litwak
P.O. Box 3226
Santa Monica, CA 90403

NAPIL

The *National Association for Public Interest Law* (NAPIL) is a coalition of public interest grant programs, run and funded by students and alumni of over forty-five law schools. Attorneys, students, and concerned citizens annually contribute 1 percent of their income or a day's pay to fund innovative public interest law projects. In 1988, NAPIL member organizations disbursed over $600,000 to more than 350 summer and year-long public interest law projects. Recently, NAPIL has launched a successful law firm campaign, which gives these employers the opportunity to contribute to fellowship programs. Through grants, loan forgiveness advocacy, and the development of public interest law career resources, NAPIL is helping the next generation of public interest lawyers pursue their commitment to social justice.

Individuals interested in supporting NAPIL's activities should write or call NAPIL at 1666 Connecticut Avenue, NW #424, Washington, D.C. 20009, (202) 462-0120.

SOURCES

Chapter 1

INTERVIEWS

Nancy Mintie, police captain Richard Batson, Meg Baum, Gary L. Blasi, LeRoy Cordova, Ed Edelman, Jill Halverson, Margaret Holub, Mark Rosenbaum.

BOOK

Stern, Philip M. *Lawyers on Trial*, New York: Times Books, 1980.

ARTICLES

Blasi, Gary L. "Litigation on Behalf of the Homeless: Systematic Approaches." *Journal of Urban and Contemporary Law*, Vol. 31 (1987), pp. 137–142.

Clancy, Frank. "Lawyers Team Up to Fight for the Homeless." *Los Angeles Times*, September 18, 1986.

Fein, David. "Law with a Human Touch." *Los Angeles News*, November 1985, p. 8.

Goldin, Gregory. "Gimme Shelter." *California Lawyer*, Vol. 7, No. 5 (May 1987), pp. 29–34.

Johnston, David. "Attorney Seeks Justice for the Poor of Skid Row." *Los Angeles Times*, January 7, 1985.

McMillian, Penelop, and George Ramos. "Homeless Fade Away as Police Move In for Arrests." *Los Angeles Times*, June 5, 1987.

SOURCES

"Briefcase." *The Los Angeles Daily Journal*, September 16, 1986.

REPORTS

"Profile of the Inner City Law Center." Los Angeles: Inner City Law Center, February 20, 1986.

COURT RECORDS

Bannister v. Board of Supervisors, Superior Court of the State of California, Los Angeles County, File No. C535833.

Blair v. Board of Supervisors, Superior Court of the State of California, Los Angeles County, File No. C568184.

Eisenheim v. Board of Supervisors, Superior Court of the State of California, Los Angeles County, File No. C479453.

Eisen v. Carlisle & Jacqueline, 417 U.S. 156 (1974).

Godinez v. Nachman, Superior Court of the State of California, Los Angeles County, File No. C491679.

Paris v. Board of Supervisors, Superior Court of the State of California, Los Angeles County, File No. C523361.

Ross v. Board of Supervisors, Superior Court of the State of California, Los Angeles County, File No. C501603.

Chapter 2

INTERVIEWS

Ed Swartz, Ralph Nader, Marvin E. Krakow.

BOOKS

Swartz, Edward M., *Proof of Product Defect*. New York: Lawyers Co-operative Publishing Co., 1985.

——*Slaughter by Product*. New York: Kluwer Law Book Publishers, 1986.

——*Toys That Don't Care*. Boston: Gambit, 1971.

SOURCES

————*Toys That Kill*. New York: Vintage Books, 1986.

ARTICLES

Hartman, Curtis. "Is This Any Way to Make a Million?" *Boston*, September 1978, p. 98.

Kindregan, Charles P., and Edward M. Swartz. "The Assault on the Captive Consumer: Emasculating the Common Law of Torts in the Name of Reform." *St. Mary's Law Journal*, Vol. 18 (Winter 1987), pp. 673–711.

Lynch, Mitchell. "Stalking Killer Toys." *Boston Business*, Winter 1985, p. 27.

Matza, Michael. "The Nader of the Nursery." *Student Lawyer*, December 1981, p. 29.

Swartz, Edward M. "Freeing the Captive Consumer." *Trial*, April 1986, p. 28.

COURT RECORDS

Iain Cunningham v. Quaker Oats Company, Fisher Price Division, U.S. District Court, Western District of New York, Civil Action No. 1973-343.

Briefs for Plaintiffs-Appellants/Cross-Appellees, Iain Cunningham v. Quaker Oats Company, United States Court of Appeals for the Second Circut, File Nos. 86-7740, 86-7742.

Depositions and documents obtained through discovery in the Buckley case.

Chapter 3

INTERVIEWS

William Parnall, Jason Kirkman, Wanita Kirkman, Judge Michael Martinez, Paul Mones, Judith Areens, and Leslie Mitchel of the National Committee for Prevention of Child Abuse.

SOURCES

BOOK

Areens, Judith. *Family Law*, 2nd ed. New York: The Foundation Press, 1985.

ARTICLES

Eber, Loraine Patricia. "The Battered Wife's Dilemma: To Kill or Be Killed." *Hastings Law Journal*, Vol. 32 (1981), p. 895.

Severo, Richard. "The Short Unhappy Life of Rubin Almeyda." *The New York Times*, September 6, 1977, p. 37.

"Study Finds Severe Abuse No Defense for Killing Parent." *Criminal Justice Newsletter*, Vol. 16 (April 1, 1985), p. 5.

Wayne State Law Review, Vol. 24 (1978), p. 1705.

Numerous press clippings on the Kirkman case from the *Albuquerque Journal*.

REPORTS

Mones, Paul. "The Relationship Between Child Abuse and Parricide: An Overview," in *Unhappy Families*, Eli Newberger, M.D., and Richard Bourne, J.D., eds. Littleton, Mass.: T.S.G. Publishing Co., 1985.

"Child Abuse Fatalities Remain High: The Results of the 1987 Annual Fifty State Survey." Prepared by the National Center on Child Abuse Prevention Research, National Committee for Prevention of Child Abuse, 332 South Michigan Avenue, Suite 950, Chicago, Illinois 60604.

"Child Abuse: Prelude to Delinquency? Findings of a Research Conference Conducted by the National Committee for Prevention of Child Abuse," April 7–10, 1984. Ellen Gray, project director. Washington, D.C.: Office of Juvenile Justice and Delinquency Prevention, U.S. Department of Justice, September 1986.

Executive Summary, Study of National Incidence and Prevalence of Child Abuse and Neglect. Prepared for the National Center on Child Abuse and Neglect, December 1987.

"Study of National Incidence and Prevalence of Child Abuse and Neglect: 1988." U.S. Department of Health and Human Services, National Center on Child Abuse and Neglect.

Especially useful was the sentencing report by Lorie E. Andersen for the National Center on Institutions and Alternatives. NCIA's western regional office is at 304 South Broadway, Los Angeles, California 90013.

San Quentin Prison Study: Maurer, A., "Physical Punishment of Children." Paper presented at the California State Psychological Convention, Anaheim.

New York University study of death row juveniles by Dr. Dorothy Otnow Lewis, published in *American Journal of Psychiatry*, May 1987.

I also relied upon coroner and police department reports; affidavit for search warrant; correspondence between William Parnall and Jason Kirkman; Jason Kirkman's letter to Judge Michael Martinez; psychological reports by Robert Zussman, Ph.D., Edward W. Snyder, Ph.D., Robert L. Karp, M.D., Jullianne Lockwood, Ph.D., James B. Franklin, Ph.D., and Dennis L. Pilgrim, Ph.D.

COURT RECORDS

In the Matter of Jason Kirkman, Respondent, Cause No. CH-86-00859, File No. C-8777.

In Re East, 32 Ohio Misc. 65, 288 N.E. 2d 343 (1972).

Roe v. Conn., 417 F. Supp. 769 (1976).

State v. Aragon, 512 P. 2d 974, 85 N.M. 401.

State v. Jones, 95 N.C. 588 (1886).

State v. Gallegos, 719 P. 2d 1268, 104 N.M. 247 (N.M. App. 1986).

State of New Jersey v. Kelly, 478 At. 2d 364, 97 N.J. 178 (1984).

Chapter 4

INTERVIEWS

Ron Meshbesher, Thomas K. Berg, Thor Anderson, Paul W. Bergstrom.

SOURCES

BOOKS

Johnson, Phillip E. *Criminal Law, Cases, Materials and Text*. St. Paul, Minnesota: West Publishing Co., 1985.

Lewis, Alfred Allan, and Herbert Leon MacDonell. *The Evidence Never Lies*. New York: Dell Publishing Co., 1984.

Moenssens, Andre A., and Fred E. Inbau. *Scientific Evidence in Criminal Cases*, 2nd ed. New York: The Foundation Press, 1978.

Wolfram, Charles W. *Modern Legal Ethics*. St. Paul, Minnesota: West Publishing Co., 1986.

Issues in Forensic Psychiatry, Washington, D.C.: American Psychiatric Association, 1984.

ARTICLES

Adcock, Thomas Larry. "The Defense That Never Rests." *Mpls. St. Paul Magazine*, July 1980, pp. 101–105.

Jones, Gwenyth. "4 Lawyers Who Spell Success in Courtroom."*Minneapolis Star*, September 2, 1977.

Ross, Deborah. "Unraveling Ron Meshbesher." *Twin Cities Reader*, Vol. 4, No. 33 (September 5–13), cover story.

Slovenko, Ralph. "The Insanity Defense in the Wake of the Hinckley Trial." *Ruthers Law Journal*, Vol. 14 (Winter 1983), pp. 373–395.

Numerous articles from the *Minneapolis Star, Minneapolis Tribune,* and the *St. Paul Pioneer Press* covering the Ming Sen Shiue case.

COURT RECORDS

United States of America v. Ming Sen Shiue, United States District Court, District of Minnesota, Third Division, File No. 3-80-72.

United States of America v. Ming Sen Shiue, 650 F. 2nd 919 (8th cir., 1981).

State of Minnesota v. Ming Sen Shiue, 326 N.W. Reporter 2nd. 648 (Supreme Ct. 1982).

Sources

Chapter 5

Book

Morgan, Lael, ed. *Alaska's Native People. Alaska Geographic,* Vol 6, No. 3 (1979), Alaska Geographic Society, Anchorage.

Articles

Carbonara, Peter. "A Burnt-Out Case." *American Lawyer*, November 1988, p. 87.

Thomas, Eric. "Challenge Attracts Peel's Maverick Defender." *Bellingham* (Wash.) *Herald*, January 7, 1986.

Toomey, Sheila. "Radical Attorney." *Anchorage Daily News*, May 1, 1988.

Court Records

Division of Corrections v. Neakok, 721 P. 2d 1121 (1986).

McKinnon v. State, 526 P. 2d 18 (1974).

Ravin v. State of Alaska, 537 P. 2d 494 (1975).

State of Alaska v. John Kenneth Peel, Ketchikan Superior Court File No. 1KE-S84-1010 CR; Juneau Superior Court File No. 1JU-S87-975CR.

State v. Browder, 486 P. 2d 925 (1971).

United States of America v. Phillip M. Weidner, U.S. District Court, Northern District of Illinois, 75 CR 17 (1975).

Statutes

Alaska Hire Law: Alaska Stat. Ann. Sec. 38.40.010 to 38.40.090 (1977).

Chapter 6

Interviews

Ralph Nader, John Richard, Donald Ross, Alan Morrison.

Books

Gorey, Hays. *Nader and the Power of Everyman.* New York: Grosset and Dunlap, 1975.

McCarry, Charles. *Citizen Nader.* New York: Saturday Review Press, 1972.

Nader, Ralph. *Unsafe at Any Speed.* New York: Grossman Publishers, 1965.

Speiser, Stuart M. *Lawsuit.* New York: Horizon Press, 1980, Chapter 1.

Articles

Auletta, Ken. "Ralph Nader, Public Eye." *Esquire*, December 1983, p. 480.

Klein, Joe. "Ralph Nader: The Man in the Class Action Suit." *Rolling Stone*, November 20, 1975.

Mintz, Morton. "Car Safety Critic Reports Being Tailed." *The Washington Post*, February 13, 1966.

Nader, Ralph. "Law Schools and Law Firms." *The New Republic*, October 11, 1969, p. 20.

Ridgeway, James. "The Dick." *The New Republic*, March 12, 1966, p. 11.

Rowe, Jonathan. "Ralph Nader Reconsidered." *The Washington Monthly*, March 1985, p.12.

Profile, *Los Angeles Daily Journal*, August 29, 1983.

"(Still) Unsafe at Any Speed." *Inc.* magazine, December 1985, p. 33.

Speeches

Address of Ralph Nader at Harvard University, March 3, 1987.

Address of Ralph Nader at Suffolk Law School, March 4, 1987.

Court Records

Goldfarb v. Virginia State Bar, 421 U.S. 773 (1975).

INS v. Chadha, 462 U.S. 919 (1983).

SOURCES

Nader v. General Motors Corp., 292 N.Y.S. 2d 514 (Sup. Ct., Special Term 1968).

Nader v. General Motors Corp., 298 N.Y.S. 2d 137 (App. Div. 1969).

Nader v. General Motors Corp., 25 N.Y. 2d 560, 307 N.Y.S. 2d 647 (1970).

Virginia State Board of Pharmacy v. Virginia Citizens Consumer Council, 425 U.S. 748 (1976).

Chapter 7

INTERVIEWS

Prosecutors Michael Chertoff, John Savarese, Gil Childers; defense attorneys Stanley Meyer, Sam Dawson, and Albert Gaudelli; *Newsday* reporter Gerald McKelvey; Anne Fairbanks Childers.

BOOKS

Brownstein, Ronald and Nina Easton. *Reagan's Ruling Class*, Presidential Accountability Group (P.O. Box 19312, Washington, D.C. 20036), 1982.

Edelhertz, Herbert, ed. *Major Issues in Organized Crime Control,* Symposium Proceedings, September 25–26, 1986, Northwest Policy Studies Center. Bellevue, Wash.: September 1987.

Peterson, Vergil W. *The Mob.* Ottawa, Ill.: Green Hill Publishers, 1983.

Talese, Gay. *Honor Thy Father.* New York: Dell Publishing Co., 1986.

ARTICLES

Billard, Mary. "Junior Gives It His Best Shot." *American Lawyer,* January/February 1987.

Collins, Nancy. "Gotcha." *New York,* May 25, 1987, pp. 28–40.

Drogin, Bob. "8 Mob Leaders Guilty." *Los Angeles Times,* November 20, 1986, pp. 1, 22.

"Inside the Mafia Commission Trial." Anonymous article purportedly written by a juror, *Us* magazine, February 9, 1987, pp. 6, 8.

Larsen, Jonathan Z. "The Avenger." *Manhattan, inc.*, February 1985, pp. 87–96.

Mokhiber, Russell. "Why We Picketed the Corporate Law Firm of Wilmer, Cutler & Pickering, Chanting 'Hands Off RICO.' " *New York Law School Law Review*, Vol. XXXI, No. 1 (1986), pp. 147–166.

"New Arrests on Wall Street." *Newsweek*, February 23, 1987.

Winerip, Michael. "High Profile Prosecutor." *The New York Times Magazine*, June 9, 1985, p. 37.

Especially helpful were Gerald McKelvey's series of articles written for *Newsday* reporting on the trial; and "The Mob on Trial," *Newsday* special reprint of articles appearing during September 1986.

Various articles in the *New York Post, Daily News*, and *Newsday* appearing July 13, 1979.

COURT RECORDS

United States of America v. Anthony Salerno, United States Court of Appeals for the Second Circuit, Brief for United States of America, File No. 87-1075.

United States of America v. Anthony Salerno *et al.*, United States District Court, Southern District of New York, File No. SSS 85 Cr. 139 (RO).

ACKNOWLEDGMENTS

I am fortunate to be married to Tiiu Lukk, an unusually gifted and literate woman whose critique of my work always improves it. She also assisted me in interviewing Ron Meshbesher and Wanita Kirkman.

My editor, Harvey Ginsberg, is not afraid to speak his mind, and his advice is always appreciated.

I am indebted to my agent, Harvey Klinger, for his suggestions and steadfast competence.

Linda Powers has earned my gratitude for quickly and accurately transcribing my interviews.

Finally, I appreciate the cooperation of my subjects, all of whom gave generously of their time.

INDEX